EDWARDIAN FICTION

Edwardian Fiction

JEFFERSON HUNTER

Harvard University Press

Cambridge, Massachusetts

and London, England

1982

Publication of this book has been aided by a grant
from the Andrew W. Mellon Foundation.

Library of Congress Cataloging in Publication Data

Hunter, Jefferson, 1947-
   Edwardian fiction.

   Includes bibliographical references and index.
   1. English fiction—20th century—History and criticism.   2. Great Britain—History—Edward VII, 1901-
1910—Sources.   I. Title.
PR881.H86   823'.912'09   81-6729
   ISBN 0-674-24030-8   AACR2

To My Father
and the Memory of My Mother

Preface

This book is a study of the forms and themes of the English novel in one unusually rich decade of its existence, the first decade of the twentieth century, which by chance coincided with the reign of Edward VII, by the Grace of God King of Great Britain and Ireland, Defender of the Faith, Emperor of India. I have confined myself more narrowly than most writers on the period to works actually published during the King's reign (January 1901-May 1910), though I have no particular quarrel with those who would extend the Edwardian years back to 1897 or forward to 1914. Quibbling over the exact boundaries of a literary period is a barren but harmless enterprise. Occasionally, as with *Lord Jim*, I have considered slightly earlier works myself. Dates given in the text are those of first English publication in book form. I have consulted and quoted from the first editions whenever possible, on the theory that generalities about the period ought to be based on the texts the Edwardians themselves read.

"Edwardian" is now a word with powerful associations, even with a train of attendant images: a table opulently laid for tea, a formal dinner party (but with mud and fog outside in the London streets), a summer afternoon in the garden of a country house. It is impossible to think about a historical period without characterizing it, hence in a sense fictionalizing it, but in thinking about the Edwardian decade, I have tried to avoid the most conventional and self-serving characterizations: those that respond less to what happened in the decade than to what later writers, for their own purposes, want the decade to have been. In practice this means defining Edwardian fiction as any fiction published within the decade, not as fiction with certain qualities, and not as fiction written by major figures only. Avoiding over-simplification means abandoning the familiar view of the decade as ruled by the triumvirate Wells, Bennett, and Galsworthy, with James at Lamb House perhaps thrown in as a distinguished survivor from the previous century, Conrad admitted as an anomalous seafaring Pole, and Forster included as a representative of fiction of the future. More voices than those six made up the Edwardian chorus.

Accordingly, unambitious and ephemeral novels are also considered here, those that appear on no one's reading list and are long out of print. Their usefulness lies in suggesting more accurate associations and images for the decade, and in throwing into relief the qualities of those novels—*Howards End, The Old Wives' Tale, The Man of Property, The Ambassadors, Tono-Bungay, Nostromo*—which are on everyone's list. The canon of Edwardian fiction does not need radical revision. It does need historical context. Forgotten novels of cowardice redeemed show how *Lord Jim* is both a book of the year 1900 and a book of eight decades later.

This study surveys the Edwardians' own ideas about their time, examines criticism and best-sellers of the period, and attempts to account for the two most salient facts about Edwardian fiction: thematic adventurousness and formal conservatism. It also explores the complications of fictional escapism: what novelists discovered when they "went abroad" imaginatively. John Masefield, G. K. Chesterton, W. H. Hudson, Erskine Childers, John Buchan, and Joseph Conrad figure largely here. Finally, the work considers the complementary "movement homeward," the mood of recessional or withdrawal resulting partly from disillusions about imperialism, partly from suspicions of human powerlessness. Here the chief figures are Henry James, Rudyard Kipling, John Galsworthy, Arnold Bennett, Hugh Walpole, E. V. Lucas, George Gissing, H. G. Wells, and E. M. Forster.

Most of the reading for and some of the writing of this book took place during a year freed from teaching duties. I am grateful to Yale University for the award of a Morse Fellowship, which made that year possible. A grant from the A. Whitney Griswold Fund, also provided by Yale, assisted materially with the preparation of the manuscript. By precept and example Professor Martin Price of Yale helped shape the first unwritten stages of this study; for that aid, and much aid that came later, I am greatly in his debt. Professor John Elder of Middlebury College also read portions of the book and helped me discover what I had to say and how to say it. Virginia LaPlante, my editor, made many helpful suggestions for revision.

To Pamela C. Hunter I am indebted in equal measure for patience and impatience, for giving me time to work and keeping me to the task.

Contents

One. The Sense of a Period

1. A Balfourian Age   3

2. From Personality to Personality   12

3. Continuities of Form   21

4. The Uncritical Attitude   35

5. Edwardian Best-Sellers   45

6. Departure   58

Two. Adventures Abroad

7. The Adventure and Romance Agency   77

8. Complications of Imperialism   99

9. The Black Panther   112

10. Conrad and Adventure   124

Three. Coming Home

11. The Theme of Recessional   155

12. Continental Rescues and Autumnal Affairs   173

13. The Backward Hunt for the Homely   189

14. This Strange Loneliness of Millions in a Crowd   215

15. The Condition of England and the Condition of Fiction   235

Notes   257

Index   275

PART ONE

The Sense of a Period

There! Peace at last! The far-off roar
  Of human passion dies away.
"Welcome to our broad shade once more,"
  The waning woodlands seem to say:

The music of the vagrant wind,
  That wandered aimlessly, is stilled;
The songless branches all remind
  That Summer's glory is fulfilled.

The fluttering of the falling leaves
  Dimples the leaden pool awhile;
So Age impassively receives
  Youth's tale of troubles with a smile.

Thus, as the seasons steal away,
  How much is schemed, how little done,
What splendid plans at break of day,
  What void regrets at set of sun!

—Alfred Austin, *The Door of Humility*

And in wild hours
A people, roaring ripe
With victory, rises, menaces, stands renewed,
Sheds its old piddling aims,
Approves its virtue, puts behind itself
The comfortable dream, and goes,
Armoured and militant,
New-pithed, new-souled, new-visioned, up the steeps
To those great altitudes, whereat the weak
Live not. But only the strong
Have leave to strive, and suffer, and achieve.

—W. E. Henley, Epilogue to *For England's Sake*

1

A Balfourian Age

The initial decade of the twentieth century, and the four years that followed it to the outbreak of the First World War, are the last periods of English literary history known by the names of their reigning monarchs. Since 1914, periods have been designated by the wars or depressions that occupy them, and when on occasion they have been given the name of a single figure, as in Hugh Kenner's *The Pound Era* or Samuel Hynes's *The Auden Generation*, that figure is a writer, not a king or queen. Significantly, the early 1950s in England have entered the historical record as the years of the Angry Young Men, not as the start of a Second Elizabethan Age.

The generation of writers who published their work between 1901 and 1910—novelists, poets, and playwrights alike—saw nothing artificial in the name "Edwardian." It was a natural choice for an age following sixty-four years universally called Victorian after the Queen who typified the taste of those years, and if Edwardians were slow to adopt their name—the *Oxford English Dictionary* records 1908 as the earliest date of "Edwardian" in its current sense—that may only indicate their resistance to any kind of labeling.[1] The Edwardians saw the particulars of their time with a vividness which prevented easy categorizations. They were aware of checks to their social and literary progress and of contradictions in their most calculated theories of art and civilization. They felt change all about them and yet could not specify the differences between their spirit and that of the late nineteenth century. As a result, the conflict between the dubiously progressive and the veraciously static became a favorite theme of their novelists. The Edwardians were excited and confused, sometimes bewildered, by their times, and openly acknowledged these turbulent feelings, though the most conservative Edwardians were ready to deny complacently that anything in England had changed with the change in sovereign, or to proclaim irascibly that everything had changed for the worse. It was the young and intellectually adventurous at the turn of the century who first recognized that they were living in a period marked off from the past, who countenanced the complex and elusive character of the period, and who sensed, in 1910 or 1914, that another and more troubling age was about to succeed the one they had just begun to understand. For the purposes of the young, "Edwardian" was an acceptable title: it made no ideological claim and committed them to nothing.[2]

The youngest and most intellectually adventurous of all Edwardians, H. G. Wells, never ceased arguing that the first ten years of the century were set apart. He half-seriously proposed that his was the Balfourian age, during which even religion sought to establish itself on doubt; everything was to be called into question; nothing was to be assumed.[3] "Balfourian" alludes to the Conservative Prime Minister's *A Defence of Philosophic Doubt* (1879), which was in fact more orthodox than skeptical. But the term alludes even more to Balfour's statesmanship, which Wells thought indecisive and altogether too doubtful and timid for the fast-changing and unforgiving political events of the era: labor unrest, militarization in Germany, the constitutional crisis over the power of the House of Lords, and above all the unresolved problem of Ireland. As a premier, Balfour was largely unsuccessful, a fact recognized in the sweeping Liberal victory of 1906. But as a figure of his age, he is wonderfully representative—far more representative, for example, than Lord Haldane, a devotee of German metaphysics who became Secretary for War after 1906, and who once silenced a Council meeting by telling some British officers that England's new model army should be a Hegelian one.[4] Very little about the Edwardian decade was as systematic as Haldane's Hegelianism.

4

In one sense Balfour was not doubtful enough for Wells, not sufficiently free-thinking, independent, skeptical. These were qualities that the age itself encouraged according to Wells: "to-day, while we live in a period of tightening and extending social organisation, we live also in a period of adventurous and insurgent thought, in an intellectual spring unprecedented in the world's history. There is an enormous criticism going on of the faiths upon which men's lives and associations are based, and of every standard and rule of conduct."[5] Though this remark was made in 1911, it applies to the whole of the Edwardian period, an intellectual spring which began more genuinely with the publication of Wells's *Anticipations* in 1901 than with the accession of Edward VII in the same year. The remark serves better than any other single passage in Edwardian literature as an epigraph for the period, despite the fact that the criticism of which Wells speaks frequently resulted in the reaffirmation of old standards. Not all Englishmen wished to exchange a familiar existence for someone else's utopia, and a few of them refused even to criticize their self-contained and apparently permanent worlds. These Edwardians appear prominently, though usually disguised as late Victorians, in the novels of Galsworthy, who felt a certain admiration for their rigidly principled and orderly lives. But Wells spoke for the excited young and the troubled old who saw that questions would have to be raised.

The drop in real wages, the appearance of militant suffragettes, the inability of authorities to cope with London slums, the spread of the motor-car industry, the growth of the Labour Party, the inefficiencies in the management of the Boer War—all of these social and political facts profoundly influenced the way Edwardian Englishmen lived, and so became the proper matter for imaginative writers as well as journalists. But as Wells saw with particular clarity, writers could not just examine facts. They had also to examine the faiths by which Englishmen apprehended facts in the first place and resisted those they most disliked or feared. The Boer War made the British general staff seem amateurish partly because myths of gentlemanly success—

Public School hero metamorphosed into dashing subaltern and then sagacious tactician—had been so current. Dick Remington, who speaks for Wells in *The New Machiavelli* (1911), is disillusioned by the war precisely in proportion to his early, illusion-filled conception of it: "the pleasant officers we had imagined would change to wonderful heroes at the first crackling of rifles, remained the pleasant, rather incompetent men they had always been, failing to imagine, failing to plan and co-operate, failing to grip."[6] As for the Woman Question which Edwardians had to face almost immediately after the war was concluded, its bitter intensity derived from a similar conflict between myth and actuality. Suffragette violence shocked Tory and Liberal alike because men had an idealized notion of what women wanted and of how they behaved.

With characteristic egotism, Wells decided that in his age a new philosophy, or a new way of responding to past philosophies, put all in doubt. This Wellsian summary of Edwardianism opposes another view of the decade, which regards it as a golden autumn or endless afternoon, an unchanging era of comfortable certainties, economic abundance, high-minded but flexible social rules, and above all unhurried leisure—a single long country-house weekend from Edward's coronation to his passing and, beyond that, to the guns of August. Such a view of the period, what C. S. Lewis might call the "dangerous sense" of the word "Edwardian," does not survive even a cursory reading of its books, but it has persisted because it has been congenial to later generations.[7] It has allowed them to feel superior to Edwardian selfishness, somnolence, and snobbery, while at the same time providing them with a refuge from political violence and confusion. The version of social history accompanying nostalgic Edwardianism is not in fact the most misleading thing about it, for the class which kept servants and perhaps lived chiefly on the earnings of shares did have an abundance of time and money rare before or afterward. Comfortably situated Edwardians could look back on a century of economic and intellectual strenuousness and feel ready to enjoy "a keener search for personal pleasure," as Canon Samuel Barnett wrote in 1897, "a disposition to enjoy our forefathers' savings."[8] But not all Edwardians were *rentiers* or comfortably situated. They were also the desperately poor encountered in Galsworthy's *A Commentary* (1908), the urban riff-raff of Conrad's *The Secret Agent* (1907), and the pushy climbers of Wells's books.

The dangerous illusion is that the Edwardian era can be comprehended by a single myth or mood or symbol, can be perfectly understood and so reproduced as a painter reproduces a landscape consistent in all its parts or as a novelist composes a period setting. Something like this illusion underlies Victoria Sackville-West's *The Edwardians* (1930), which attempts to comprehend the decade by describing the manners, affectations, and evasions of one social class. It takes as its field of action that characteristically "Edwardian" scene, a country-house party in 1905. The house, Chevron, offers pleasures in an Edwardian abundance: food and drink, bridge, flirtation, political gossip, or alternatively the placid continuity of a settled agricultural order where there are no hard-to-place Londoners, no Jewish financiers, no women of the King's Smart Set, but rather the gamekeeper and blacksmith, secretary and scullery maid, farm laborer and upper servant, each keeping his place and contributing his efforts to the maintenance of the whole structure. That this order of things should be unchangeably upheld becomes the task of Sebastian, the son of the house. Along with Chevron he inherits certain obligations—trying to make the land pay, courting a dull woman of good family, carrying on a series of love affairs with predictably disillusioning results. By the novel's end he is almost committed to a life exactly like those of his forefathers, but at the last moment he is saved by an outsider, the explorer Anquetil, who plucks him out of England to a three-years' expedition abroad. Sebastian's escape is a personal victory, a release from conventions that would have stifled him. Yet what he leaves behind is the moral center of the book. Chevron's autumnal grandeurs more than compensate for the heir's defection and its own smugness and hypocrisy. Sackville-West affects to criticize the country-house world she has created, but she dwells in it with loving forbearance.

The Edwardians simplifies a decade which was less ignorant and more critical than it implies. It also simplifies the Edwardian novels of which it is an imitation. Only one or two characters in Edwardian fiction, such as Roger Naldrett in John Masefield's *Multitude and Solitude* (1909), do what Sebastian does, which is to react against one role imposed on him by helplessly accepting another, for which he is spectacularly unqualified. Significantly more Edwardian characters see change, not permanency, as the essential social fact of their time; they define their relation to change by a conscious choice of old or new roles; and they avoid entrapment by altering their expectations, not by escaping to the jungle. Into the group fall Wells's Dick Remington and George Ponderevo (*Tono-Bungay*), Galsworthy's Richard Shelton (*The Island Pharisees*), and perhaps Bennett's Clayhanger (*Clayhanger* and *Hilda Lessways*). These characters are "doubtful" in Wells's sense of the word; they are properly Balfourian and properly Edwardian.

As for the country house and its weekend parties, it unquestionably appears in novels of 1901-1910, often as opulently as it does in *The Edwardians*, but the most genuinely Edwardian house party of all happened in fact, not fiction. To celebrate Christmas 1899 and the coming of the new century, the American novelist Stephen Crane and his wife Cora invited a large party of guests, including Wells and his wife, to Brede Place, a magnificent but antique manor near Rye. The Cranes had been lent the house and perhaps were unaware of its limitations as a place for entertainment, for they invited far too many guests for the available bedrooms, and most of the crowd had to bring their own bedding and be accommodated in makeshift dormitories. Sanitary facilities were also limited, and accessible only through what became the Girls' Dormitory, so that in the morning, Wells remembers in his *Experiment in Autobiography*, the wintry countryside "was dotted with wandering melancholy, preoccupied, men guests." The party was "an extraordinary lark": dancing, reveling each night till two or three, literary conversation, late breakfasts of beer, eggs, bacon, and sweet potatoes from America, an improvised ghost play in the hall.[9] This gathering at Brede indicates the mood of the decade to follow: the inheritance from the past is casually accepted and haphazardly adapted to new conditions; the conventions are in part observed, in part ignored in a new spirit of social freedom; an enlivening American influence makes itself felt; and over all there reigns a spirit of adventure, of new wine about to burst old bottles. There is even, to complicate the spirit of adventure as it was regularly complicated throughout the succeeding decade, a sharp, intermittent sense of melancholy, brought about in this case by the awareness that Crane was too sick to live much longer.

The Cranes' party is a symbolic moment—almost a public declaration of Edwardianism. There is an equivalent moment, though on a more intimate scale, in a dinner party which took place toward the end of the decade. This also comes to us through Wells. At the dinner party—described in *The New Machiavelli* as happening at "Lord Tarvrille's" but occurring in fact at Harry Cust's, the editor of the *Pall Mall Gazette*—the upper stories of the house catch fire and the guests go on with their meal.[10] Sparks fly, water cascades from the ceiling, the drips being caught in bowls, the servants hand round bath towels with the port, but the conversation never lags.[11] "Talk so interesting that the dinner went on, though Cust was obliged to absent himself for a few minutes . . . Talk to accompaniment of engine throbs, swishing, tramping etc. Guests obliged to move table further up room out of puddles. Dinner lasted until midnight in dining-room, when they went to drawing room to view the place gutted."[12] Superficially a comment on English *sangfroid* or pigheadedness in the face of calamity, the party actually testifies, and is so treated in Wells's novel, to the excitement of new ideas. The dinner guests keep up the ritual not for its own sake but because it permits them to talk, and by talk they firmly believe they will come to an understanding of change.

Edwardians without country houses or dinner parties yet had to hand a convenient, cheap medium for the exchange of ideas. The Edwardian novel was uniquely suited to the intellectual spring Wells saw going on about him. It could analyze the "tightening and extending" social organization; it could expose outmoded standards of conduct; and above all it could dramatize the questioning of "the faiths upon which men's lives and associations are based"—old faiths held on to confidently or desperately, new faiths formulated for the new century. From the writer's point of view, the novel, "so flexible in form, so all-embracing in theme," was the natural outlet of expression for a time with "tremendously complex social needs and interrelations," in Richard Burton's words of 1902.[13] For its vast army of readers, fiction was the most familiar means of learning to cope with change—though it succeeded best in this task when it avoided direct lecturing and relied on its familiar devices of humor, pathos, satire, romance, and suspense. Best-sellers, to be sure, confirmed prejudices and insisted on old pieties; but the Edwardians' best fiction forced them to examine, however reluctantly, the ideas by which they lived. It awakened new feelings, but through accustomed and therefore effective methods: it concentrated on character and so affirmed their deep-seated belief that ideas mattered only in relation to people. It usually supplied a narrative progress from complication to solution, thereby suggesting that the experience of living was comprehensible, if not always happy or educative. That an Edwardian heroine married at the end of a novel might substantiate old ideas about feminine purity or furnish another way to admire the New Woman, depending on the handling of heroine and matrimony, but it would always imply that human affairs, in fiction as in life, formed understandable patterns. In an era of rapid change such patterns were highly valued, and if patterns were sometimes wrongly interpreted, that might be the fault of the reader as much as the novel. Galsworthy's *The Man of Property* (1906) is set in the 1880s, so its hero Soames Forsyte has no acquaintance with Edwardian novels, but it is unlikely that any fictional treatment of

10

marriage could unsettle the cold egotism which makes Soames's wife Irene hate him. Rather, his reading provides an automatic corroboration of his marital tactics: "Like most novel readers of his generation (and Soames was a great novel reader), literature coloured his view of life; and he had imbibed the belief that it was only a question of time. In the end the husband always gained the affection of his wife."[14] No Edwardian reader could believe that after finishing Galsworthy's book. No Edwardian reader of Wells or Forster, James or Conrad, could come away from his reading with all his prejudices intact, all his faiths confirmed.

2

From Personality to Personality

The Edwardian period began with the writing of obituaries for Queen Victoria. Her passing was deplored in solemn poetic phrase and symbolically interpreted as the passing of an era—for once, not a cliché, but an accurate historical judgment.[1] The old sovereign was the past, and the new sovereign, as he made clear immediately, was the future. There were changes in Edward VII's court: a new sophistication and cosmopolitanism, a relaxation of domestic proprieties, and a vastly expanded range of royal pleasures to emulate or admire from afar. At this moment of change, the old century, by coincidence, changed to the new, encouraging further retrospection and prophecy. Englishmen who thought about national affairs could see in the Boer War, which had been going on since 1899 and was to continue until May 1902, a turning-point in the history of the empire. Yet they could agree on no general lesson to be absorbed from its mismanaged early battles or from its later strategies, successful but morally tainted, of farm burning and concentration camps. Something in the national spirit was changed, the English noted in diaries and speeches, but what the change was they could not easily say, even with the aid of prompt histories by Arthur Conan Doyle and the bitter war stories of Rudyard Kipling.[2]

No comparable event, symbolic or actual, marks the beginning of Edwardian fiction, nor any significant debut; Wells, Conrad, Bennett, and Galsworthy had all published their first work before 1900. Moreover, there were well-established novelists, from Henry James at one extreme of ambition and achievement to Hall Caine at the other, whose Edwardian books seemed indistinguishable from their books of the 1890s. James's art had indeed broadened and deepened with the publication of *The Wings of the Dove* in 1902, but most readers were so baffled by the style he had been elaborating since *What Maisie Knew* in 1897 that they failed to recognize the changed scope of the last three novels.

Writing in 1907, the belle-lettrist Osbert Burdett begins his study *The Last Ten Years of English Literature* with the dictum that literature does not pass from period to period but from personality to personality, and he suggests Oscar Wilde's death in 1900 as a starting-point for the writing of the new age. With Wilde's death, according to Burdett, decadence became a worn-out fashion, the mannerism of a clique. But he also remarks that Wilde's paradoxical style was passed on intact to the Edwardian G. K. Chesterton.[3] Such period-blurring observations are standard in turn-of-the-century criticism, which had no theoretical commitment to innovation *per se*—Burdett complains bitterly of the "malady of modernism"—and which liked to help readers by connecting the old with the new, the familiar with the strange.

The connections were easy enough to make. Consistently in matters of form and occasionally in matters of substance Edwardian literature was continuous with the writing of the past, even the immediate past, which for the Georgians and the self-consciously modernist writers of the 1920s became a burden or irrelevance. Lytton Strachey quietly belittled a whole century by showing, in *Eminent Victorians* (1918), exactly what personal eccentricities and moral compromises in Cardinal Manning or Florence Nightingale went to make up Victorian eminence; the young T. S. Eliot dissociated himself from Tennysonianism; Ezra Pound bid farewell to "old Hippety-hop o' the accents," Browning; D. H. Lawrence scorned the old stable ego of character; but H. G. Wells, the apostle of the new as the Edwardian decade began, modeled much of his science fiction on the productions of George Chetwynd Griffith, the late-Victorian author of imperial, adventure, and scientific romances, including *The Outlaws of the Air* (1895), which had a direct effect on Wells's *The War in the Air* (1908). Wells confessed the debt, by having his heroes read Griffith. He turned to books when his imagination, resourceful and free-ranging as it was, could not keep pace with his compulsion to publish—a compulsion producing some seventeen books during the Edwardian years.

Other, less driven writers turned to the past for inspiration rather than material. Kipling, for instance, who seemed to Henry James to spring out of nowhere, an "infant monster," sprang actually from Walter Besant's *All in a Garden Fair* (1883), which Kipling credits with rescuing him from depression, providing him with a model of artistic creativity ("a young man who desired to write; who came to realise the possibilities of common things seen, and who eventually succeeded in his desire"), and sending him away from India to measure himself against "the doorsills of London."[4] In a more general way Kipling acknowledged the help his parents—especially his father, the accomplished draftsman and curator of Indian art John Lockwood Kipling—had given him. Another who did so was the novelist William Babington Maxwell, who testified that "Most of the knowledge I possess of how to write . . . and, indeed, the fact that I commenced to write at all, I owe to my mother"—the mother being M. E. Braddon, the Victorian sensation novelist.[5] Though the Edwardian period saw the publication of Samuel Butler's *The Way of All Flesh* (1903) and Edmund Gosse's *Father and Son* (1907), it was not entirely unfilial.

The discoverer of the vein Mrs. Braddon mined so profitably, Wilkie Collins, died well within the Victorian period, in 1889, but his concoctions of mystery, crime, and sensation continued to be produced by Edwardians, especially by E. Phillips Oppenheim, who became still more successful than Collins by toning down his grotesqueries and emphasizing the glamorous settings in which his heroines were threatened and intrigues carried on. With Oppenheim, continuity results less from a sharing of tastes than from a calculated duplication for commercial purposes. He identified a best-selling genre and set out to adapt it for the contemporary market.

Dickens, a more overwhelming novelistic personality than

Collins, found not a few Edwardian disciples. After a life devoted to scholarship and ceramics William De Morgan in 1906, at the age of sixty-seven, suddenly published *Joseph Vance: An Ill-Written Autobiography*, and followed it with *Alice-for-Short* in 1907. These two sentimental and tediously whimsical novels reveal how Dickens could be misunderstood in the first years of the century, despite excellent critical studies by George Gissing (1898) and G. K. Chesterton (1906). They are exercises in family cheerfulness, Cockney vitality, and colorful, essentially virtuous poverty, and though they are in no sense trivial or formulistic, they fail utterly to reproduce Dickens' sense of evil and imaginative boldness. They are entertainments and so suited to those Edwardian readers, perhaps a majority, who preferred Dickens' humor to his social vision, failing to see that the targets of his anger were still in business—the Circumlocution Office now installed in the War Department, Mr. Podsnap reincarnated in the Lord Chamberlain's Examiner of Plays—and who, led by a new school of slum-visiting Gradgrinds, wanted their social criticism to be based on hard fact, preferably statistical, not the imagination.

What was admired and imitated, in the case of Dickens, was a manner. The "Dickensian" spirit of humor and pathos could be applied to plots and locales Dickens himself had not attempted, and when it was so applied by writers of some originality, it could be stimulating rather than constricting, a way of freeing the imagination. Chesterton's skill in manipulating comic caricatures, his verbal flamboyance, his underlying sentimentality, and perhaps his dark and tumultuous London owe something to Dickens, though the resemblances tend to be less visible than Chesterton's own idiosyncrasies—the taste for paradox and medievalism, the obsessive need to portray obsession. Dickens' eccentrics have their *idées fixes*, such as King Charles's head or Mr. F's Aunt's misanthropy, but these are comic props: Chesterton's characters are wholly defined by delusions that turn into *beaux mensonges*. "Humanity as a whole is changeful, mystical, fickle, delightful," writes Chesterton in *The Napoleon of Notting*

15

Hill (1902), and with all the adjectives except "mystical" Dickens would have agreed.[6]

Wells was more comprehensively indebted to Dickens, in part because, like Shaw, he understood Dickens' radicalism more thoroughly than Chesterton or other writers, in part because he was so much like Dickens in personality. He learned from the older novelist much as George Eliot learned from Jane Austen or Henry James from Turgenev, in a respectful apprenticeship that was really a form of self-discovery. Wells and Dickens shared a hatred for social restraints, a distrust for established power whether in the entrenched bureaucrat or the meddling reformer, an enormous ambition to reach over the mechanisms of government and touch the public directly, and a general agreement on the means fiction ought to use to achieve its ends. For example, they believed in imaginative freedom for its own sake, an improvisatory method of working, and an occasional outburst of authorial anger, even at the cost of a loose formal structure—the fluid puddings and baggy monsters that James deplored. This generous conception of fictional form explains some of what Wells meant when he spoke of his determination to make *Kipps* (1905) a "great novel on the Dickens plan"—that is, an unfettered work of the imagination which would be allowed to make discoveries as it went along.[7] Wells and Dickens were attuned to the popular taste. They were eager to adapt for their work features of the new literary forms of their day—detective fiction for Dickens, scientific romance for Wells. Sharing similar backgrounds of middling poverty, casual schooling, and parental irresponsibility alternating with bouts of fierce control, they formed their novels around similar plots of entrapment and escape, and employed a similar range of characters: servants, impecunious schoolmasters, small shopkeepers, journalists, middle-class parents, and rebellious offspring. "It is a pity you will keep up this foolishness about Dickens," Wells writes to Bennett in 1901, meaning that Bennett cannot be convinced of Dickens' greatness and potential helpfulness to young authors trying to forge a fictional style.[8] Bennett stayed foolish; he had a genuine preference for French literature and a provincial's dislike of being thought indebted to a novelist as unsophisticated and English as Dickens.

Dickens had been dead thirty years by the turn of the century. The figure of Thomas Hardy stood much closer to the Edwardians, though indeed he had ceased writing novels after *Jude the Obscure* in 1895, having earned enough money by then to return to writing poetry.[9] Hardy tantalized the Edwardians with his fictional silence and challenged them to imitation. Their failure to respond successfully, whereas they had flourished by imitating Dickens, shows that Hardy was not so easy to understand as Dickens, or all too easy to understand in a limited way. Edwardian writers copied what they could see in Hardy, his recording of passionate experience in a picturesque rural setting. Mary P. Willcocks' *A Man of Genius* (1908) is about the coast of North Devon—a part of Wessex Hardy had obligingly neglected—in the same sense that *The Return of the Native* is about Egdon Heath. It chronicles the rise to prominence of Ambrose Velly, whose triple allegiance to his art, his family, and his passions suggests the story's classical subtitle, *A Story of the Judgment of Paris,* and generates the chief conflicts of the plot.

Velly is a Jude who starts with a few material advantages and eventually succeeds in life, his aspiration being to architecture rather than scholarship or divinity. He is a hero of considerable complexity torn, like Jude, between two more simply drawn heroines, the passionate Thyrza Braund and the educated Damaris Westaway. Thyrza unthinkingly accepts the workaday realities of her life and believes in folk ritual; Damaris wants to rise above her lot but falls victim to the disease of modernism. Unable to find a conventional outlet for her energies, she eventually returns Thyrza to Velly and settles for a renunciatory, spiritual relationship to the now famous architect. In his masterpiece, an oratory, she sees a shining star of hope, and on that vague note of decorous joy the novel ends, as far from Hardy's spirit as possible. Most of *A Man of Genius* is superior to its ending, and Willcocks reproduces with considerable skill those aspects of

Hardy which are incidental and reproducible, such as an interest in rural churches, the use of dialect, a chatty knowingness about folklore, a taste for classical allusion, but her novel inevitably follows the bent of her own mind, which is pious and sentimental, rather than Hardy's, which is skeptical and passionately angry about the limits placed on human happiness. Jude's architectural masterpiece—the only one he is permitted to build—is the Christminster colleges done in gingerbread cakes, and in *Tess of the D'Urbervilles* the stars shine down, not with hope on a woman's renunciation, but with frosty indifference on her suffering.

Eden Phillpotts' Dartmoor novels are as comprehensive of their region as Hardy's of Wessex. They circle around and around its heaths, isolated farm cottages, and granite tors, seeming to exhaust all the possibilities of passion it contains at a pace too slow for any single work. *The Secret Woman* (1905), a novel extravagantly admired by the young Arnold Bennett ("fine, classical, and indeed great"), is representative of the whole series.[10] It is a story of weak fathers and strong daughters on the pattern of *Tess*, of rivalry in love between father and son, of hidden guilt on the part of the "secret woman" and of final tearful repentance —all told with scrupulous attention to local institutions, accents, and ways of life. Its set pieces of landscape description have a certain authority, even though the novel opens with a learned simile more awkward than any Hardy attempted: Dartmoor is "many-breasted as Artemis of the Ephesians; but since her bosom is of granite, we compare her more properly to that other Diana of the Greeks, sister of Apollo, she who in her virgin lap brings blessings." Yet Phillpotts, like Willcocks, never attempts Hardy's placement of characters against a landscape that carries symbolic meaning—that mirrors or contrasts sardonically with their mood, dramatizes their sense of freedom or bewilderment, or makes obvious their isolation. Hardy's heir in this symbolic technique was Conrad, as in the scene of Marlow's leaving Lord Jim in Patusan, the latter's white face and clothes shining against the jungle and dark sky. Phillpotts' placement of characters in the scene is more apt to be tritely moralizing: "While Salome, with a primrose between her lips, heard love in the dingles of Halstock, her sister walked steadily along to a trying ordeal."[11] The other great power in Hardy, missing in both Willcocks and Phillpotts, is a sensitivity to time and change. Hardy's Wessex is never pastoral, invulnerable, or unconnected with the rest of England. On the contrary, it is shown as being invaded by railways, raw new buildings, new agricultural machines and methods—in short, as being altered out of recognition by industrialism. Admittedly, as late as 1905 Dartmoor was in comparison with most of Wessex untouched by industrialism, but Phillpotts' treatment of it as much as its actual barrenness keeps it inviolate in the novels. Like Willcocks' North Devon or Sackville-West's Chevron, it is a region of the mind deliberately kept unchanged for the pleasure of readers needing fictional retreats. Phillpotts and other fictionalizers of the quaint lived in a decade when the industrializing process Hardy described had been accomplished, and the need of their time was precisely for an escape, temporary and artificial though it might be, from the consequences of that process.

The House with Green Shutters (1901), by the Scottish novelist George Douglas, is arguably the best single Edwardian novel in the Hardy manner. For one thing it displays a personal style of its own in the description of setting and especially of character. Douglas pursues his fictional premises to their conclusions without much regard for conventional expectations. Consequently he is sometimes crude or awkward, as Hardy was, but the crudities stem from the effort to say something original. The novel is a lowland Scottish version of The Mayor of Casterbridge, an eventually tragic study of the downfall of John Gourlay, a bullying carter who makes himself master of a small town, encounters opposition, overextends himself, and is finally murdered by his son in a drunken fit. At this point the tragedy topples over into melodrama. The son, pursued after the crime by his father's vengeful eyes, kills himself; the sister, dying of tuberculosis, kills herself; the mother, dying of cancer, kills herself. The working

19

out of retribution becomes ludicrously relentless, but at least in its grim finale the novel avoids the sentimentalism of the Kailyard School of J. M. Barrie, Ian Maclaren, and S. R. Crockett, which at the end of the nineteenth century threatened to romanticize the English view of Scotland permanently. Bennett comments on this fact in a letter of 1901: "You see Scotland in it [Douglas's novel] for the first time in your life."[12]

This turn of phrase occurred repeatedly in the letters and essays of the Edwardians as they tried to explain what they found exciting about the literature of their period. Seeing Scotland "for the first time" was more important for Bennett than seeing the influence of Hardy or anyone else, and this preference was general for the decade. Young writers would not deny the fact of continuity—Bennett acknowledged on many occasions the debt he owed to nineteenth-century French novelists—but what struck them above all, in their own work or that of others, was the feat of presenting a new reality. The Edwardian tendency was to look beyond matters of style, influence, and form to the substance of fiction. Although this tendency produced some formless books, some unconscious and therefore clumsy imitations of older writers, it produced also the most original fiction of the period.

3

Continuities of Form

In Willcocks' *A Man of Genius* Damaris Westaway has one other consolation besides admiring Velly from afar. She writes a novel called *A Man of Genius,* and Velly, "though no critic," recognizes as the "peculiar quality" of the work "its insistence on the movement of life, on its changing life and shadows. Just as colours in the *plein air* school of painting shift and wane on the solid shapes of the landscape, so the characters of *A Man of Genius* shone through varying lights, unlike the solid entities of the Victorian novelists."[1] Willcocks presumably hoped readers would recognize these qualities in her own novel, for there are signs throughout of her identification with Damaris, but the novel as written hardly displays them. Among Edwardian novels, *A Man of Genius* is unusual in commenting on itself, but typical in its conservatism of method.[2] Like dozens of other fictions of the period, it describes exactly those scenes the readers expected to have described and omits nothing obligatory. Its chapters are of a conventional length and end with customary devices of resolution or suspense. It alternates in a regular way between description and dialogue. It is interested in telling the story effectively and intelligently, not in presenting variously misleading or revealing points of view. It is, in short, as solid as Hardy or any other Victorian novelist in its handling of character and its rendering of the "movement of life" by the means closest to hand, the movement of plot; and if the varying lights of fictional impressionism sometimes play over its surface, they do not obscure the firm outlines, studied composition, and forthright coloring of the whole. Victorian portraiture makes as just an analogy to *A Man of Genius* as does the *plein air* school.

The general continuity of method between Victorian and Edwardian fiction arises from an attitude to fiction-making shared by most practitioners, not just by journeymen like Willcocks. It is an attitude of caution, modesty, and self-imposed discipline, and it rests on a complex of assumptions, largely unexplored but nonetheless influential, about the differences between narrative and other forms of literature, the rate at which literary methods ought to change, the peculiarly English qualities of the novel, and the relation between fiction and its marketplace. Why should the methods of fiction change, any number of Edwardian novelists might have asked, when fiction was so conspicuously successful in its aim of interpreting real life? Why change the narrative devices used by admired novelists of the recent past and adaptable, as far as anyone could see, to new circumstances and subjects? Why import a foreign liking for theory into an act as simple and natural as telling a story? Why risk misunderstanding when the rewards of communication were so great? Why tamper with a form almost universally acknowledged to be the characteristic and dominant one of its time?

Certainty about the answers to these questions could and did lead to absurdities, such as the belief that the methods of fiction had been discovered once and for all and thus could be summarized and taught in the form of a handbook; Walter Besant's *The Pen and the Book* (1899) was one such handbook. But certainty about fiction could also lead to a confidence in writing, an assurance of being understood, which was the right of hacks, who interpreted technical conservatism as reliance on formula, and serious novelists alike. Despite some minority critical views, despite the manifest achievement of Continental novelists whom Arnold Bennett, George Moore, Ford Madox Ford, Maurice Baring, and Henry James were laboring to introduce to England, and despite the obvious changes going on in the organization of their society, Edwardian novelists went on organizing and narrating their books more or less as nineteenth century writers had done. A few Edwardians might regret the traditionalism and wish for innovation, but they would not actively dispute the fact that the Victorians knew what a novel was and could be. Even E. M. Forster, after writing four Edwardian novels which in method do not break with the past (as *A Passage to India* would do in 1924), generalizes in *Aspects of the Novel*, a little sadly, that the novel tells a story.

The contemporary sense of what a novel does has been enormously complicated and expanded, and it is now difficult to read Edwardian fiction without wishing for more experimentation in form—more Balfourian structures for containing the Balfourian age. After Virginia Woolf and D. H. Lawrence, Bennett and Galsworthy seem plain, even though their plainness is the result of a consciously limited technique, not of limited imagination or the factual obsessions of a dull decade, as is sometimes claimed. The plainness derives from a technique deliberately limiting itself to proven narrative methods for fear of upsetting the implied fictional contract between writer and reader.

Perhaps this is a matter for regret. It is certainly a pity that Bennett, who in *The Old Wives' Tale* did all he could with the naturalistic novel on the French model, failed to negotiate other fictional contracts and experiment with other modes of serious fiction. That he had the imaginative resources for such experimentation is shown by fantasias like *The Grand Babylon Hotel* (1902) which, slick though they are, suggest what he might have done with the form of the symbolic fable. Somewhere inside Bennett there was a sardonic *Zuleika Dobson* or a provincial *Secret Agent* waiting to be written. Wells's situation was also regrettable, especially to Wells himself. He was never quite comfortable with the fictional forms he knew he had mastered, his chafing against their limitations being particularly clear in the preface to *A Modern Utopia* (1905). Wells's book reviews of 1895-1897 show him thinking hard about the contemporary state of the art of fiction.[3] But this thinking gained him more frustration than certainty, and he failed to devise a fictional form, improved if not actually utopian, for his new fictional purposes.

This improved form might have coped with his discursiveness and his acute sense of character, which come too often into conflict in his books or have to be relegated to separate sections.

Yet regrets of this sort about Edwardian fiction are essentially irrelevant. Novelists of the period should not be condemned for missing opportunities which can be read back into the artistic situation; they need to be judged on their own merits, which are those of writers skillfully exploiting well-understood techniques. Would dislocations of time, for instance, necessarily improve *The Old Wives' Tale?* The chief virtue of Bennett's novel is that it is told plainly; the fictional devices employed, such as patterns of contrast, balancing slow narrative with rapid summary, and the finding of significance in seemingly trivial details, are matched exactly to the quality of Bennett's creative imagination. The novel could not be narrated in a more Jamesian or Joycean way without losing its integrity, the integrity of a scrupulously honest mind determined to say all it can about the ordinariness of life. Or in Galsworthy's case, should one wish for *ficelles* in his novels, given the expert control of tone and management of scene he displays in his undisguised authorial commentary? The answers to these questions seem obvious, but not a few later critics have wanted to rewrite Edwardian novels in another mode, somewhat in the manner of Henry James wanting to rewrite the novels of Wells, while at the same time claiming that such a wish was the highest form of praise he could bestow. Or they have simply left writers like Bennett, Wells, and Galsworthy out of discussions of novelistic form. In *The Craft of Fiction* (1921) Percy Lubbock regularized James's working methods into a manual of discipline, but to do so, he had to ignore Edwardian writers other than James, because he could not take them on their own terms.

Edwardian novelists need to be taken on individual terms, because some were more interested in the purely formal management of their art than others, and a few were determined not to be plain at all. Consider the most basic principle of the novel, the fact, as Forster puts it, that it tells a story. Edwardian fiction is

24

patently constrained to tell a story and organized around a definite plot. One of the salient traits of the middle-brow fiction of
the decade is its procrustean ability to shape the most recondite
and refractory materials into conventionally plotted novels
which end, as likely as not, with the obligatory wedding-bells
and even an occasional pronouncement that the hero and heroine are destined to live happily ever after. But in a few Edwardian novels a struggle against the tyranny of the plot takes place,
and though this struggle was not victorious by 1910—no more
so than the struggle for women's suffrage or the Irish struggle for
Home Rule—it was an important phenomenon of the time.

There are three varieties of struggle against the tyranny of
plot. The first is a "struggle" only in the most figurative sense.
This is the tendency to admit more into a novel than can be comprehended in a conventional plot; that is, to be digressive, essay-
istic, and faithful only to the wayward impressions of the author.
"Impressions" is the key term. In the Oxford Chancellor's Essay
for 1905 Alexander Maxwell surveys the "Condition and Pros-
pects of Imaginative Literature at the Present Day" and declares
that the novel is the dominant form of literary expression, that
realism in its exaggerated form ("as Zola conceived it") is dead,
and that it has been largely replaced by "impressionism," by
which is meant not the shifting lights of Willcocks' *plein air*
school, nor yet the allegiance to memory rather than fact that
Ford Madox Ford would champion in his reminiscences, but the
modern novelist's relative freedom from plot. Modern novels,
Maxwell says, are not stories but studies, and their interest lies
less in the movement of the tale than in the representation of
character and society. The modern novelist, no longer being
bound by plot, is able to deal with life in isolated phrases, to assume all shapes and moods and tongues.[4] The Edwardian im-
pressionists in this sense are E. V. Lucas, Leonard Merrick,
Walter de la Mare in *The Return* (1910), Wells on occasion, and
pre-eminently George Gissing in *The Private Papers of Henry
Ryecroft* (1903), where action is almost entirely replaced by
reverie and speculation. The worst that can be said of these ami-

able books is that they lack ambition. Their authors seem casually unaware of getting by without a plot, since plot and other matters of structure are less important to them than the veracity of their judgments or the fineness of their phrasing.

The second type of struggle against the tyranny of plot in Edwardian novels actively contends against the limits of a conventional narrative, or against the reader's expectation of such a thing. In *Nostromo* Conrad distorts the time scale of his story so as to avoid the pattern of suspense and resolution associated with ordinary adventure plots; in *Howards End* Forster makes the wedding-bells come awkwardly early for the characters and the reader; in *The Island Pharisees* Galsworthy insists that what is important is what does *not* happen; in *The Napoleon of Notting Hill* Chesterton replaces the cause-and-effect sequence of plot with the principled whimsy of his imagination, in a large-scale paradox to match the small-scale stylistic paradoxes going on all the time in his prose. In these novels thematic meaning is conveyed by the formal device of conspicuously avoiding a formal device. The lack of an ordinary plot is meant to wrench the reader's understanding into new channels, which means in Conrad's novel that the reader is to share the author's skepticism about the significance of events as mere events, and in Galsworthy's that he is to see how problems of society are too large for ordinary devices of resolution. Conrad and Galsworthy can attempt such indirection only because they are writing for an audience expecting a plot. Their irregularity stands out sharply against a "standard" background of regularity, a fact linking them with Edwardian playwrights and poets, who benefit equally from being in a position to defeat expectations and depart tellingly from the conventional, as Shaw does in the provocative length of *Man and Superman* (1903) and Ezra Pound in the rhythms of *Personae* and *Exultations* (1909).

The third and most interesting type of Edwardian struggle against the tyranny of plot shifts attention away from the narrative to the narration, implying that the most challenging human problem is not how to act but how to understand, how to know, and how to communicate. These works focus on the drama of the telling. They are the achievement most conspicuously of James, whose prefaces to the New York Edition catalogue the ways in which meaning may be captured by the appropriate fictional consciousness and reflected to the reader, and whose three great Edwardian novels—*The Wings of the Dove, The Ambassadors* (1903), and *The Golden Bowl* (1904)—dispense with all but the politest outward conflict in order to concentrate on the all-absorbing inner conflict between what is felt and what is known, what is known and what is revealed, and what is revealed and what is the truth.

If other Edwardians lacked James's specific ambition, which was to discover and expound a whole theory of narration, they at least shared his fascination with the personal and artistic difficulties of knowing. Wells's fascination is apparent in George Ponderevo, the narrator of *Tono-Bungay* (1909), who knows that the process of remembering his past is inevitably a process of selective interpretation and distortion. The Ponderevo who writes the novel never lets the reader forget that he is "creating" the youthful Ponderevo as he goes along; *Tono-Bungay* is thus the Edwardian version of *Great Expectations*.[5] Anthony Hope, the author in the 1890s of *The Prisoner of Zenda* and *Rupert of Hentzau*, published an Edwardian novel, *The Great Miss Driver* (1908), which illustrates the distinction between mere plot and plot as the creation of a characterized narrator, in this case the ironical male secretary to the powerful and unconventional heiress of the title. E. V. Lucas' *Listener's Lure: An Oblique Narration* (1906) is an epistolary novel as subtly constructed as the subtitle asserts. It reveals in delicate stages of hesitancy and commitment how a middle-aged man allows himself to realize he is falling in love with a younger woman.

The Great Miss Driver, Listener's Lure, and *The Golden Bowl* represent vastly different achievements, but merely as novels, they share the need for an organizing factor or motive force. Thus from none of them does plot disappear entirely. The full-length novel could not escape a certain conventionality in form, simply because it was full-length. As it represented a major investment of time and artistic imagination, it had to rely on a tested and familiar structure. More experimentation of all sorts was possible in shorter fiction. Because the short story or tale or "blest nouvelle" was conceived as a single, consistent work of art, it tended to give its practitioners an unusual awareness of formal possibilities—possibilities, say, of circular structure, symbolic patterning, the hastening of pace Ford called *progession d'effet*, abrupt openings and closings, or simply a sharpened critical consciousness about telling, about narration itself. The most rewarding Edwardian experimentation involved the drama of the telling in a quite literal and specific sense. The teller, no longer a disembodied voice, was given shape and character and often a good deal more: prejudices, sensitivities, a realistically presented understanding that speculated boldly into the mysterious sources of action or broke off in doubt. Furthermore, the teller was made to speak not into the void but to a group of listeners: men sitting and smoking quietly on a verandah in the dark, people on a boat, a circle of genteel guests around a drawing-room fire, three soldiers waiting idly on a hilltop and trying unsuccessfully to fight off boredom with a story. The Edwardians, that is, favored tales framed not by some fictionalized provenance—the discovery of a manuscript in an old chest, a written confession, a recovered bundle of documents—but rather by the fictionalized circumstances of its telling. The substantive story is merely "overheard" by the reader.

The Edwardians hardly invented this variety of the frame-tale, but they exploited it brilliantly. It suited their taste for assimilating and perfecting the techniques of the past, and it allowed them to link perceptiveness with character, much as the dramatic monologue had allowed Victorian poets to link moral consciousness with circumstance. Above all, it permitted them to acknowledge, perhaps even to mourn, the passing of a particular kind of human simplicity. According to the German critic Walter Benjamin, writing in 1936, the art of storytelling had come to be more and more remote from the experience of modern man; the storyteller himself was a distant figure, the inhabitant of a lost past in which it was still possible to exchange experiences and give counsel. Although the First World War was the ultimate cause of the storyteller's decline, because it dramatically devalued the store of human wisdom and sent its participants home "silent—not richer, but poorer in communicable experience," there were earlier, more literary causes, including the rise of the novel and of printed information in general, the widespread dissemination of information, and the growing complexity of life that stories had to reflect.[6] Edwardian Englishmen were so placed in history as to be forced to see these early changes and the resulting decline of the storyteller with particular clarity. They noted, partly because Hardy had made it one of his subjects, the lapse of communal memory. They witnessed events inaccessible to older forms of understanding. They grew to distrust the speaking voice, which might lie or twist reality to suit its own purposes; they were psychologists and beginning to be moral relativists. They lost faith in wisdom as their fathers had lost faith in God.

For all these reasons they knew that the simple act of exchanging experience between people could no longer serve their purposes. In their time storytelling became a lost art, and they reacted to the loss with a complex art of their own, or of their own perfecting—the narrative frame-tale. Over and over again in these Edwardian fictions the encounter between speaker and listener is fixed in permanent language, as if to demonstrate to future generations that people once spun tales while others listened, while at the same time the relation between the frame and its tale is complicated with ironies or psychological nuances required by the intellectual situation. The frame-tale permitted Edwardians to be simple and sophisticated at the same time, to be nostalgic and up-to-date; it allowed them to preserve what they knew was ceasing to be possible. When in 1908 Henry James looked back on the origin of one of his best-known frame-tales, "The Turn of the Screw" (1898), he noted that it was written at a time when the "beautiful lost form" of the ghost story or

29

the fairy tale seemed unavailable to the serious artist. The charm of those things "for the distracted modern mind" was "the clear field of experience . . . over which we are thus led to roam; an annexed but independent world in which nothing is right save as we rightly imagine it." No one would call James's mind distracted, but he knew he was living in a morally and psychologically cluttered world, and so in "The Turn of the Screw" he made no attempt to provide a "clear field of experience," a ghost story pure and simple. He provided instead a deliberately ambiguous story of a strained consciousness which might produce ghosts, and he surrounded the whole "sinister romance" with an imagined narrative scene. He made "The Turn of the Screw" a frame-tale: a complicated thing posing as a simple thing, an "excursion into chaos" which yet remained, "like Blue-Beard and Cinderella, but an anecdote."[7] There is no clearer statement of the double opportunity, for looking backward and looking forward, provided in the Edwardian frame-tale.

As it happens, "The Turn of the Screw" is so occupied with the governess' mind that it almost forgets its ostensible form. A James tale with a more prominent framing is the later short story "Maud-Evelyn" (*The Soft Side,* 1910). Here a Lady Emma narrates the story of a young man, Marmaduke, and the recently deceased daughter of a couple he has met, Maud-Evelyn. In Marmaduke and the parents' obsessive imagination, Maud-Evelyn grows up, becomes Marmaduke's wife, and is duly sanctified in the fane of her carefully preserved room, "a temple of grief and worship." This is the theme of "The Altar of the Dead" grotesquely transformed in its exposition by Lady Emma, who misses none of the ironies of the situation, such as Marmaduke's rejection by another woman and his possible fortune-hunting motives. Her cynicism suggests the appropriate view to take of Marmaduke and his bride of quietness and yet fails to explain his character, making the point of the story that some obsessions are so incomprehensible and troubling that they must be dismissed with laughter.

A similar narrative contrast—a conventional, uncomprehending frame surrounding a violent or macabre event—is used with crude ironic effectiveness in a volume of stories far obscurer than *The Soft Side*, the *Unprofessional Tales* (1901) by "Normyx," a pseudonym for Norman Douglas and a collaborator, probably his wife. In "The Ignoble," for example, a circle of listeners is kept ghoulishly entertained by the tale of an impoverished French noblewoman, bedridden with severe rheumatism, who is devoured by her starving cats. The story ends with the listeners looking out uncomprehendingly into the night: "The young moon had already gone to rest, but the snow, between the sombre patches of shadow, glittered tremulously with the reflected scintillations of a myriad stars. There was a stillness in the atmosphere that promised good sport for the morrow."[8] Another tale, "Nerinda," is on a theme rather like that of "Maud-Evelyn" —a man's obsession with the statue of a young girl in the museum at Pompeii leading to madness and murder—but it is in the form of a confessional journal, not a tale related to an audience, and it shows all too clearly what subtleties are lost when the drama of the telling and the listening is replaced by the melodrama of the doing.

The most consistent and ambitious Edwardian users of the narrative frame-tale were Conrad and Kipling. They both had lived and worked in places where stories were more naturally told than read, and where eloquence and a measure of mystification in the telling were valued, so they looked on storytelling with a more informed nostalgia than their contemporaries. Furthermore, as writers in England they both were outsiders— Conrad because he was a foreigner, Kipling because he was a colonial. From their sense of exclusion, which persisted despite literary and social success, came a profound interest in the bonds that unite human beings, and from that came an equally profound skepticism about the bonds of communication between teller and listener, writer and reader. They knew the looseness of this literary bond, which they would never have called a "contract," and yet they were fascinated by its unspoken rules and secret signs of recognition—as fascinated as they were, in other moods, by the marks that make Lord Jim "one of us" or the arcana of Freemasonry. Their work is devoted impartially to the narrator's compulsion to make his or another's experience understandable—"to make you *see*," Conrad puts it with emphasis in the preface to *The Nigger of the "Narcissus"*—and to the misunderstanding, hostility, or mere indifference which so often rewards the narrator.

The stories in Kipling's *Puck of Pook's Hill* (1906) and his *Rewards and Fairies* (1910), which use the same general frame— two children receiving lessons in English history from various figures of the past—make unremarkable use of the form, as do the Kipling frame-tales expressing his fondness for complication in literature as in machinery ("The Captive," "The Bonds of Discipline"). Kipling's genius seems to have been stimulated only when he discovered a mordant incongruity between the tale and its narrative setting, as in "A Deal in Cotton" (*Actions and Reactions*, 1909), where a young Englishman returned from Africa tells a bloody tale of slave-driving and cannibalism while his mother plays "Once in Royal David's City" on the organ; and even more in "Mrs. Bathurst" (*Traffics and Discoveries*, 1904). This is an intricate tale—intricate even for Kipling—about a sailor's unlikely and unexplained love for a kind barmaid; he loses her, sees her in the background of a news film shown at Cape Town, attempts to find her by walking the length of Africa, and dies, with an unidentified companion, by the side of a railway. Both have been mysteriously carbonized. It is not a subject any other writer could have handled without absurdity, but in Kipling's narrative frame it becomes a study of how men are drawn to and then away from something alien in their experience. An oddly assorted, brilliantly sketched group of idlers listen to the story while taking shelter from the sun on a South African beach, their eyes roving constantly over the land and water, as if to avoid looking too closely into the tale as it is being unfolded to them. In its way "Mrs. Bathurst" is as impressive as Kipling's better-known "On Greenhow Hill" (*Life's Handicap*, 1891), a delicate juxtaposing of story, the death of a young English girl, and frame, the Indian hilltop setting where snipers wait to ambush a native marauder.

Conrad's frame-tales are not so much impressive as over-whelming. They trap the reader in the circle of shadowy listeners for whom the narrator Marlow reminisces, ever more weary and dubious as the night goes on, permitting the reader no escape from the accumulating disillusionments of Conrad's meaning, which is as inherent in frame as in tale. In Conrad, indeed, the distinction between frame and tale, vehicle and tenor, becomes blurred. What Conrad conveys via the frame-tale is not neces-sarily profound. There is no puzzle in understanding how the re-peated cries of "Pass the bottle" in "Youth" (1902) dramatize a middle-aged habit of cherishing and devaluing a lost romanti-cism; or in understanding in "Amy Foster" (1903) how the good doctor who relates the tale to a friend must defend himself against the deepest implications of what he is perceiving, the essential human loneliness:

> The Doctor came to the window and looked out at the frigid splendour of the sea, immense in the haze, as if en-closing all the earth with all the hearts lost among the pas-sions of love and fear.
> "Physiologically, now," he said, turning away abruptly, "it was possible. It was possible."⁹

Heart of Darkness (1902) is more complicated. With an in-genuity that would have astounded Conrad, critics have teased out what the story implies about evil, the corruption of high ideas, the insufficiencies of European culture, and the ignoble means by which sanity is preserved; yet even now it may be doubted that the darkness of which Conrad wrote is fully illumi-nated. Darkness is unquestionably a part of Conrad's telling. To his companions on the yacht moored in the Thames, Marlow speaks of trying to help Kurtz, and then he breaks off to wonder if he is being understood:

> "Do you see him? Do you see the story? Do you see any-thing? It seems to me I am trying to tell you a dream—

making a vain attempt, because no relation of a dream can convey the dream-sensation, that commingling of absurdity, surprise, and bewilderment in a tremor of struggling revolt, that notion of being captured by the incredible which is of the very essence of dreams . . ."

He was silent for a while.

". . . No, it is impossible; it is impossible to convey the life-sensation of any given epoch of one's existence—that which makes its truth, its meaning—its subtle and penetrating essence. It is impossible. We live, as we dream—alone . . ."

He paused again as if reflecting, then added:

"Of course in this you fellows see more than I could then. You see me, whom you know . . ."

It had become so pitch dark that we listeners could hardly see one another. For a long time already he, sitting apart, had been no more to us than a voice.[10]

Long before Benjamin's essay, Conrad foresaw the decline of storytelling, and he imaged it in this passage as the fading of communal vision into darkness, the faltering of a voice into silence.

4

The Uncritical Attitude

Heart of Darkness is perhaps the finest example in the period of coincident form and meaning. When Conrad adapted the narrative frame-tale for the novel *Lord Jim* (1900), he made it a means to a larger end, psychological analysis. Marlow's relation to Jim reveals in both men the defenses meant to ward off the dangers of imagination, but it does so only at the cost, which Conrad was willing to pay, of puzzling some critics. The usual complaint made about Conrad during the period was that he fails to tell a story in logical order but zigzags back and forth, and that he inflates modest short stories into pretentious novels.[1] But to long for logical order in *Lord Jim* is to fail to see what the book is about.

This particular misjudgment suggests why the Edwardian critical establishment often failed to see what formally innovative fiction was about. Critics of all sorts, from penny-a-line book reviewers to successful men of letters like Richard Garnett and Sir Walter Besant, tended to rely on a sort of gentleman's agreement as to what the form of the novel should be. The novel tells a story, the novel tells a story in a logical order, the novel subordinates manner to matter—unexamined postulates like these were sufficient for the business of criticism and for the higher task of defending the genre against those who found it pedestrian, commercial, or artistically impure.[2] During the decade the novel was championed ably but generally; it was praised for its aesthetic simplicity, while specific issues of narration and artistic control were slighted. Like the House of Commons reviewing the English Constitution or English Liberalism reviewing the British

Empire, critics took pride in something they preferred not to examine too closely.

Edwardian England lacked the prerequisite for any comprehensive and intellectually rigorous study of form, namely a genuinely critical attitude. Such was the judgment of Ford Madox Ford. He was in an exceptional position to recognize the slovenly habits and inherent possibilities of the novel, since his intense aestheticism, his pre-Raphaelite family background, and his own unusual talent predisposed him to question academic tastes and challenge critical complacencies. Ford was a good European at a time when Englishmen tended to prize their insularity; he encouraged Wells and collaborated with Conrad; and in 1908 he became the first editor of the best of all Edwardian literary journals, the *English Review*.[3] Ford was too careless a businessman to stay editor of the *English Review* for long, but under other direction it kept up its standards. In its pages appeared the last short stories of Henry James, Wells's *Tono-Bungay*, and a stream of essays and reviews by Ford himself, which were collected in the 1911 volume *The Critical Attitude*.

In that book Ford takes to task a characteristically optimistic opinion of Wells, that the motor-car was a welcome development because it would make Englishmen think. Ford's retort to Wells is blunt: nothing will make the English think. They are too passive, too sentimental, too tradition-minded. They are entirely without the proper critical attitude, which requires a willingness on the part of the critic to define and insist on standards, and a conscientious desire on the part of the author to examine the tools of his trade and, by avoiding the opposed traps of the merely factual and the merely inventive, to supply "a picture of the way we live."[4] The critical attitude is for Ford synonymous with literary art, which he found at the end of the decade almost entirely confined to the novel, and sporadic even there, being evident in six novelists only: James, Conrad, George Moore, Galsworthy, Kipling, and Wells. The first three are chided for various failings but are at least wholly concerned with their art.

Galsworthy falls just short of this ultimate literary conscientiousness, while Kipling and Wells are included in the group of six only by virtue of their forceful personalities. Arnold Bennett is also meritorious, though too doggedly realistic, too trapped by the merely factual, to meet Ford's standards for literary art.

Tendentious though Ford's ranking system may be, it judges novelists strictly as novelists, it displays a shrewd critical intelligence at work, and it is based on a well thought-out, consistent system of fictional standards. *The Critical Attitude* knows what it wants, and in this respect it contrasts instructively with Sir Walter Besant's *The Art of Fiction,* which does not know what it wants, or wants contradictory things. Besant was a far more typical critic than Ford. Well-intentioned, diligent, talented—he was the author of numerous historical romances—Besant yet cannot "define and insist on standards." His critical attitude is colored by a moral attitude and based, at bottom, on postulates which would have proved inconsistent if carefully examined.

The new edition of *The Art of Fiction* (1902) expands only slightly on a lecture delivered in 1884. It poses three main principles: fiction is an art, the equal of painting, sculpture, music, and poetry; as an art, fiction is governed by general laws, which "may be laid down and taught with as much precision and exactness as the laws of harmony, perspective, and proportion"; and no laws or rules may teach fiction to those not naturally gifted.[5] In other words nature and nurture are both involved in the creative process, though Besant's emphasis rests clearly on nurture. He lists the laws governing the novel, that "tremendous engine of popular influence." Anything purely invented, not experienced, is worthless; since the sole aim of modern fiction is to portray humanity and human character, the design must be in accordance with the customs and general practice of living men and women. That is, the characters must be real. Historical novels are acceptable because men and women are "pretty much alike" in all ages. The drawing of each figure, whether period or contemporary, is to be clear in outline; nothing should be admitted which does not advance the story; situations must be presented as dramatically—that is, as forcefully—as possible; and attention must be paid to careful workmanship, to style.

In all this there is nothing exceptionable, and nothing that Zola could have disagreed with; but Besant's realism turns out to be oddly qualified. The modern English novel, he notes, leaving "as opposed to the modern French novel" unspoken, almost always starts with a conscious moral purpose; it preaches a higher morality than is seen in the actual world. And in its preaching nothing works better than a cheerful countenance, a hearty manner. So much for Zola. Over the decades few English critics or novelists have been able to reconcile the claims of moral earnestness and realism to their entire satisfaction. George Eliot, for example, was pulled in opposite directions by the Dutch painting and the *Westminster Review* sides of her nature, and a similar indecision between portraying people as they are and portraying them as they ought to be appears in Wells, who wrote novels to accomplish the first function and romances to accomplish the second. The disturbing thing about Besant's criticism is that it does not notice the inevitable conflict between the "general practice of living men and women" and a "higher morality than is seen in the actual world." Besant makes demands on fiction which no serious Edwardian novel could fulfill: not *Nostromo* (1904), not *The Golden Bowl*, not *Where Angels Fear to Tread* (1905), not *Ann Veronica* (1909). None of these works he could have read—he died in 1901—but they would hardly have changed his views of the art of fiction, lacking as they do a hearty manner.

Longman's Magazine of September 1884 carried a witty and moving response to Besant's original lecture. Also called "The Art of Fiction," it introduced to the debate on the English novel a voice already well known from fiction, reviews, and essays, but never before so clearly and authoritatively heard, the voice of Henry James. James grants Besant's premise that "the only reason for the existence of a novel is that it does attempt to represent life," and then proceeds to show what very different things the two writers mean by the realistic art of fiction. For Besant and others, "art means rose-colored window-panes, and selection [of fictional subjects] means picking a bouquet for Mrs. Grundy"; for James, art means an absolute freedom to choose subjects and methods. The experience included in a novel is "never complete; it is an immense sensibility, a kind of huge spider-web of the finest silken threads suspended in the chamber of consciousness, and catching every air-borne particle in its tissue." As for the educative responsibility of the novelist, his work must indeed have moral energy, but its essence is "to survey the whole field."[6] Nothing human may be omitted. Preaching is not mentioned; observation, courage, and dedication are.

The English novel of 1884 seemed to James excessively diffident, but he felt that new fictional enterprises, undertaken with a new artistic seriousness, were in store. The untheoretic era, the era of naive fictional puddings, was over; the era of discussion had opened. Novels were to be as consciously composed as paintings. Encouraged by what he took to be the state of criticism, confident in his own creative powers, James predicted that the novel was about to come into its own.

He returned to this topic in 1899, bringing his views up to date. In an article titled "The Future of the Novel," James surveys the situation of the novel as the Edwardian age was about to begin and finds much that is encouraging. The flood of novels swells and swells, James finds, "threatening the whole field of letters, as would often seem, with submersion." The appeal of fiction is universal because it offers experience so easily, so painlessly, and there is no reason to doubt that future readers will continue to be "trapped"—perhaps a reference to his previous image of the spider-web—by its versatility: "It can do simply everything, and that is its strength and its life. Its plasticity, its elasticity are infinite." "So long as life retains its power of projecting itself upon [the reader's] imagination, he will find the novel work off the impression better than anything he knows . . . Till the world is an unpeopled void there will be an image in the mirror."[7]

Wells himself could not be a more optimistic prophet—but James then adds qualifications, conditions, doubts. The novel will continue, but individual novelists seem at the moment to be failing. A "facile flatness" has replaced the mystery of the great novels of the past, most modern productions cease to exist within a year, and the novels that survive do so because they cater to an immense new audience, "millions for whom taste is but an obscure, confused, immediate instinct."[8] Whatever image in the mirror is likely to please them may be meretricious or vulgar. The metaphor of a threatening flood of novels begins to seem ominous.

For James, the critical attitude is a matter of regarding fiction as an artistic discipline, experimenting with new forms, and refining taste into something more reliable than a confused, immediate instinct. Like Ford, he deplores the present lack of a critical attitude, but more specifically even than Ford he makes the lack a national one. He acknowledges what for Edwardian commentators would become a truism, but for him seems a discovery: the future of fiction is intimately bound up with the future of the society that produces and consumes it. "A community addicted to reflection and fond of ideas will try experiments with the 'story' that will be left untried in a community mainly devoted to traveling and shooting, to pushing trade and playing football." If the novel ceases to experiment, if it thinks it has found its finished form, it is doomed to negligibility.[9]

The Edwardians who would bear the responsibility for encouraging reflection and experimentation were not the denizens of what Shaw would call Horseback Hall, or the tradesmen and football players, but the critics and writers who alone were in a position to guide the confused national taste away from a good strong story and toward some appreciation of arrangement and narration. The responsibility James calls for should not have been burdensome. He commits the community of letters to nothing save thinking about fictional form—not to his own narrative methods, not to his opinion of the modern novel, not to his harmless snobberies about football and pushing trade. The call is simply for a lessened reliance on the novel's "elasticity" and a heightened awareness of its "plasticity," its suitability for being molded and shaped at the hands of the controlling artist. But the call went unheeded by those who might have profited by it.

In 1899 James's position in the English community of letters was unsure. He was isolated, not entirely by his own choice, and not entirely in a way he could separate from the personal loneliness of his existence as a man without a close family and as an American, though a Europeanized one, in England. Both personal and professional isolation seem to be hinted at in a turn-of-the-century letter to Morton Fullerton: "The port from which I set out was, I think, that of *the essential loneliness of my life*— and it seems to be the port also, in sooth, to which my course again finally directs itself!"[10] As the Edwardian decade progressed, the unsuccessful playwright and moderately successful novelist tried to mitigate his loneliness by becoming more deliberately sociable. He cultivated literary neighbors and gave advice to the young; he received homage in Lamb House; he made himself, in short, into the universally admired, if not universally read, Master. But he still remained apart—apart from Kipling, from Conrad, from Wells, from Hugh Walpole. The letters he sent out in great quantity to these fellow practitioners, attempting to be helpful, convey only a conviction of unbridgeable distance.

That distance is most obvious in the James-Wells correspondence. Here James gives Wells the praise and encouragement due one practitioner from another, at the same time trying to instill in Wells the proper critical attitude, the proper sense of responsibility for shaping the national taste. Inadvertently, though, James's terms of praise confess how little hope he has of converting the younger man. James the disciplined novelist and Wells the most interesting "literary man" of his generation are writers of a radically different kind. In order to write *Kipps*, for example, which is "not so much a masterpiece as a mere born gem," Wells had merely to dive "straight down into the mysterious depths of observation and knowledge" and retrieve something already fashioned. The life depicted in the book is vivid and sharp—but raw.[11] *The New Machiavelli,* according to James, casts a light as if from "a far-flaring even though turbid and smoky lamp, projecting the most vivid and splendid golden splotches, *creating* them about the field—shining scattered innumerable morsels of a huge smashed mirror." In this book and others Wells also displays his "capacity for chewing up the thickness of the world in such enormous mouthfuls, while [he] fairly slobber[s], so to speak, with the multitudinous taste."[12] The smoky lamp, golden splotches, smashed mirror, and slobbering mouthfuls are grotesque enough, but still less so than James's labored critique of *In the Days of the Comet* (1906). In that book the reader is not allowed, in effect, to "take refuge . . . in the waiting-room of The Crematorium, with a saddened sense of the dread Process going on *adjacently*—one is in the presence of the heated oven and one hears and feels the roar and the scorch of the flames. That is your Book—magnificently crematory, in other words magnificently direct and real (though perhaps with too little of the waiting room.)"[13] The imaginative transformation of Wells's writing is thus completed. From a "mere born gem," it has become the heated oven of a crematorium, in a pattern that extends and exaggerates James's earlier imaginative transformation of Kipling, from "the young Bard," to "the star of the hour," then "the infant monster," and finally "the little black demon."[14]

James's letters to Wells and other younger writers are consistently playful, so that his crematorium imagery may well have been intended as ironically as is his offer in another letter to collaborate with Wells in writing a book about the exploration of Mars (James had just read *The First Men in the Moon*).[15] But to explain all of the oddity away as mere playfulness—or as the chronic convolutedness of James's late style—is to miss the point of the James-Wells "debate," which is that it was not really a debate at all, but rather a process of self-definition, and therefore an intensification of James's artistic loneliness. By associating Wells with fictional rawness, an art not contrived but improvised, James indirectly described his own fiction as an art wholly contrived, serious, and responsive to the critical attitude. The fact is that James needed to protect himself from Wells and the slobbering multitudinous taste he feared that Wells was pleasing. In the letters James's ever more Mandarin compliments and ever more strained metaphors are the defense mechanisms of an artist who had not only to define his differences from Wells in subject and method but also, in some measure, to render ironic his genuine astonishment at the originality and success of the younger writer.

Wells's resentment at the Master's ponderousness would grow until it produced the satiric attack *Boon* in 1915, but during the first years of the century Wells genuinely admired the artistic rigor of James, and he admired it the more as he realized how unlikely it was that he would achieve it himself. He encouraged Bennett to read James, much as he encouraged him to read Dickens, announcing grandly in a letter of 1902 that *The Wings of the Dove* is a book to read in and learn from, though confessing that he has not yet been able to get through the novel.[16] Bennett proved resistant. Eight years later, in the course of a review of James's *The Finer Grain* (1910), Bennett notes that he has never been a James enthusiast, having read no more than a quarter of the Master's work. There follows a balance-sheet accounting of the novelist. On the credit side, James is a fine writer, marvelous craftsman, and excellent critic; he savors life with eagerness. On the debit side, he lacks emotional power, has an oversophisticated sense of beauty, views life timidly and conventionally, and has limited curiosity. *The Finer Grain* itself is uninteresting.[17]

The sad thing about James's position in the Edwardian decade was not that the rigorous standards of his art kept him isolated from best-selling novelists like Hall Caine. James rejoiced in the fastidiousness which prevented his being influential at their level. "Hall Caine would have made it large as life and magnificent," he writes to Ford, commenting on the *scène obligatoire* he himself so carefully omitted from *The Wings of the Dove*, the final confrontation between Milly and Densher.[18] The sad thing was that James had so little influence on novelists like Wells and Bennett. Even if they wished to reject the particular limitations of James's novels, the undoubted timidity and oversophistication, they might have worked with James (and Ford) in diffusing a critical attitude through the community of letters, and that attitude might have been a more representative and generous one than James could define by himself.

Instead, Wells and Bennett went their own ways, relying on their own, separate notions of what the novel was and could become. The Edwardian critical establishment might conceivably have mediated between James and other novelists, but it was, with one or two exceptions, unable to value James and so inimical to his call for literary conscientiousness.[19] In 1902 Richard Burton comments on "the invertebrate method of a Henry James," who dismisses "the notion of any plot or argument at all for the story, which may be high art, but is chilling in effect upon the patrons."[20] In 1904 W. L. Courtney mourns the "fate of those who have a morbid conscientiousness in their work—the sad case of Mr. Henry James . . . inertia and languor in style . . . ambiguity of meaning, involution of sentence, and an impossibly fantastic psychology."[21] Between such critics and James, planning the New York Edition of his work in the quiet isolation of Lamb House and systematically distilling a lifetime's experience of fiction into its stately prefaces, there could be no possibility of debate—and therefore no real chance for raising and invigorating critical standards. In the first decade of the century, Ford identified artistic virtue, Besant laid down laws, James spoke for conscious composition, book reviewers praised and damned, but all in vain. Edwardian fiction had to manage its achievements without the help of an Edwardian critical attitude.

5

Edwardian Best-Sellers

To the Edwardians, there could be nothing wrong in principle about naming a decade after its reigning king, but the literary-minded must sooner or later have regretted being connected in even a nominal way with Edward VII. Like a great many of his subjects, the king was resolutely unliterary, and he vastly preferred sporting to intellectual pursuits. This fact is recorded in the "Circe" chapter of Joyce's *Ulysses,* an encyclopedic guide to the period in general and to 1904 in particular, where Edward appears fantastically garbed but doing something perfectly characteristic of him, witnessing a boxing match ("Cheerio, boys. We have come here to witness a clean straight fight and we heartily wish both men the best of good luck.")[1] Though there were no sympathies between Edwardian literature and the taste of its eponym, with one variety of fiction at least the king was familiar. It is known that as Prince of Wales he was much given to reading those "silly little novels (half farces)" on sale at railway stations, and that as king he was an extravagant admirer of Marie Corelli.[2] The silly little novels, the best-sellers, the minor and ephemeral productions of the age in general are more literally "Edwardian" than anything James or Wells wrote, and since Edward's taste was so widely shared by his people, the books he liked have a claim to be considered in a literary history of the period. One way to recover the life of Edward's decade is to consider the part of its literature which has now died.

George Dangerfield has remarked that major writing rarely gives the exact flavor of its period, whereas very minor literature "is the Baedeker of the soul, and will guide you through the curious relics, the tumbledown buildings, the flimsy palaces, the false pagodas, the distorted and fantastical and faery vistas which have cluttered the imagination of mankind at this or that brief period of its history."[3] This seems undeniable, since major writing is still read and discussed, and therefore belongs to the present as much as to the specific past which created it; major writing is the creation of writers who were ahead of their time because they speculated more boldly, tolerated fewer myths, and observed events more perceptively than their contemporaries. Minor writing lives and dies wholly within one period, of which it is therefore representative. A Baedeker gone out of date, it is the best guide to monuments which have now been swept away or seem inexplicable, and which even at the time were being underestimated and despised by leading spirits. Minor writing is historically serviceable, whether the "monuments" it explains are figurative or literal.

In a literal sense, it is in reading the minor Edwardian novels and essays about imperialism, national identity, and the myth of the Navy that one comes to an understanding of Sir Aston Webb's Admiralty Arch (1910), which to the modern onlooker seems to guard Trafalgar Square from the Mall with massive pointlessness. Edwardian minor literature is a guide to the figurative monuments of the age as well—its speculations, controversies, and ephemera. This literature is particularly revealing because it exaggerates and overdramatizes, treating issues with intense seriousness. Consider Marie Corelli's overblown fantasy *The Devil's Motor*, in which Satan appears over the earth amid "the stench and muffled roar of a huge Car" to call all mankind to Hell. "Come, tie your pigmy chariots to the sun," says the Father of Lies, "and so be drawn into its flaming vortex of perdition . . . Progress and speed!" Men and women are seduced by this demonic slogan, the Car is splashed thick with human blood, and mankind is led over the edge of a cliff to an abyss, leaving a completely purified earth and God setting his seal on the closed history of the world.[4] That an automotive apocalypse like this could be taken seriously enough to be published twice, first in a miscellany of 1901 and second in an expensive illustrated 1910 edition of its own, suggests that the motor-car did indeed offend Edwardian sensitivities in a significant way, by blighting the landscape with its associated industry and by upsetting notions of how fast man should move, how fast man's life should change.[5] It suggests also that there is nothing reactionary about Forster's dislike for the Wilcox motor in *Howards End*. He was sharing a widespread attitude, and his symbol for the new Wilcoxian England on the horizon, the "throbbing, stinking car," was well-chosen and expressive.

The minor literature of most relevance falls into two types, coterie fiction and best-selling novels. The types blend together but are roughly distinguished by the audience for which each was written. Coterie authors worked in strictly defined, highly conventional specialities addressed to an identifiable readership of enthusiasts. They were able to "subsist quite happily with the little sect" they found, or which found them. They lived "safely in their islands," according to Wells, writing in 1901 of a compartmentalization of fiction which followed as a corollary of the breaking up of society into distinct social and cultural groups. Wells thought this compartmentalization would intensify in the twentieth century.[6] The metaphor of islands is particularly congenial to the period, with its reawakened consciousness of England as an island and its painful need to choose between expansionism and insularity.

The other aspect to compartmentalization that Wells notes is the division of literature into serious books and best-sellers. In the past the "boom" book was genuinely read by everyone, but the boom book of the early twentieth century, "So-and-so's Hundred Thousand Copy success," is simply unthinkable to some sections of the reading public, who are appalled by the suggestion that vast sales indicate a vastly important book. "One gets used to literary booms, just as one gets used to motor cars, they are no longer marvellous, universally significant things, but merely something that goes by with much unnecessary noise and leaves a faint offence in the air."[7] Wells himself was not above booming his own books, even to the extent of nagging Frederick

47

Macmillan to use sandwich men as advertisements for his fiction.[8] And in *Tono-Bungay* at the end of the decade Wells wrote the great Edwardian exposé of booming, in both its outward or advertising aspect and its inward or self-deception form.

Most of the coteries "to subsist quite happily" after the turn of the century were not Edwardian inventions. They went back to fictional successes of the nineteenth century, extending and exploiting audiences developed then. Into this group falls the Edwardian fiction of fantasy or whimsy, as practiced by Kenneth Grahame, E. Nesbit, Saki, Ronald Firbank (*Odette: A Fairy-Tale for Weary People*, 1905), Max Beerbohm (*Zuleika Dobson*, 1911), and James Stephens (*The Crock of Gold*, 1912). Whimsy of a different sort was offered in Ernest Bramah's *The Wallet of Kai Lung* (1900), in which a wandering Chinese storyteller narrates the exploits of various heroes and villains in a Mandarin style of elaborate periphrasis and flowery compliment. This testament to the period's vogue for Chinoiserie was successful, but not so successful as to keep Bramah later in his career from turning to a still better-selling genre of coterie fiction, the detective story.

In prefatorial remarks to "The Turn of the Screw" James writes of the new-fashioned "psychical" ghost story as being "washed clean of all queerness as by exposure to a flowing laboratory tap," and therefore promising little in the way of "the dear old sacred terror." But something of the old terror was offered in Edwardian works like M. R. James's *Ghost Stories of an Antiquary* (1904), Algernon Blackwood's *The Empty House* (1906), and Oliver Onions' *Widdershins* (1911). These books were written for a limited but steady readership, who evidently preferred subtlety to horrifics. In James's terms, they preferred "the tone of suspected and felt trouble" to "the offered example, the imputed vice, the cited act, the limited deplorable presentable instance."[9] But few readers could have been prepared for the kind of subtlety employed in the best two Edwardian tales about ghosts, James's "The Jolly Corner," first published in the *English Review* (1908), and Kipling's "They" (*Traffics and Discoveries*, 1904).

Both stories are without any taint of the laboratory tap; both arise from powerful emotions in their authors; both make the tone of "felt trouble" a means of psychological investigation.

"The Jolly Corner" suggests that it is better to live in the present than be haunted by the past. This lesson was plenteously refuted by the Edwardian authors of historical romance, who offered their readers a familiar kind of nostalgic escapism. They provided the past in the form, in Wells's words, of "healthy light fiction with chromatic titles, 'The Red Sword,' 'The Black Helmet,' 'The Purple Robe.' "[10] Bennett was simply wrong when in 1903 he told aspirants to fiction that the historical novel was an exhausted form and the market for it was flat.[11] The market was not exhausted, and there were plenty of expert practitioners to exploit it, among them Maurice Hewlett, Stanley Weyman, Henry Seton Merriman, Marjorie Bowen, Henry Christopher Bailey, Sir Arthur Conan Doyle, and Ford Madox Ford, whose trilogy *The Fifth Queen, Privy Seal,* and *The Fifth Queen Crowned* (1906-1908) is the best of Edwardian works in this genre. The reader of *The Fifth Queen* does not so much escape to England in the sixteenth century as become trapped there along with the characters who, like all characters in Ford's fiction, are either willing but unable to escape from their predicaments, or else able but unwilling.

The Edwardian silver-fork novel carried that early Victorian genre to new intensities of snobbish enticement and so to huge new sales. The best example from the decade, Elinor Glyn's *Three Weeks* (1907), clearly passes over the line separating coterie work from best-seller. It is a best-seller pure and simple. The plot, a young man's affair with an experienced older woman, is that of *The Ambassadors,* but to put James's characters next to Glyn's is to realize the gulf that separates fictional revelation from best-selling sensation. Glyn's hero, a young English gentleman-huntsman, the product of Eton and Oxford, falls in love with the wrong woman, the daughter of a mere parson, and is consequently sent off by his parents to forget. Switzerland is thought to be proof against entanglements and intrigues (Conrad had not yet published *Under Western Eyes*), but there the hero meets a *femme fatale* dressed in obligatory dishabille and with a rose between her teeth. She first tries to warn him away ("Paul . . . You are young, so young—and I shall hunt you—probably. Won't you go now—while there is yet time?"), then promises she will teach him "how-to-LIVE" and seduces him on a tiger-skin rug. After giving herself to her young lover for three weeks, she leaves him to try intrigues in some Balkan state, where she is killed, leaving Paul with a lock of his newborn son's hair, a golden collar for his dog, and despair. This costume drama is designed entirely for the sake of the costumes, for the sake of parading wealth before the envious reader, who is coyly invited to think she belongs to the world of Paul and his Tiger Queen: "Do you know the Belvedere at the Rigi Kaltbad, looking over the corner to a vast world below, on a fair day in May, when the air is clear as crystal and the lake ultramarine?"[12]

Such a question is wonderfully indicative of the Edwardian admiration for wealth, which leaner decades have translated into an Edwardian attainment of wealth, as though *Three Weeks* and best-sellers like it were merely transcribing everyday reality instead of providing glamorous escape. George Orwell's 1947 view is representative:

> There never was, I suppose, in the history of the world a time when the sheer vulgar fatness of wealth, without any kind of aristocratic elegance to redeem it, was so obtrusive as in those years before 1914. It was the age when crazy millionaires in curly top-hats and lavender waistcoats gave champagne parties in rococo house-boats on the Thames, the age of diabolo and hobble skirts, the age of the "knut" in his grey bowler and cutaway coat, the age of *The Merry Widow*, Saki's novels, *Peter Pan* and *Where the Rainbow Ends*, the age when people talked about chocs and cigs and ripping and topping and heavenly, when they went for divvy week-ends at Brighton and had scrumptious teas at the Troc. From the whole decade before 1914 there seems to breathe forth a smell of the more vulgar, un-grown-up kinds of luxury, a smell of brilliantine and *crème-de-*

menthe and soft-centred chocolates—an atmosphere, as it were, of eating everlasting strawberry ices on green lawns to the tune of the Eton Boating Song.[13]

This piece of impressionistic writing, a mythologizing view like that of Sackville-West, is yet not wholly inaccurate in its portrayal of Edwardian money-consciousness. To *The Grand Babylon Hotel,* one of the books Bennett wrote in order to become really successful, he added the subtitle *A Fantasia on Modern Themes,* suggesting that the book's fascination with "the value and the marvelous power of mere money, of the lucre which philosophers pretend to despise and men sell their souls for," was a particularly modern, an Edwardian concern.[14] Money consciousness was an admitted fact of the decade, and it may have been no less stimulating to novelists than hard social facts. After all, it must have been comforting to think that fiction might be not only the medium by which wealth was depicted, but the very means by which it was achieved. A note of honest greed comes into Bennett's voice as he contemplates the marketability of his art: "Never before, despite the abolition of the three-volume novel, did so many average painstaking novelists earn such respectable incomes as at the present day. And the rewards of the really successful novelist seem to increase year by year."[15] Bennett is austere in comparison with Besant, whose *The Pen and the Book* (1899), which has the Podsnapian subtitle *Written for the Instruction and Guidance of Young Persons Thinking of the Literary Life,* boasts that a respectable man of letters may now command an income and position equal to those of the average doctor or lawyer, while a writer who rises to the top may enjoy as much social consideration as a bishop. But then in Besant's view there is something inspirational, even homiletic, about the life of letters: "It is the function of literature to be always dispersing clouds that are always gathering: and it is a most certain law of humanity that it will infallibly sink lower if it is not continually lifted higher." Or there is something personally redemptive, as in Besant's sketch of the career of a modern Chatterton: poverty, reading, writing for magazines and newspapers, a volume of poetry or fiction, and finally solid prosperity and eventual distinction as the literary editor of a great morning newspaper.[16]

The emphasis on wealth in the age's best-seller points, then, to a particularly Edwardian philistinism, but there is nothing particularly Edwardian about the phenomenon of the best-seller itself, which was the creation of nineteenth-century industrial, educational, and marketing improvements: mass-production printing, increased literacy, serial publication in magazines and newspapers, publication in parts, cheap one-volume reprints, the growth of libraries, and the machinery of advertising and reviewing. Throughout its long and continuing career the best-seller has not had to depend on any one historical consciousness. It has needed only a tacit agreement between writers and readers as to what kind of fiction should be written and purchased, an agreement routinely covering such allied issues as the demands to be made on the reader's attention, the kinds of sexual and political frankness to be avoided, the conventions of storytelling to be employed, and even the proper amount of fiction to be furnished. Bennett suggests in 1903 that long novels are most popular with both publishers and readers, as the most successful works of the day, by Caine and Corelli, are also the longest.[17]

In the end, these conventions depend upon the view a period takes of all its fiction, not just the best-selling variety, and it may be that an Edwardian view of fiction made it easy to reach compromising formulas for the best-seller. James, Conrad, Ford, and even Bennett in moments when he ceased to think about his potential income, were laboring hard throughout the decade to make the novel fully serious and respectable, but they could do little with the persistent attitude that the novel, as a form, could not be traduced by its vulgarization in the best-seller because it was itself inherently vulgar, or at least trivial: light entertainment for the bored female or the burdened male, the "Weary Giant," as Wells says sarcastically. No troublesome realities, no facts, but rather romance, humor, and excitement: these qualities the novel was to bring to its readers, preferably in an easy chair at the close of the day. Critics of what Chesterton called the "Hammock school" ("I read this book in a hammock: half asleep in the sleepy sunlight") were essential collaborators in this attitude.[18] Judged against such standards, *Three Weeks* hardly seems egregious in proffering its Belvederes and ultramarine lakes.

Best-selling authors could be surprisingly frank in revealing how far their artistic aims were lowered. Jeffrey Farnol, author of the exceptionally best-selling *The Broad Highway* (1910), begins his book with an "Ante Scriptum" in which the narrator-to-be, Peter Vibart, talks over the work in prospect with one of those opinionated tinkers who throng the byways of picaresque. The tinker is pleased to hear that in the story there are going to be a highwayman, a pugilist, a one-legged soldier of the Penin-sula, an adventure at a lonely tavern, a flight through woods at midnight pursued by desperate villains—and a most extraordi-nary tinker. This is a potentially Quixotian moment of confu-sion between fiction and reality, or at least between frame and tale, but fictional reflexivity is not Farnol's concern. Instead, he wants to use the tinker, who sells novels as well as scissors, as a figure for the great book-buying public. "I've read a good many nov-els in my time," the tinker says. "I've made love to duch-esses, run off with heiresses, and fought dooels—ah! by the hun-dred—all between the covers of some book or other and enjoyed it uncommonly well—especially the dooels." He finishes his exordium with the advice not to be overingenious in trying to please the public; just give them "Love . . . and plenty of it," mixed with a little artful bloodletting.[19] That is exactly what Farnol provides, apparently confident that readers will not be insulted to have their vicarious longings spelled out for them so much in advance and so openly.

Farnol may have rated his readers too simply, however. The popularity which best-sellers by definition have always enjoyed stems partly from their capacity to provoke relatively compli-cated but never articulated responses in their readers. Among these are skepticism and sentimentality, realism (a sense of what life is like) and fantasy (the desire to live in capital letters and in luxurious Swiss surroundings), convention and adventure, morality and pleasure. Contradictory responses like these make the reading of a best-seller a highly energized and absorbing process, yet they are not carried so far as to threaten basic certainties or to disrupt the rapid movement of the plot, which finally takes precedence over everything else. In the best-seller plot controls ideas, and the resolution of the plot provides a parallel resolution, often a forced or artificial one, for the reader's complicated response to ideas. That is, in the final scene the reader is granted release from whatever ambiguities the rest of the book may have thrust on him. He is reassured that, after all, crime does not pay, or that virtue is its own reward, or that God helps those who help themselves.

Edwardian best-sellers are particularly apt to rely on such resolutions. They entertain dangerous ideas and then fall back on conventionality at the last moment, thus providing "the approved pruriency of a work that [is] shocking by innuendo" while avoiding at all costs "the possible unpleasantness of a work that shock[s] because it [is] too literal."[20] Not every work plays with fire in this way. *The Broad Highway* sticks to a simple formula and so gets along without any ideas at all. But *Three Weeks*, a more typical example, glories in the passionate freedom of its hero and heroine and openly flouts the conventional notion of sexual morality. It is a novel written expressly in defense of love, Glyn testifies in her autobiography, and as a therapeutic escape for both writer and reader: "I drew, out of my vivid imagination, material to satisfy my own unfulfilled longing for romantic love, and so, out of my own poverty, I was able to provide the riches of imaginary fulfilment and pour them out into the love-starved lives of thousands of others whom I did not know."[21] There is an engagingly naive selflessness about this claim, especially in connection with Farnol's cynical calculation of what readers want, and yet it does not quite square with the finale of *Three Weeks*, in which the adulterous Queen is killed and the wages of sin explicitly invoked: "For Paul had come the tears. But for her—cold steel and blood. And so, as ever, the woman paid the price."[22] It is possible to see a protest against the double sexual standard in this statement, or perhaps, with a subtler irony, Glyn is paying lip-service to what she knows has become a moral cliché. But nothing else in the book suggests that kind of ethical authority. In *Three Weeks* Glyn is simply adventurous and prudent at the same time. Her heroine is glamorized over three hundred pages and condemned, albeit sympathetically, in the last paragraph, with the result that as the reader puts the book down, she savors the complementary emotions of envy and self-righteousness.

A similar principle is apparently at work in the novel by the best-selling author Sidney Revel in Wells's *Kipps*. Titled *Red Hearts a-Beating*, the novel is "a tale of spirited adventure, full of youth and beauty and naive passion and generous devotion, bold, as the *Bookman* said, and frank in places, but never in the slightest degree morbid."[23] To be frank without being morbid, in other words to be hypocritically unconventional, is a special achievement of Guy Thorne's *When It Was Dark* (1905), which boldly imagines that Christ's resurrection stems from an ancient deception, and hence that Christianity is a gigantic fraud. In the end the resurrection is triumphantly reaffirmed when the whole crisis is traced back to a scheming master-criminal. The world returns from moral chaos to faith and normality, but meanwhile the reader has been thrilled by the forbidden thoughts of atheism triumphant. Relatively speaking, this is an imaginative and daring venture on Thorne's part; other popular religious thrillers, beginning with the most lurid of them all, Marie Corelli's *The Sorrows of Satan* (1895), do not permit even a hypothetical denial of Christianity or a momentary slackening of hatred for godlessness. To Leonard Bast in *Howards End* (1910), Margaret is initially "one of those soulless, atheistical women who have been so shown up by Miss Corelli."[24] To be sure, the characters of these novels routinely experience private crises of belief, but just as routinely they are granted final peace, and in the most rhetorically grandiose cases they are granted it in the final sentence: "For always, when night falls, she sees the form of a man praying who once fled from prayer in the desert; she sees a wanderer who at last has reached his home."[25]

Whether it plays with fire or merely endorses comfortable certainties, the religious best-seller of the period is a sadly philistine affair. Compared with a late Victorian work like Mrs. Humphry Ward's *Robert Elsmere* (1888), a crisis-of-faith novel which engages seriously with important issues, the Edwardian productions are rigid, cliché-ridden, occasionally frantic, and disposed to feed on sectarian prejudices and hatreds. Corelli's *The Master Christian* (1900) imagines Christ returning to earth disguised as a young boy ("Manuel") and rejecting the "pagan" practices of the Roman Church. The whole novel is informed by Corelli's hatred for anything Continental and Catholic—in fact anything un-English and un-Protestant. To Corelli, Paris is "godless . . . hollow to the very core of rottenness . . . a witches' caldron in which Republicanism, Imperialism, Royalism, Communism and Socialism, are all thrown by the Fates to seethe together in a hellish broth of conflicting elements—and the smoke of it ascends in reeking blasphemy to Heaven."[26] An appendix to the novel lists confession among the "Relics of Paganism in Christianity As Approved by English Bishops."

Chesterton was moved to respond to polemics of this sort, not yet as a Catholic, his formal conversion taking place in 1922, but as a wit. *The Ball and the Cross* (1909) first laughingly dismisses the antiatheistical Corelli school: "Oh, I have heard all that . . . I have heard that Christianity keeps the key of virtue, and if you read Tom Paine you will cut your throat at Monte Carlo."[27] It then proceeds to fictionalize the opening essay of Chesterton's volume *Heretics* (1905), in which he attacked the habit of saying one's personal philosophy does not matter. Chesterton creates a fantasy about a running battle between MacIan the devout Catholic and Turnbull the devoted atheist. They decide to settle their differences in a duel but are almost immediately forced to join forces in a fight against ordinary English society, which refuses to believe men could fight a duel about the existence of God—which refuses, that is, to believe that one's personal philosophy matters. The society Chesterton satirizes seemed to him to have become dogmatically relativistic and unable to take anything seriously. But *The Ball and the Cross* does take religion seriously. The two heroes go all over the nation, from island resort to country manor-house, in search of Englishmen who will treat faith as a life-and-death matter, and the book ends with a nightmare vision of England transformed into the regimented tyranny of "Professor Lucifer," with all deviates, both serious believers and serious atheists, declared insane.

In spite of this dystopian view, *The Ball and the Cross* is reassuring, for it demonstrates that one Edwardian novelist at least could treat religion in an imaginative and intelligent way. Chesterton was an exception in a prevailingly secular decade.[28] His position was the intermediate and lonely one between the best-selling writers, who believed firmly enough but could only confirm sectarian prejudices in their fiction, and the serious novelists, like Wells, James, and Conrad, who were willing to attack prejudice on all sides but had ceased to believe—and who, unlike Hardy, had also ceased to be angry about their state of unbelief.

6

Departure

"I am tired of the novelist's portrait of a gentleman, with gloves and hat, leaning against a pillar, upon a vague landscape background. I want the gentleman as he appears in a snap-shot photograph, with his every-day expression on his face, and the localities in which he spends his days accurately visible around him."[1] So Edmund Gosse complained in 1892, in an essay which accepts without murmur the "tyranny" of the novel even while it resents the fact of the novel's subjection to genteel cliché. In less than a decade H. G. Wells among others would provide Gosse with his everyday gentleman as seen in a snapshot photograph; meanwhile, other voices were being raised in protest to the worn-out themes of Victorianism. Henry James, for example, declared himself contemptuous of turn-of-the-century fictional costumery ("all the loose and thin material that keeps reappearing in forms at once ready-made and sadly the worse for wear") and was ready, as a thrifty and industrious writer, to turn that contempt into something salable.[2]

James's odd tale "The Story in It" (*The Better Sort*, 1903) contains a debate about the presentation of the virtuous woman in British-American and in French fiction. The British-American novel is too naive about sexual themes, the debaters decide, seeming "really to show our sense of life as the sense of puppies and kittens"; while the French "give us only again and again, for ever and ever, the same couple."[3] On both sides of the Channel, then, James found those novels attempting to deal with the "immense omission in our fiction, the great relation between men and women," convention-bound and unable to break free. In his own novels James exerted himself for the liberation of his art in the way best suited to his gifts, by intensifying and idealizing the British-American sense of life as "puppies and kittens" and juxtaposing it against a French or Italian sexual ruthlessness; that is, by dramatizing with a newly subtle method his old theme of America and Europe, innocence and experience, romance and adultery. But James's fiction remained largely uninfluential during the Edwardian era; all he could do to help the novel-reader weary of the same old couple, the same old material, the same old gentleman, was to write his own inventive fiction.

The worn-out themes came from worn-out novelists. Frank Swinnerton, the man-of-letters, memoirist, and novelist, remembered 1899-1900 as years of profound disillusionment in the community of writers and readers: "We were old, we were fat; we had lost our teeth and our collective soul. We were certainly uneasy and full of self-criticism. The term 'Little Englander,' once abusive, was adopted by humanitarians to express the ideal of a contracted Britain shining with small, isolated virtue." For those publicly opposed to the smug little England, the imperialists, there was Kipling—but at the turn of the century Kipling had begun to seem less astounding. The subjects of his stories had grown increasingly smaller and more mechanical, and his poetry, after the immense triumph of "Recessional," had become jingoistic and slightly vulgar. "The Absent-Minded Beggar" (1899) had raised a quarter of a million pounds, but as a poem, it was markedly inferior to "Recessional," and it was published in the *Daily Mail*, not the *Times*. The Aesthetic Movement, meanwhile, that cult of weariness and sensation-seeking from the 1890s, was lingering feebly on in the works of the belle-lettrist Richard Le Gallienne and the editor and novelist Henry Harland, but without exciting interest or respect. Asked if he had read a new book by Le Gallienne, a journalist of the early 1900s replied dismissingly, "Oh, I put my hand up its pages."[4]

According to Swinnerton, what rescued the Edwardian novel from this inertia was a perception, new and suddenly invigorating in 1901, "that, even if one disliked them, one could not and should not ignore facts." Not ignoring facts stimulated a new effort directed at "the sober recording of life, with English humour, English tolerance (sometimes called 'compromise'), and English concern for the ethics of personal conduct. Precise verisimilitude was to be its main strength."[5] Swinnerton's championing of verisimilitude at the expense of imagination, with its emphasis on sobriety and dutifulness, is a little misleading, for it suggests the sudden forced enlistment of novelists in a campaign to expose slum conditions or chronicle the dreariness of working-class life—to fictionalize sociology. That function of writing was indeed prominent in 1901, the year of Wells's *Anticipations*, but not all novelists then or subsequently were inclined to follow the lead of the reformers. Swinnerton himself began his career as a novelist with *The Merry Heart* in 1909, a cheerful and shamelessly unreforming novel of family life, and he did not fictionalize facts in the sense of grim social facts until *Nocturne* (1917).

As the decade wore on, the conscientious fact-gathering of Galsworthy, the Fabian Socialists Sidney and Beatrice Webb, and the whole Mrs. Humphry Ward-Marcella-slumming school, as Wells called it in order to emphasize its ties to late Victorian reform fiction, changed into something vaguer and more intrinsically liberating. The great Edwardian discovery was that fiction might include a whole new range of personal and social observation, observation not necessarily rooted in politics but responsive simply to the planned and unplanned developments of the decade: the New Woman beside the old-fashioned woman, the disillusioned or incompetent officer beside the tanned and dutiful subaltern at the outposts of empire, the working journalist beside the *rentier*, imperial misgivings beside national confidence, private operations of the mind beside public expressions or actions, and the people of the abyss (or merely of the lower-middle class) beside Gosse's "gentleman" with his "every-day expression" and accurately observed locale. The disposition to notice facts may in the first instance have induced novelists to notice political realities previously ignored or concealed, but it soon led them to other fields for fictional exploitation, such as utopianism, fantasy, scientific invention, the relations of the sexes, and the study of the city. After recovering from their fin-de-siècle weariness, Edwardians looked about them and discovered a plenitude of fictional subjects not yet honestly attempted. With these they extended and enriched their art of fiction.

What distinguishes Edwardian fiction from the fiction of the 1890s on one side, and the formally experimental novels of postwar modernism on the other, is exactly this tendency to expand into new subjects. One of the advantages of not having a critical attitude of the sort Ford prized was that it permitted Edwardians an elastic sense of what they were doing and could do fictionally, and in practice they were willing to stretch the notion of "the novel" very far to accommodate what they saw as potential subjects, though naturally novelists differed in assessing the capacity of fiction to discourse on all subjects or examine all levels of society. At the end of the Edwardian decade Forster wrote bluntly of one of the novel's limits: "We are not concerned with the very poor. They are unthinkable, and only to be approached by the statistician or the poet."[6] This troublesome remark in *Howards End* expresses an important disagreement with the general ambitiousness of Forster's time, which on all sides, politically conservative as well as politically liberal, was marked by an enthusiasm in tackling new subjects and overturning old expectations about matters proper to prose fiction. It is difficult to think of any Edwardian novelist besides Forster, or perhaps James, whose fiction is based on a systematic art of exclusion, who could have written in any of his books, "We are not concerned." The age was concerned with everything that came its way, from the first awakening of interest in psychoanalysis (Algernon Blackwood's *John Silence: Physician Extraordinary*, 1908), to the growing naval threat of Germany (Erskine Childers' *The Riddle of the Sands*, 1903), to the recently promulgated doctrine of Zionism (M. P. Shiel's *The Lord of the Sea*, 1901). The works of one prodigious novelist alone, Wells, are a reliable guide to the major intellectual, political, and scientific developments of the decade: the Woman Question, though awkwardly conflated with the mishaps of Wells's romantic life, in *Ann Veronica;* the dangers of biological experimentation in *The Food of the Gods* (1904); the return of Halley's Comet in *In the Days of the Comet;* the strange loneliness and incomprehensibility of life in great cities in *The New Machiavelli;* the excesses of commercial imperialism in *The First Men in the Moon* (1901); the potentials of advertisement and heavier-than-air flight in *Tono-Bungay.*

There was, of course, contemporary objection to the expansion of the novel into new areas, which in some cases was objection to the areas themselves. R. A. Scott-James's *Modernism and Romance* (1908) remarks, "In this twentieth century we find that every class of things, every sphere of life, every phase of thought, every branch of knowledge has its corresponding votaries in literature." So far, so good, but the tone of disapproval creeps into Scott-James's voice as he continues to survey the new "Democracy of Letters": "Every class of persons and of things, every typical sentiment and cynicism, is represented in that chaotic and widely dispersed body of writers who produce the books and journals of to-day." The implication is that some persons and some opinions ought to stay unrepresented, since their fictionalization leads to chaos, or worse, license, the seemingly inevitable result of freedom to write on any subject. For Scott-James the novel, "the natural medium for every kind of self-expression," leads the way into reprehensible individualism.[7]

Edwardian fiction abounds with similar opinions less suavely expressed. Ann Veronica's father, threatened ideologically by Radical politicians and personally by his daughter's growing rebelliousness, lashes out at "these damned novels. All this torrent of misleading, spurious stuff that pours from the press. These sham ideals and advanced notions, Women who Dids, and all that kind of thing."[8] There is more in this caricature than disdain for stout British pigheadedness; it reveals Wells's ill-concealed resentment at those who would retard progress or limit the novel's field of action. The sexual outspokenness of *Ann Veronica,* or what seemed outspokenness in 1909, provoked a severe reaction and perhaps contributed to the difficulties Wells soon had in finding a publisher for *The New Machiavelli.* This novel was refused by Macmillan, who had the excuse not only that it was as "scandalous" or "realistic" as *Ann Veronica* (*The History of Mr. Polly* in 1910 had excited hopes among the prudish that Wells was returning to a gentler, more "English" tone), but also that it was an obvious roman-à-clef, with the "Baileys" equaling Sidney and Beatrice Webb; the "Pentagram Circle" equaling the Co-efficients, a group of advanced thinkers which had started meeting in 1902, at Beatrice Webb's suggestion, to discuss the affairs of empire; and "Isabel Rivers" equaling Amber Reeves, with whom Wells was carrying on the most intense of his prewar infatuations. "Subterranean people," a species of literary savages to match the underground Morlocks of *The Time Machine* (1895), was Wells's term for the self-appointed censors of *The New Machiavelli,* which he deemed "coldly chaste" according to "the standards of Maurice Hewlett or Mrs. Humphry Ward."[9]

Edwardian novelists had in fact less difficulty with censorship than Edwardian playwrights, if by "censorship" is meant outright prohibition of publication or confiscation of copies. Some novels were condemned—Balzac's were a frequent target, as Zola's had been in the previous decade—and others, like *Ann Veronica,* were refused by libraries, vilified in reviews, or subjected in other ways to unofficial though often effective censorship.[10] But novelists had at least no central, all-powerful, and irremediably philistine authority to appease, as was the case with dramatists and the Lord Chamberlain's Examiner of Plays. Novelists had merely to satisfy the individual sensibilities of publishers and of printers, both of whom were liable to prosecution under the Obscenity Statute, as Joyce found when he tried to publish the *Dubliners* stories in 1906. Edwardian novelists on the whole were able to get their work into print; Wells did find a publisher for *The New Machiavelli*—an American one first, then John Lane in 1911—and he and other novelists were able to devote much energy, in such matters as signing petitions and lobbying for parliamentary investigation, to the cause of their more practically afflicted colleagues the dramatists. This is not to argue that no practical damage was done to fiction by Edwardian censorship. The loss or delay of even one book is a sensible loss, and *Dubliners* was delayed eight years by the prudery and political cautiousness of its would-be publishers and printers. There was also the incalculable cost of the abortion of daring ideas in the expectation of censorship.

In "The Art of Fiction" James had declared that the novel was no longer condemned outright as immoral; that is, it was losing the stigma attached to it as a vulgar, inferior, and excessively pleasurable genre and was about to come into its own as a medium of expression as receptive to exacting manipulation as any other. This, for James, was the essential challenge presented to the novel, the challenge by which it would rise to pre-eminence or sink into genteel insipidity, and though in "The Future of the Novel" he also acknowledged the important matter of the novelist's freedom to respond to "delicate issues" and the susceptibilities of the young, he never lost sight of what was for him a holy cause: the novel as a controlled and entirely untrivial form, a deeply contrived artistic response to experience. It is hardly surprising, then, that James felt bewilderment when into his delicate spider-web of the finest silken threads came crashing the idea-crammed and often ungainly fictions of Edwardians like Kipling and Wells.

"I am not quite sure that I see your *idea*—I mean your Subject, so to speak, as determined or constituted: but in short the thing is a bloody little chunk of life," wrote James to Wells on the publication of *Love and Mr. Lewisham* in 1900, though he went on, generous in spite of his incomprehension, to wish Wells's novel "a great and continuous fortune."[11] The bloody little chunk of life versus the delicate spider-web of sensibility is the substantive issue to which the "debaters" Wells and James devoted themselves when they were not exchanging metaphors. In the simplest terms, James argued for a cautious admission of ideas and ideologies into the house of fiction, for control in their expression, (ideas "determined or constituted"), for adherence to agreed-on standards, and for the subservience of subject-matter to medium. Wells argued for the greatest possible receptivity to the new, for structural flexibility, and for the subservience of medium to subject-matter. Wells wanted more room—more room for Wells. "I want to write novels and before God I *will* write novels," he wrote to Bennett in 1900. "They are the proper stuff for my everyday work, a methodical careful distillation of one's thoughts and sentiments and experiences and impressions."[12] Eleven years later he turned this ambition into a definition of the novel's essential freedom: "the novel I hold to be a discursive thing; it is not a single interest, but a woven tapestry of interests." The phase of narrowing and restriction is over; "there is every encouragement for a return to a laxer, more spacious form of novel-writing."[13]

Yet in the midst of his impatience to make fiction reflect his turbulent times, Wells had to pay attention to the Jamesian strictures. Censure from book-persecuting Morlocks was one thing; censure from the Master, from an aesthetic point of view, was another. How could Swinnerton's invigorating "facts" and the loose novelistic structures best suited to the transmittal of facts be reconciled with artistic standards? There was no one answer, nor even one answer for each particular novelist; but Wells and all other serious writers of the period had to grapple with the question as best they could, attempting to answer it if not among themselves then for themselves, individually and tentatively. For as the decade threw up more and more subjects for possible treatment, agreement on principles of limitation or ordering grew to seem less and less likely. James's criticism of Wells emphasizes his formlessness, lack of definition, rawness, loudness, but never the validity or excitement of Wells's ideas themselves. The ideas James admires, though his admiration takes the form of ever more ingenious periphrases. Throughout the correspondence between the two novelists James's sophistication demonstrates, as if in mocking or envious comparison, Wells's freshness.

Freshness, the most elusive of literary qualities and the one most obscured by the passage of years, was a quality praised in Wells by others than James—by Bennett, for example, who in a 1902 article admires his friend's gift "of seeing things afresh, as though no one had ever seen them before." In a deft compliment Bennett invokes the angel of *The Wonderful Visit* (1895) and the mermaid of *The Sea Lady* (1902) who, like their creator, never take anything as a matter of course.[14] The note of envy in Bennett is perceptible. He aimed at the Wellsian freshness while at the same time seeking to avoid the Wellsian artistic straining, immaturity, and arrogance—the tendency of Wells, so to speak, to put forth ideas as though they had never before been heard on earth. Like Swinnerton, Bennett felt a weariness at the turn of the century and longed for invigoration; like Swinnerton again, he saw the prospect of that invigoration in new fictional subjects rather than new forms. In an article of 1901 Bennett admires the aesthetic perceptiveness and "inclination to wander" of a minority of readers, but he casts his lot definitely with the majority, who are holding "to the straight path" in putting subject matter before treatment.[15]

A sense of weariness is the burden of Bennett's important essay "The Fallow Fields of Fiction," which also appeared in 1901, just at the point when Edwardian freshness was beginning to be a distinctive achievement. Bennett commiserates with those whose business it is to examine the whole output of modern fiction, for they must necessarily be depressed and wearied by the heavy sensation of its sameness, its futility, its lack of enterprise. Reading novels is like visiting the Royal Academy: why must there always be the same scene of two men and a maid? There is altogether too much emphasis on love sentimentally expressed, and the division of fiction into types, namely the domestic, historical, criminal, theological, and bellicose, is too rigid.[16]

A new start is called for. Bennett speaks of dining in an Italian restaurant in Victoria Street, then wandering outside in search of fictional material: "We dined early, and the sun was still above the sky-affronting roofs of the thoroughfare when we passed into Victoria-street with the intention of perceiving London as though it were a foreign city."[17] That simple statement provides a major key to Edwardian fiction, both to the motives that underlie its creation and to the forms in which the creation is expressed. London seen as a foreign city, new and fresh; the city as an economic or political fact for the first time properly acknowledged; the city as an abyss, imperial encampment, or arena of telegrams and anger; the city as a place for adventure; the city altered out of all recognition and ready to be relearned by those who have been away from it, the returned imperialist or the businessman from abroad; the city "framed" or "photographed" in an act of conscious imaging which might paradoxically make it more veracious. All these possibilities, which are what the Edwardian decade made of London once it took Bennett's advice to view the city as though it were foreign, are implicit in the mere advocacy of seeing afresh, seeing artifically—that is, seeing with the kind of fictional artifice that refuses old myths and insists on new ones. Artifice and seeing afresh are in fact synonyms brought together by the pun in "novel," a pun Bennett seems on the point of discovering in an 1897 passage from his Journal:

And then, in King's Road, the figures of tradesmen at shop-doors, of children romping or stealing along mournfully, of men and women each totally different from every other, and all serious, wrapt up in their own thoughts and ends—these seemed curiously strange and novel and wonderful. Every scene, even the commonest, is wonderful, if only one can detach oneself, casting off all memory of use and custom, and behold it (as it were) for the first time; in its right, authentic colours; without making comparisons. The novelist should cherish and burnish this faculty of seeing crudely, simply, artlessly, ignorantly; of seeing like a baby or a lunatic, who lives each moment by itself and tarnishes the present by no remembrance of the past.[18]

The trick is to use art to seem artless, and neither Bennett nor any other Edwardian novelist manages the trick with consistent success. After all, writers do not want to seem too much like a baby or a lunatic. The strangeness they find in the streets tends in their works to become comprehensible, even educative. In Bennett's essay of 1901, the immediate result of looking at London in a "novel" way is to see the Westminster Cathedral, then under construction, and think of the magnificent novel that could be written about its raising, its architect, and its history. This is the Bennett who would devote immense artistic energy to the story of a house-building in *Clayhanger* (1910) and who, in doing so, would have distinguished Edwardian company: Wells in the story of the Ponderevo houses in *Tono-Bungay*; Galsworthy in *The Man of Property*; Kipling in "An Habitation Enforced" (*Actions and Reactions*).

Bennett suggests other possible topics for novelists: if not the romance of an urban cathedral, then perhaps the romance of a parish council, or "the romance, the humanity, and the passions of a great railway system." Who better than the past and future chronicler of industry in the Five Towns could have fictionalized such a topic? In 1897 Bennett had written to Wells, "It seems to me that there are immense possibilities in the very romance of manufacture—not wonders of machinery and that sort of stuff—but in the tremendous altercation with nature that is continually going on."[19]

Bennett's putative romances of cathedral-building, parish councils, and railways remind one inevitably of the most sweeping criticism ever made of Edwardian fiction: "Every sort of town is represented, and innumerable institutions; we see factories, prisons, workhouses, law courts, Houses of Parliament; a general clamour, the voice of aspiration, indignation, effort and industry, rises from the whole; but in all this vast conglomeration of printed pages, in all this congeries of streets and houses, there is not a single man or woman whom we know." That is the voice of Virginia Woolf, whose 1923 essay "Mr. Bennett and Mrs. Brown" seems to grant the Edwardians exactly what they claim for themselves and then to demonstrate the artistic pointlessness of such an achievement. Woolf announces that she is responding to a complaint of Bennett that the younger, Georgian generation of novelists has failed to create real characters. She agrees that the character-making power has evaporated, but blames this failure on novelists of the Edwardian age, including Wells, Galsworthy, and Bennett himself. In order to do this, Woolf confesses, she must oversimplify: she must "do as painters do when they wish to reduce the innumerable details of a crowded landscape to simplicity—step back, half shut the eyes, gesticulate a little vaguely with the fingers, and reduce Edwardian fiction to a view."[20] Woolf does figuratively what Sackville-West would do fictionally in *The Edwardians* a few years later, which is to foreshorten, to reduce, to rob the decade of some of its variety by taking "Edwardian" in a conventional sense.

With confessedly half-shut eyes and reduced view, then, Woolf claims that the works of Wells, Bennett, and Galsworthy give a wealth of things and a dearth of character. In her failure to see a single man or woman whom she knows there is a veiled snobbism, a hint that the Edwardians failed to supply Woolf with a single man or woman whom she would feel comfortable knowing. Her "we" is nearly as excluding as Forster's "we" in the "we are not concerned" of *Howards End;* and just as Forster, for all his broadmindedness, cannot avoid condescending to Leonard Bast, whose flat is "an amorous and not unpleasant little hole," so Woolf cannot avoid condescending to a character like Kipps, whose life is necessarily led among a clutter of things in which he takes an intense bourgeois interest. Woolf's disdain for Kippsian things is like T. S. Eliot's attitude in Part III of *The Waste Land,* where the denizens of a fallen London are blamed for living amid the wrong sort of furnishings: food in tins, drying combinations, unlit stairs. The world of drying combinations is what engages the sympathy of Edwardian writers, and Kipps's fascination with things is precisely Wells's point. Kipps has nothing else to be fascinated with. Woolf blames Wells for devoting his time to a counter-jumper and Bennett for devoting his to a homebody like Hilda Lessways. Woolf thus devalues the Edwardian sense of human limitation.

Woolf attributes the Edwardians' failure in characterization to their being daunted by the great characters of Victorian fiction and preoccupied by the material and social forces that mold character: the factories in which people work, the houses in which they live. In an analysis of *Hilda Lessways,* the second novel in the *Clayhanger* series, Woolf comments that Bennett, "being an Edwardian," begins by describing "accurately and minutely the sort of house Hilda lived in, and the sort of house she saw from the window. House property was the common ground from which the Edwardians found it easy to proceed to intimacy." This stress upon "the fabric of things" stemmed from the Edwardian need to improve the fabric of things; Bennett and his contemporaries "have given us a house in the hope that we may be able to deduce the human beings who lived there," and "to give them their due, they have made that house much better worth living in."[21]

Woolf and her contemporaries must construct their own and more figurative house of fiction, because "in or about December, 1910, human character changed . . . All human relations have shifted—those between masters and servants, husbands and wives, parents and children." The material basis of life will no longer do as the basis of fiction, life itself having become more immaterial, more diffuse, more subject to purely psychological forces. To illustrate the need for changed approaches, Woolf postulates a Mrs. Brown, who is pictured entering Woolf's railway carriage and hence the realm of possible fiction. What would the Edwardian triumvirate make of her? Wells would forget her for a utopian vision of a better world; Galsworthy would see a pathetic social example; Bennett would give her antecedents and environment in great detail.[22] Not one of the treatments would do justice to her essence, her mysterious inner being, her psychological reality.

There is no denying the fact that the older novelists sometimes wrote in these dismissive ways. But Woolf's charge is less a genuine criticism than a form of self-definition. By disparaging other writers' alleged versions of Mrs. Brown, Woolf clears a space for her own attempt at the character. She dispatches the past to a safe place in order to define more clearly what her own fiction must be like. Literary iconoclasm of this sort was a defining gesture of the modernists, and merely as an intention, it sets them apart from the preceding generation. Wells, Galsworthy, and Bennett were willing to depart from a past of circumscribed fictional subjects but not from a whole tradition of fiction-making. That tradition enabled them to make their actual versions of Mrs. Brown more aesthetically satisfying than the figures Woolf sketches on their behalf. The Baines sisters in *The Old Wives' Tale*, for example, stem at once from Bennett's observation of life in the Potteries and his admiration of *La Comédie Humaine*, from which he learned not only a doctrine of determinism-by-things but a way of cherishing the slow passage of ordinary life. If Bennett spends an inordinate amount of time minutely describing the houses in which the sisters live, that is because they are ordinary women, and houses are their only means of self-expression.

Once the cause of their limitation, the pathos of their materialism, is understood, the Baines sisters and Kipps and the rest of the Edwardian fictional company may be known as intimately and thoroughly as Woolf's Mrs. Dalloway and Mrs. Ramsay. Such a knowing entails a willingness to take the characters on their own terms, in the objectified and spiritually impoverished form in which their creators issued them, clinging to their houses and possessions, thinking predictable thoughts, entangling themselves more hopelessly in the fabric of life even as they seek to escape from it. The Edwardians deserve credit for extending the fictional imagination to those who had rarely been thought worthy of narrative: the unpicturesque, the unromantic, the unadventurous, the unexceptional.

For that matter they deserve credit simply for extending the imagination to so many different characters, some of whom were thrust into being by the actual events of the decade, some of whom symbolize a turning away from event to the more accommodating realm of fantasy. No Edwardian writer took Bennett up on his suggestions to write about the architect of Westminster Cathedral or a booking-clerk in a railway station. But there is Edwardian fiction about guilt-ridden clergymen in Ireland, popular jockeys, diplomats, amateur spies, journalists dignified and undignified, housewives who gamble, gentlemen in retirement, anarchists, ship-wrecked children, travelers in Arabia, a dictator of the world, aesthetes, hearties, returned colonials, smart heroines, the inventor of an antigravity substance, suffragettes, and international criminals. Most though not all of these characters are seen freshly, as "for the first time"; they are seen with a consciousness that they benefit the novel by allowing it to participate in the Edwardian enlargement of life.

Confronted with the new multiplicity of fiction, which they wished to put in some kind of order, critics in the period relied on the familiar labels "romance" and "realism," the poles between which, they argued, all novels migrate.[23] The problem is not that these terms are meaningless for Edwardian writing. James's preface to *The American* (1877), one of those composed during his Edwardian years of retirement, demonstrates that the terms could have exact and useful meaning. The real represents "the things we cannot possibly *not* know, sooner or later, in one way or another," whereas the romantic stands for the "things that, with all the facilities in the world, all the wealth and all the courage and all the wit and all the adventure, we never *can* directly know; the things that reach us only through the beautiful circuit and subterfuge of our thought and our desire."[24] James restores the terms to usefulness by rescuing them from superficiality (romance as "being a matter indispensably of boats, or of caravans, or of tigers"), and by showing their pertinence to the work of all serious novelists. In practice the serious Edwardian novelists, dramatizing tendencies toward romance and realism in the various longings of their fictional characters, often stress the pathos of never quite being able to know the beautiful things of romance. Wells's Mr. Polly, whose only escape from an unsympathetic wife and a small shopkeeper's life is daydreaming, represents romance radically limited by the imaginative materials at hand. Much the same might be said of Forster's Leonard

Bast, who wishes to romanticize his flat as Ruskin romanticized Venice, but is defeated by its stuffiness and his own fatigue. The contrary urge is dramatized in Galsworthy's Richard Shelton in *The Island Pharisees* (1908), who lives to thrust realism, the things we cannot possibly not know, in front of the English Liberal conscience.

The problem with the terms is that "romance" and "realism" were taken in too absolute a sense and were made part of an inexorable literary cycle. Romance was seen as yielding to realism, and *vice versa,* in a presumably unending process. But such a progression is too tidy. The Edwardian years were realistic and romantic at the same time, the tendencies being in simultaneous reaction to each other, often among the books of a single author. One case is that of Phyllis Bottome, who published *The Master Hope,* a high-spirited love story, in 1904, and followed it a year later with *Raw Material: Some Characters and Episodes among Working Lads.* Perhaps the epigraph from Kipling that Bottome chose for her novel ("Thou canst not choose Freedom and go in bondage to the delight of life") suddenly made her think realistically about the "delight of life" available in the East End.

The Edwardians lived through a decade with few clear-cut movements of any kind and with an abundance of polarities: the city versus the country, little England versus the empire, Peter Pan versus the Five Towns, the life of telegrams and anger versus the life of personal relations. They were not so foolish as to believe that one extreme would give way completely to its opposite, and hoped instead for a middle ground between extremes. This would not necessarily be that most cautious and English of concepts, a compromise. In its most courageous form it might be what Margaret Schlegel calls for in *Howards End,* "a continuous excursion between realms," an unshaken faith in the possibilities of connection. The Edwardians knew that at the very least they had to acknowledge the contradictions inherent in their era, and some among them acknowledged that fact with cheerfulness, as though it were a new and exciting thing to be pulled in different directions. To quote Wells, in the guise of his character Capes, the lover of Ann Veronica: "Life is two things . . . Life is moral-ity—life is adventure. Squire and master. Adventure rules and morality—looks up the trains in the Bradshaw. Morality tells you what is right, and adventure moves you."[25] In Capes's ex-citement—he has snatched Ann Veronica away from her dread-ful family and is standing with her on an Alp—he pontificates, but his sense of contemporary life is accurate, however pompous his words.

In this polarity-ridden or -blessed period, then, a novel called *The Dream and the Business* may be taken as representative by virtue of its title alone. The matter of the novel is also represen-tative—not, it must be said, of the best fictional art of the dec-ade, but of ramshackle Edwardian ambitiousness in general. This 1906 work by "John Oliver Hobbes" (Pearl M. T. Craigie) begins with an old-fashioned triangle involving an artist, a busi-nessman, and a young woman, a fierce Nonconformist. But complications quickly turn this fiction of two men and a maid into something far more interesting, though also more shapeless. Among the topics covered are religious controversy (the Catho-lics of the novel attempt to convert the Protestants, and *vice versa*), the morality of marriage (there is a sudden revelation of bigamy, as in *Clayhanger*), the political maneuverings of Glad-stone's ministry, the cruelty of the divorce laws, the moral short-comings of the Stage, and the conflict between the life of art and the life of duty. In the end nothing works out well, none of the expected happy marriages takes place, and no issue is brought to a conclusion. Clearly, whenever *The Dream and the Business* is confronted with a choice of alternatives, it insists on both, which is to say it attempts to discuss more than it can understand. In this sense, if in no other, it offers a parable about all of Edwar-dian fiction.

PART TWO

Adventures Abroad

Time, and the ocean, and some fostering star,
In high cabal have made us what we are,
Who stretch one hand to Huron's bearded pines,
And one on Kashmir's snowy shoulder lay,
And round the streaming of whose raiment shines
The iris of the Australasian spray.
For waters have connived at our designs,
And winds have plotted with us—and behold,
Kingdom in kingdom, sway in oversway,
Dominion fold in fold . . .
So great we are, and old.

—William Watson, "Ode on the Day
of the Coronation of King Edward VII"

7

The Adventure and Romance Agency

Carruthers is a bored young gentleman trapped in an out-of-season London by his duties at the Foreign Office. During the day he reads telegrams and makes a few desultory minutes, and during the night he regrets not having accepted invitations to certain country-house parties. A slumming expedition to the East End and a visit to a music hall only intensify his suffering. Suddenly a letter arrives asking him to join his friend Davies on a yacht in the Baltic, and in the space of a few hours Carruthers has obtained leave, made the necessary nautical purchases, and embarked on a steamer for Flushing. The boat slides "through the calm channels of the Thames estuary" and passes "the cordon of scintillating lightships that watch over the sea-roads to the imperial city like pickets round a sleeping army." Carruthers' world is opening up. He has been ironic and melancholy, but on his friend's yacht in the open air a new series of emotions is going to seize him in spite of all his man-about-town defenses:

> Close in the train of Humour came Romance, veiling her face, but I knew it was the rustle of her robes that I heard in the foam beneath me; I knew that it was she who handed me the cup of sparkling wine and bade me drink and be merry. Strange to me though it was, I knew the taste when it touched my lips. It was not that bastard concoction I had tasted in the pseudo-Bohemias of Soho; it was not the showy but insipid beverage I should have drunk my fill of at Morven Lodge; it was the purest of pure vintages, instilling the ancient inspiration which, under many guises, quickens thousands of better brains than mine, but whose essence is always the same: the gay pursuit of a perilous quest.[1]

77

Domini Enfilden, vaguely restless and dissatisfied by her life, travels to North Africa in search of sensation. In the hotel at Beni-Mora she is unable to sleep. Cardinal Newman's *The Dream of Gerontius* is at hand, but Domini hears the wind rustling outside and goes to the window:

> She felt the brave companionship of mystery. In it she divined the beating pulses, the hot, surging blood of freedom.
>
> She wanted freedom, a wide horizon, the great winds, the great sun, the terrible spaces, the glowing, shimmering radiance, the hot, entrancing noons and bloomy, purple nights of Africa. She wanted the nomad's fires and the acid voices of the Kabyle dogs. She wanted the roar of the tom-toms, the clash of the cymbals, the rattle of the negroes' castanets, the fluttering, painted figures of the dancers. She wanted—more than she could express, more than she knew. It was there, want, aching in her heart, as she drew into her nostrils this strange and wealthy atmosphere.
>
> When Domini returned to her bed she found it impossible to read any more Newman.[2]

George Ponderevo and his uncle Teddy, the great magnate of Tono-Bungay, are sitting in their London office listening to a strange explorer-buccaneer tell a stranger tale of the valuable mineral deposit he has discovered on a remote island. The explorer smiles and scrutinizes them through the smoke of a cigar, then begins to piece his story together:

> He conjured up a vision of this strange forgotten link in the world's littoral . . . He gave a sense of heat and a perpetual reek of vegetable decay, and told how at last comes a break among these things, an arena fringed with bone-white dead trees, a sight of the hard-blue sea line beyond the dazzling surf and a wide desolation of dirty shingle and mud, bleached and scarred . . . A little way off among charred dead weeds stands the abandoned station,—abandoned because every man who stayed two months at that station stayed to die, eaten up mysteriously like a leper . . . He talked of the Dutch East Indies and of the Congo, of Portuguese East Africa and Paraguay, of Malays and rich Chi-

nese merchants, Dyaks and Negroes and the spread of the Mahometan world in Africa to-day . . . Our cosy inner office became a little place, and all our business cold and lifeless exploits beside his glimpses of strange minglings of men, of slayings unavenged and curious customs, of trade where no writs run, and the dark treacheries of eastern ports and uncharted channels.[3]

These passages—from Erskine Childers' *The Riddle of the Sands* (1903), Robert Hichens' *The Garden of Allah* (1905), and H. G. Wells's *Tono-Bungay* (1909)—are parables of escape from the dark, confining streets of London, the burden of intellectualism and melancholy, and the boredom of routine. In different ways they dramatize a widespread desire to move away from the known to the unknown, from the social to the personal, or from realism to romance, as those terms were conventionally understood. The passages lie at the heart of a whole Edwardian literature of mystery and adventure, a literature which with exotic settings and compounded dangers gave Englishmen of the period the profoundly satisfying illusion that it was complicating life, whereas in reality it simplified it, by removing the ordinary controls placed over life and making life wholly amenable to the imagination. In romance, according to James's formula, "nothing is right save as we rightly imagine it." Romantic literature rejected the pragmatic, comprehensive philosophy of Wells's Mr. Capes ("Life is two things . . . Life is morality—life is adventure") and with it the Edwardian regard for polarities, asserting as a matter of faith that life was only one thing. In all periods, of course, romance has asserted the bracing simplicity of life. The vast Victorian literature of adventure, such as that written by R. M. Ballantyne, Frederick Marryat, Thomas Mayne Reid, Rider Haggard, and Robert Louis Stevenson, is in this sense indistinguishable from Edwardian adventure books. But in the same measure as Edwardians grew more certain of the Balfourian qualities of their decade, their fictional adventures abroad grew more artificial, escapist, and un-Balfourian.

Momentarily in some books, constantly in others, the literature of adventure denied what Edwardians knew was really the truth about the world in which they were placed. In that sense it was treacherous, as darkly and alluringly treacherous as Wells's eastern ports and uncharted channels. But the fact of the treachery could be only partially recognized and admitted. The need for adventure was too insistent. Many Edwardians were in the position of Domini Enfilden. Want was aching in their hearts, and the want was for more than they could express. Adventure revealed itself in glimpses, romance came to them veiled—or it receded before them like the horizon. "It lies a little distance before us," says the narrator of the most self-consciously romantic Edwardian novel of all, "and a little distance behind—about as far as the eye can carry. One discovers that one has passed through it just as one passed what is to-day our horizon."[4]

This is a sailor's image, and with its tone of disillusioned weariness it seems to belong naturally to Conrad, who may indeed have written the sentences, which are taken from *Romance* (1903), his collaboration with Ford Madox Ford. Other Edwardians—Bennett, Wells, Kipling—tended to see romance in different places, lying about them on the land, in the streets, in machinery, in the railways or half-built cathedrals, but at one time or another nearly all Edwardians did in fact see romance. Their sensitivity to ordinariness drove them to see it. The fanciful Chesterton went a step further, viewing romance not as the most elusive of human moods but as a commodity, a manufacture, a marketable enterprise of urban ingenuity. He expressed this view in *The Club of Queer Trades* (1905), a collection of short stories mocking the intuitive powers of an amateur detective named Basil Grant. One of the "crimes" Grant investigates turns out to be a well-planned performance of the "Adventure and Romance Agency" which, according to one of its operatives, "has been started to meet a great modern desire":

> On every side, in conversation and in literature, we hear of the desire for a larger theatre of events—for something to waylay us and lead us splendidly astray. Now the man who feels this desire for a varied life pays a yearly or quar-

terly sum to the Adventure and Romance Agency; in return, the Adventure and Romance Agency undertakes to
surround him with startling and weird events. As a man is
leaving his front door, an excited sweep approaches him
and assures him of a plot against his life; he gets into a cab,
and is driven to an opium den; he receives a mysterious
telegram or a dramatic visit, and is immediately in a vortex
of incidents. A very picturesque and moving story is first
written by one of the staff of distinguished novelists who
are at present hard at work in the adjoining room.[5]

This brilliant conceit is a more suggestive one than seems possible in the midst of Chesterton's relentless whimsicality. The
Adventure and Romance Agency satirizes the artificial romanti-
cizing of London as it was carried out by the amateur adventurers of Stevenson's *New Arabian Nights,* but at the same time
it takes seriously the urban restlessness on which the *New Arabian Nights* was based. This restlessness was anything but artificial in 1905. Chesterton did not exaggerate when he spoke of the
"great modern desire" for romance, and he was transparently
symbolical when he created the agency, with its staff of distinguished novelists at work on scenarios in the adjoining room, as
a response to this desire. In the first decade of the century there
was a real if unincorporated agency of this kind. It consisted of
the writers of adventure fiction, Chesterton included, who in return for regular payments provided regular installments of the
startling and the weird. The only inaccurate thing about Chesterton's conception is that it makes adventure writing a completely
cynical business, whereas in fact it was often genuinely exciting
to its practitioners. In the manner of Elinor Glyn taking comfort
in her own emotional fantasies, the Edwardian adventure novelist used his fiction to expand his own life, to meet men "vivid,
real, with strong outlines, with intense hopes, and [the novelist]
entered into their desires and hopes, and made them more than
his own."[6] Liberating imaginations on all sides, the Edwardian
Adventure and Romance Agency put the results of imagination
within the covers of a book and so found a way, as Cardinal

81

Newman could not, to keep millions of Domini Enfildens away from the window and concentrating on the text.

The Club of Queer Trades takes place in modern-day London and so is unrepresentative of the fictions of this agency, which with some other exceptions—such as Chesterton's *The Man Who Was Thursday* (1908) and Conrad's *The Secret Agent* (1907), both of them anarchist novels—preferred a foreign setting. The foreignness could be a matter of geography; a matter of period, as in the decade's historical romances or Wells's scientific romances, which escaped from the present in two different directions; or a matter of both, as in *Wilderspin*, the tale of the discovery of America which George Moffat is writing in Ford's *The Benefactor* (1905). *Wilderspin* is "full of the open air, of the sea; yes, certainly of romance; of kindness, too, and a certain good-hearted braveness."[7] Ford himself published such a book, *The "Half Moon": A Romance of the Old World and the New*, in 1909. Whatever the form of the foreignness, outward movement from the placid certainties of contemporary English life was a requirement for Edwardian adventurism. In geographically romantic books, the movement had at the very least to reach across the Channel to the Continent, where for decades the characters of English novels had gone to be educated or wicked. In *Baccarat* (1904) by "Frank Danby" (Julia Frankau), the young French wife of an English lawyer returns to her homeland on holiday and loses both her money and her reputation at the tables; the sexual adventurism in this work matches the fighting and exploring of more conventional adventure stories. In the best-selling *Beloved Vagabond* of W. J. Locke (1906), the French-Irish hero Paragot, manager of the Bohemian Lotus Club in London, exhausts the possibilities of romance in England and sets out for France and Hungary, where he wanders freely, playing the violin, and adopts a homeless waif, Asticot, the Jim to his Long John Silver. In the typical manner of best-sellers, however, *The Beloved Vagabond* hedges about Paragot's Bohemianism. Unconventional and absinthe-soaked he may be, but he is also an old Rugbeian and a brilliant architect who has abandoned his career for the sake of a woman. Paragot is a secret aristocrat, like one of Kipling's gentleman-rankers, and the adventurism hanging about him is of the reassuring sort that only pretends to get away from English standards of behavior. It comes as no surprise that Paragot was the creation of an adventure novelist who was also the secretary of the Royal Institute of British Architects.

The favored locales of Edwardian adventurism—real adventurism, not just Paragot's violin-playing—were much further from England than the Continent, more remote from English experience, and created by the imagination working on stories and descriptions handed down by explorers and novelists of the past. Exotic lands held out to Englishmen the promise of lost simplicities; abroad, away from England and its problems, they could find undiscovered territory, physical danger, cleaner choices between courage and cowardice, signs of identity to be taken in at a glance (to Marlow and Conrad, Lord Jim is immediately "one of us"), and welcome rituals of discipline. These are the elements of a myth of adventurism, one of the "faiths" on which Edwardian lives and associations were based. This myth George Ponderevo remembers when, in describing his boyhood explorations of the Kentish countryside, he notes how "All streams came from the then undiscovered 'sources of the Nile' in those days, all thickets were Indian jungles."[8] And it is this myth that Carruthers turns to when at the beginning of *The Riddle of the Sands* he tries to convey the sense of his isolation in an abandoned London. He thinks of the figure of the "obscure Burmese administrator," whose fate is like his own, and whose rituals can keep him up to the mark: "I have read of men who, when forced by their calling to live for long periods in utter solitude—save for a few black faces—have made it a rule to dress regularly for dinner in order to maintain their self-respect and prevent a relapse into barbarism."[9] Carruthers imitates this particular ritual, with "an added touch of self-consciousness," and so keeps himself fit for the experiences to come. In much the same way the Assistant

Commissioner in Conrad's *The Secret Agent* regards London as a jungle and himself as an explorer in that jungle, in order to keep himself fit for the task of tracking down the anarchists.

In a shrinking world with fewer blank spaces on the map, Edwardians emulated as best they could the exploits of nineteenth-century voyagers; they traveled, and so had personal experience as well as a myth to guide them when they wrote about exotic places. John Buchan tramped over the Scottish moorland described in books like *The Watcher by the Threshold* (1902); H. M. Tomlinson went up the Amazon in a tramp steamer in order to write *The Sea and the Jungle* (1912); Conrad sailed in the seas and up the rivers of his tales, though he also depended heavily on books for description and historical background.[10] The most glamorous Edwardian traveler, R. B. Cunninghame Graham, "Don Roberto," based his sketches firmly on his personal knowledge of Spain, South America, Scotland, and North Africa. But the myth of adventure touched all these travelers by shaping their vision in certain ways and urging them to recall one set of images rather than another. Edwardians saw what an inherited set of literary convictions encouraged them to see. In particular, the myth encouraged them to see desert or mountain or jungle or ocean scenes as devoid of humanity. When it had nothing but its own preferences to guide it, Edwardian adventure writing characteristically imagined an empty landscape, and it set moving across this landscape, under a vast sky, the lonely figure of the adventurer. For Cunninghame Graham, who seems influenced by Hardy as well as his friend Conrad, the loneliness led to a proof of man's helplessness: "Cooped underneath the sky, like butterflies shut up by schoolboys under a finger-bowl, we can but flutter, or if we fly, rise only to the middle of the glass. What we can do, is to look out as far as possible through the imprisoning crystal and set down what we see."[11]

The "imprisoning crystal" finely expresses the melancholy accompanying Cunninghame Graham's belated romanticism, but it is not the right phrase for his fellow novelists, who as a rule felt the opposite emotion, a sense of freedom and uninhibited movement, when they forgot for a moment the crowds of London which actually surrounded them, the parceled-off and tightly restricted spaces of a settled England, and imagined, as they did in book after book, a depopulated earth. Edwardian adventures keep returning to Eden. It is there in H. De Vere Stacpoole's *The Blue Lagoon* (1908), the story of two children lost in a shipwreck and marooned on a South Pacific island with a garrulous and bibulous old Irish sailor, who is their mentor or retainer-figure.[12] This Eden has space only for the young and the very old; the middle-aged, who belong to the real world, are banished. Eventually the old sailor dies, and the children are left alone to grow up, to mate, and to have a child, that is, to become wholly innocent versions of Adam and Eve. In Conrad and Ford's *Romance* John Kemp and Seraphina finally escape from the Cuban cave where they have been imprisoned and find themselves alone in the jungle: "We might have been an only couple sent back from the underworld to begin another cycle of pain on a depopulated earth."[13] The politician Melmont in Wells's *In the Days of the Comet* awakes in a world purified by the comet's tail to feel himself "a new Adam" on the earth. Marlow and his companions in *Heart of Darkness* are "wanderers on a prehistoric earth" which is theirs to be possessed "at the cost of profound anguish and of excessive toil"; they recall the exile from Eden rather than Eden itself.[14] Finally, in *Nostromo*, an Adamic figure is placed in an empty landscape, a landscape surviving a metaphoric apocalypse, but with no Eve to comfort him:

> At last the conflagration of sea and sky, lying embraced and asleep in a flaming contact upon the edge of the world, went out. The red sparks in the water vanished together with the stains of blood in the black mantle draping the sombre head of the Placid Gulf; and a sudden breeze sprang up and died out after rustling heavily the growth of bushes on the ruined earthwork of the fort. Nostromo woke up from a fourteen hours' sleep, and arose full length from his lair in the long grass. He stood knee deep amongst the whispering undulations of the green blades with the lost air of a man just born into the world. Handsome,

robust, and supple, he threw back his head, flung his arms open, and stretched himself with a slow twist of the waist and a leisurely growling yawn of white teeth, as natural and free from evil in the moment of waking as a magnificent and unconscious wild beast. Then, in the suddenly steadied glance fixed upon nothing from under a forced frown, appeared the man.[15]

Nostromo's glance fixed upon nothing brings the knowledge that he has after all not swum to Eden but to Sulaco, which is going to have questions about the silver he has taken to safety, and which will require from him human deviousness, not animal innocence. His glance marks the distance between adventure fiction as it was usually conceived and Conrad's version of it in *Nostromo*.

The force behind the empty landscapes in Edwardian books is the sheer pressure of numbers in Edwardian life. The function of the landscapes is to provide a clear field of experience for heroic action, or for sexual action in the case of books like *The Blue Lagoon*, which are responding to a strait-laced society. Nostromo and Decoud come as close to heroic action as Conrad's irony will permit when they drift alone with the silver across the gulf and slip past the Monterists' ship in the dark. Carruthers and his friend Davies sail in secrecy among the desolate sand-flats of the Frisian coast, discovering there a German plan to invade England. In both exploits there is a shadowy human enemy to be outwitted, but the immediately threatening enemy is darkness, too much wind or not enough of it, the sea. From this "elemental" struggle of the human will against nature is generated tale after tale of initiation and regeneration.

The tales of initiation relate the passage of a young man, by symbolic ordeal, into the select company of those who, as Marlow puts it in *Lord Jim*, have learned the "few simple notions" necessary for survival, physical and moral. Both aspects of survival are essential. In Conrad's novel Captain Brierly passes all the physical tests but fails the moral one, or thinks he has failed it, and so commits suicide. *The Riddle of the Sands* combines the tests in an unusually interesting way. Carruthers needs to learn not only how to handle a boat and conduct himself in a gale—tasks set for children in dozens of juvenile initiation dramas, as in Kipling's *Captains Courageous*—but also how to value such physical accomplishments. As he passes through his initiation, he grows steadily more stoical and action-minded, steadily less ironic and urban. While the yacht "Dulcibella" is cruising in the Baltic, Carruthers relies on the city for a simile: the "throbbing of screws filled the air like the distant roar of London streets. In fact, every time we spun round for our dart across the fiord I felt like a rustic matron gathering her skirts for the transit of the Strand on a busy night." He thus brings London into the world of adventure as before he brought the world of adventure into London. But by the end of the book, when Carruthers has been fully initiated into the adventure world, such metaphorical displacements cease. The former Foreign Office gentleman, now speaking with a blunter accent, simply wants to get out into the wind and weather: "the close heat of the room and its tainted atmosphere, succeeding so abruptly to the wholesome nip of the outside air, were giving me a faintness." Davies, meanwhile, undergoes his own symbolic ordeal in a flashback; he has already mastered physical tasks and knows their value, and in the narrative proper he is given the harder task of spiritual regeneration. He must cease to be a restless wanderer and unsuccessful naval candidate and become a loyal servant of England. In language reminiscent of Marlow on Lord Jim, Carruthers reports that Davies, once set on his "dutiful road" of detecting and exposing the German scheme, grips "his purpose with childlike faith and tenacity. It [is] his 'chance'."[16]

John Masefield's *Multitude and Solitude* (1909) is a novel of regeneration-by-adventure on a much larger and less successful scale. The title, suggesting an abstract contrast between the crowds of London and the empty landscape of adventure, alludes more directly to the condition of the hero, Roger Naldrett, who is isolated within a superfine sensibility wherever he happens to be. Naldrett, a playwright and *littérateur*, wanders the

London streets disconsolately after his tragedy is greeted with boos. He speculates about the crowds, feels a vague discontent, counters the discontent with irony, and exultantly rededicates himself to art and the woman who has inspired it. Later his beloved, Ottalie, drowns in an accident, and Naldrett comes away from her death thinking that "art is very frightful when it has not the seriousness of life and death in it." Some chance "messages," which he interprets as signs from the dead Ottalie, implant the idea of sleeping sickness in his mind, and at this juncture the African explorer and medical researcher Lionel Heseltine obligingly enters the scene. His function is to pluck the hero away from the city to the bush, to "the little lonely stations of scientists and soldiers, far away in the wilds," where people have time and space to investigate the "high and tragical things of life and death."[17]

In Africa, Naldrett and Heseltine grow sick with malaria and are abandoned by their native bearers. The landscape is now literally emptied for them, and they seek physical and psychological refuge in a ruined fort, which seems to them, in a standard Edwardian allusion, "like a Roman camp, like military virtue, order, calm, courage, dignity." At last, having contracted the sleeping sickness they have come to study, they face the ordeal of fear: "The old savage devil of the dark was there; the darkness of loneliness, the loneliness of silence, the immanent terror of places not yet won, still ruled by the old unclean gods, not yet exorcised by virtue." At his worst moment, however, Naldrett is inspired by the memory of his love: "He must be Ottalie's fair mind at work still, blessing the world." He then concocts a serum which heals and preserves them for an eventual escape.[18]

There is a marked difference in quality between the London scenes of this novel, which are subtle, inventive, and delicate, and the African scenes, which are patched together from the features of every jungle adventure story ever written. Masefield, the Poet Laureate to be, knew a great deal about London and nothing about Africa other than what he could get out of the myth of adventure, which he seems to have accepted as truth or as working principle, together with its repertory of themes and images and its faith in a heroism stronger than any darkness or loneliness. Naldrett is a Kurtz saved by the jungle; Ottalie is a Kurtz's Intended who needs no lie from Marlow to become the inspiration for her beloved's cause. Yet it is precisely Masefield's differences from Conrad that qualified him for journeyman work in the Adventure and Romance Agency. The Edwardian taste was not displeased by the sort of idealism Masefield provided. "An artist had no right to create at pleasure, ignoble types and situations, fixing fragments of the perishing to the walls of the world, as a keeper nails vermin," says Naldrett at one point.[19] This creed explains why *Multitude and Solitude* is a fable of escape and not, like *Lord Jim*, a novel of regeneration-gone-wrong or, like *Heart of Darkness*, a study in concentric disillusions.

Naldrett and Heseltine, or Carruthers and Davies, form partnerships for the redemption of themselves in particular and of the idea of heroism in general. Two other types of adventurous hero appear in Edwardian fiction, the team player and the superman, both of whom are staunchly unneedful of being redeemed. Nor does either type require empty landscapes, their field of action being instead a city, a community, the whole of Europe, or even the earth. In these settings the romantic contention between man and nature is replaced by a variety of new contentions, realistic or fantastic, but always involving communities of people. The fiction of team players and supermen brings adventure home from the jungle and puts it in the encampment or street. By so doing, it frees adventure from settings and gestures which by the early twentieth century had grown weary, as *Multitude and Solitude* indicates.

In his study *The Adventurer* Paul Zweig complains of the confusions clustering around the word "hero" and suggests that two words are needed to refer to the two major types of heroism in literature, the moral and amoral, or responsible and buccaneering. The "hero," as Zweig defines him, is a virtuous man demonstrating qualities of courage, loyalty, charisma, and selflessness.

He is a leader who defines the established order and whom followers, or readers, may admire without reservation. The "adventurer," on the other hand, is idiosyncratic, rebellious, a law unto himself, exciting rather than respectable, a "phenomenon of sheer energy" who is constantly endangering his followers and himself as well as his enemies.[20] Paragot, according to this scheme, is a cautiously raffish adventurer, Davies an apprentice hero, Nostromo an adventurer unhappy about the role of hero thrust on him.

The Edwardian team player is pre-eminently a hero, by virtue of belonging to a self-consciously heroic group—a corps of volunteer leaders or a ruling caste. His heroism in fact depends on the support he derives from the group, into which, in extreme cases, his identity may be so merged that he becomes a simple anonymous toiler. That is, his heroism may be superficially unheroic. Such is the case with the sailors of Conrad's ship "Narcissus." They are neither leaders nor aware of themselves as a group, but in their single-minded and innocent devotion to duty they express a genuine heroism. That heroism is pathetic in outward aspect except when it is focused on their representative, Singleton, the helmsman with the significant name, the Palinurus of the modern merchant marine. As a crew, Conrad's sailors preserve their ship from destruction, in spite of the corrupting individualism of Donkin and Waite, then melt into the slums of London, their corporate identity dispersed, their heroism lost. *The Nigger of the "Narcissus"* begins a literary tradition skeptical about individual heroes and warily confident about the virtues and fidelities of small groups.

At a higher level of idealization are the dutiful soldiers and colonial agents of Kipling's fiction, who work together to preserve an empire from destruction, occasionally in the spirit of heroic defenders of a city besieged by hostile armies, more often in the cheerful style of amateurs playing up and playing The Game. The Game is what Kim joins when he leaves the meditative discipline of the Lama Teshoo for the secret struggle against the Russians in Afghanistan, and The Game is the metaphor underlying Kipling's story "Little Foxes: A Tale of the Gihon Hunt" (*Actions and Reactions*). Here English officials in Ethiopia organize a fox hunt in the bush, gain the admiration of the natives, and turn the hunt meetings into impromptu outdoor tribunals for rendering title judgments on land disputes. The virtues of sport properly regularized and ritualized are translated into the virtues of good government, and though Kipling is nearly as reluctant as his horsey characters to admit it, there is a kind of heroism in that translation, a casual, stoical English heroism which prefers to appear as something else, such as pukkadom or good sportsmanship.

The empire served by these particular heroes is the turn-of-the-century one visible in vast red-colored areas of the map, but in other Kipling stories the empire may be of the past or future. The past empire is strikingly like the present one. Three stories from *Puck of Pook's Hill*—"A Centurion of the Thirtieth," "On the Great Wall," and "The Winged Hats"—are detailed recreations of Britain as part of a Roman Raj, where Simla is turned into Aquae Sulis (Bath), subalterns into centurions, marauding Pathans into marauding Danes, the bazaars of Lahore or Peshawur into the decadent, pleasure-loving city at the base of Hadrian's Wall. Hunting remains hunting, as does its ethos, though the quarry changes. Parnesius, the centurion who tells these stories to the listening child Dan, advises him that "a boy is safe from all things that really harm when he is astride a pony or after a deer."[21] In his outpost at the frontier of a great but troubled empire Parnesius has the comradeship of a brother officer, Pertinax, and the occasional co-operation of the Picts, who are like the sometimes faithful, sometimes treacherous subjects of a Hindu native state. When in a battle with the Danes Parnesius rescues one of the enemy, a fellow Mithraist, from drowning, he is sent a necklace in return, a gesture asserting, as Kipling's ballad of 1889 put it, that "there is neither East nor West, Border, nor Breed, nor Birth, / When two strong men stand face to face, though they come from the ends of the earth!"[22]

The point of the stories is not merely these equivalents between one empire and another, but the loneliness of imperial service. Parnesius and Pertinax are heroic because they suffer without complaining, as do dozens of district officers in fever-ridden Indian villages, as do thousands of Tommies in South Africa. The Romano-Britons are "Sons of Martha" to whom belief is forbidden and from whom relief is far; they are "Pro-Consuls" who "dig foundations deep, / Fit for realms to rise upon"; they are the "Wage-Slaves" who simply do the work. In the best-known poetic terms of all, they have taken up the White Man's burden, which to Kipling was a felt weight and not a phrase:

> Take up the White Man's burden—
> Send forth the best ye breed—
> Go bind your sons to exile
> To serve your captives' need;
> To wait in heavy harness
> On fluttered folk and wild—
> Your new-caught, sullen peoples,
> Half devil and half child.[23]

Exile and service would be less onerous if they made the empire permanently secure, but Kipling warns his heroes that they will have to watch "Sloth and heathen Folly" bring all their work to nought. He was pessimistic so long as he dealt with the actual empire he knew, however disguised in Roman forms, and with men capable of suffering. But imagining a perfected future, which promised men grown as durable and efficient as machines, Kipling could be breezily confident. A caste of unsuffering technocrats have taken over the government of the world in his "With the Night Mail: A Story of 2000 A.D." (Actions and Reactions), which tells of a dirigible carrying mail across the Atlantic. War is abolished and scientific miracles are commonplace, all because the "Aerial Board of Control" confirms or annuls "all international arrangements and, to judge from its last report, finds our tolerant, humorous, lazy little planet only too ready to shift the whole burden of public administration on its shoulders."[24] This is the heroism of organization, which Chesterton saw coming in the essay "Mr. Rudyard Kipling and Making the

World Small," observing that Kipling's real poetry and true romance was "the romance of the division of labour and the discipline of all the trades."[25] "Discipline" is a suitably workaday
word for the workaday saintliness of the A. B. C. (even the
acronym is as basic as possible), and yet Kipling imagines its efficiency with a starry-eyed, dreamy joy. The A. B. C. is only a
short step away from Wells's equally glittering ideal, the corps of
world rulers in *A Modern Utopia* (1905), the "Samurai," who
are well educated, ascetic, and dedicated—everything Wells
himself was not (in the same way the heroes of Shaw's plays,
who are at least potentially world rulers, are wholly unShavian,
except in their verbal brilliance). Both Wells's Samurai and Kipling's A. B. C. are best considered reactions to actual English
inefficiency; they are dreams of a future from which Muddle and
How Not To Do It have been banished forever. They also represent a strain of vicarious power worship seen in its purest Edwardian form in the crippled W. E. Henley, the editor and poet
of "Invictus," who was a notorious admirer of manly heroism.
According to Wells, Henley was the guiding light behind the
Samurai canon of behavior.[26]

Zweig's adventurer too had his Edwardian avatar, who may
be called, using the Nietzschean terminology in vogue throughout the decade, the superman. For the superman there could be
no question of team play, group fidelity, or even the personal
rituals of initiation or regeneration. His function was simply to
exercise power on a grand scale, to redefine adventure as a quan-
titative achievement. He challenged novelists to invent plots
commensurate with his Nietzschean dimensions, and the Edwardian novelist who responded most extravagantly to the challenge was M. P. Shiel. Shiel was an influence on Wells, his *The
Purple Cloud* being an acknowledged source for *In the Days of
the Comet*, but as the author of three strange fantasies of heroism, Shiel deserves consideration on his own account.[27] In *The
Lord of the Sea* (1901), which is typical of all three, a sturdy
English farmer, Richard Hogarth, falls into the clutches of an
evil Jew named Frankl, simultaneously falls in love with Frankl's

daughter Rebekah, is wrongly convicted of murder and imprisoned, escapes, grows stupendously wealthy, and seeks revenge by making himself "lord of the sea," the commander of floating fortresses which exact tolls from the world's shipping. Sea battles follow (these draw on the contemporary interest in naval rearmament), and Hogarth becomes regent of England, only to be brought down by the calumnies of his old enemies and the discovery of his tainted past. Subsequently, having learned that he is Jewish, Hogarth becomes fervently Zionist and sails for Palestine, where he is hailed as the Messiah and rules as judge over Israel for sixty years.

The Lord of the Sea is part *Daniel Deronda* and part *Count of Monte Cristo*, part anti-Semitic diatribe and part Zionist tract. It shares with the two other books an elaborate and pointless narrative frame, purporting to have been taken by dictation from the ravings of a wealthy woman whom a doctor has hypnotized; on his deathbed the doctor hands his notes over to a fictional editor. Shiel seems determined to match the energies of his hero with authorial energies of his own, and the only thing that holds the novel together is its idea of a superhuman adventurism as the expression, the glorification, of power. *The Lord of the Sea* hints that only an overweening and amoral power can heal the divisions of the modern world. By way of epigraph, it reports the Earl of Rosebery as saying, "I sometimes wish that we had a Dictator—a Man who would see what is needed, and would do it."

If Edwardian politics produced no dictator, Edwardian commerce produced numbers of his counterpart, the great industrial magnate, and Edwardian fiction magnified this figure into another version of the superman, the megalomaniac businessman. He came onto the fictional scene in Anthony Hope's *The God in the Car* (1894), which is about a South African mining king, and he reappeared throughout the Edwardian years and the 1920s as a mover of men and a consumer of the world's riches, as in Bennett's *The Grand Babylon Hotel* and other fantasias.[28] Finally, in the 1930s he became the symbol of capitalist evil, epitomized in the sinister munitions manufacturer of Graham Greene's *A Gun for Sale.* The most famous Edwardian magnate is Teddy Ponderevo in *Tono-Bungay,* who through advertising blows up a catchy name and a highly alcoholic product into a vast commercial enterprise, an empire in more than name. Anglo-Saxon commercial energy, says Ponderevo, has "put things in our grip —threads, wires, stretching out and out, George, from that little office of ours, out to West Africa, out to Egypt, out to Inja, out east, west, north and south. Running the world practically." And running it, if need be, by force: Ponderevo knows that the romance of modern business consists of men fighting like brigands, of "Conquest. Province by province. Like sojers." He thinks in these terms because he has been reading Nietzsche and studying Napoleon, because everyone around him flatters his vanity (his mistress calls him her "god in the car," after Hope's novel), and because it is after all true that the swindle or fiction he has created has put a vast number of things into his Napoleonic grip. Ponderevo is connected to the world, not isolated in it. No crystal imprisons him. The very sky over his head is uneasy about his grasp, as if fearing his next coup. At least that is how his nephew imagines the sky as being painted in what he judges the right portrait of Teddy: an uneasy sky, a throbbing motor-car with chauffeur in the background, a secretary with importunate papers.[29]

Competitive big business—in Ponderevo's appropriate malapropism, "the career *ouvert* to the Talons"—was one of two radically disturbing forces in Edwardian society. The other was the growth of a technocratic establishment, which brought a newly powerful superman on the scene, the engineer. Edwardian engineers are more considerable figures than, say, the Ironmaster Rouncewell in *Bleak House* or the inventor Doyce in *Little Dorrit,* who may represent alternatives superior to the traditional English system of patronage and circumlocution, but who are in Dickens' time not yet seen as threats to the established order. They are met with misunderstanding rather than animosity, and finally they go off safely to the industrial North or the Continent to carry on their pursuits. In Edwardian fiction, and particularly in the scientific romances of Wells, science and technology enter much more boldly into English life, promising great achievements in social engineering but also raising enormous doubts.

It was typical of Wells not to know what he wanted to say in a book until he was well into it, and *The Food of the Gods* (1904), which focuses most sharply on these ideas, starts as a light-hearted comedy, with much incidental silliness and several Dickensian eccentrics. Two scientists, Redwood and Bensington, invent a chemical growth stimulant with which they create giant chickens, then accidentally giant wasps and giant rats. The experimenters cannot control the biological process they have provoked or the commercial enterprise of a doctor who in the best Ponderevo style decides to turn the stimulant into a commodity ("Boomfood"). Redwood gives Boomfood to his son, others do likewise, and eventually a race of giants is created. Much humor attends their awkward growing up.

Halfway through the book the tone suddenly changes as Wells begins to take the giants seriously. They come to symbolize the laboring proletariat kept in subjection by the ruling classes when, at a time of strikes, the starving workers cheer one of the giants for stealing food. After that the giants become heroic workers for change who are opposed by government functionaries and petty conservatism in general. The giants are young, in the standard Wells dichotomy, while their opponents are old. Furthermore, the giants, being linked to the engineer Cossar, father of three of them, stand for a future meaningless to the conservatives, who hate Cossar merely for being technological: "An engineer! To him all that we hold dear and sacred is nothing. Nothing! The splendid traditions of our race and land, the noble institutions, the venerable order, the broad slow march from precedent to precedent that has made our English people great and this sunny island free—it is all an idle tale, told and done with. Some claptrap about the Future is worth all these sacred things."[30]

The plot centers on the struggle between a giant named Caddles and the complacent village of Cheasing Eyebright, where he is raised by the local Lady Bountiful and the patronizing vicar. War breaks out, Caddles is killed, and in the ensuing battles Wells invests his sympathies in his race of giants who, unlike their enemies, are happy, loving, and militarily efficient. As if infected by the giants' expansive mood and taste for sweeping views, Wells grows apocalyptic at the close: while the old way of life is coming to a violent end, the new way of life is glimpsed in the silhouette of a heroic young giant standing against the horizon: "For one instant he shone, looking up fearlessly into the starry deeps, mail-clad, young and strong, resolute and still. Then the light had passed and he was no more than a great black outline against the starry sky, —a great black outline that threatened with one mighty gesture the firmament of heaven and all its multitude of stars."[31]

The rhetoric here, like that of the final paragraphs of Wells's prophetic books, is celebratory, but it also hints at worries about the immense power exercised by the giant. He casts a black outline against the stars, and his gesture is threatening. The giant warriors whom Wells has been admiring are frighteningly efficient at tearing down the past, even while they are ignorant about the future they want to construct. They have come out of an experiment gone wrong, and no one knows what their destiny will be. Their power is incomprehensible and literally superhuman, and like Ponderevo's, it is the dangerous power of the adventurer, who is subject to uncontrollable forces within himself and therefore a threat to others. The power of the giants is the most fantastic and troubling idea produced by the Edwardian myth of adventure, and it marks the point beyond which the myth could no longer be wholeheartedly believed—not because it necessarily led to ludicrous imaginative excess, as with Shiel, but because it became more subversive than myths are allowed to be. Edwardian adventurism in this book of Wells implies a future much less reassuring than that so carefully diagramed in *A Modern Utopia*. In other works of the period, adventurism ran into realities of history and politics which made it morally questionable. After a point, the myth of adventurism required an imaginative commitment which no Edwardian writer—not even Wells the futurist and romancer—could give it. In *The Food of the Gods* there is a description of the scientist Bensington which comments admirably on two things, the growing unease of the whole Edwardian era about the escapist visions it demanded for its entertainment, and the strange mixture of adventurism and uneasiness in the mind of Wells himself:

> This little spectacled man . . . would have again a flash of that adolescent vision, would have a momentary perception of the eternal unfolding of the seed that had been sown in his brain, would see as it were in the sky, behind the grotesque shapes and accidents of the present, the coming world of giants and all the mighty things the future has in store—vague and splendid, like some glittering palace seen suddenly in the passing of a sunbeam far away . . . and presently it would be with him as though that distant splendour had never shone upon his brain, and he would perceive nothing ahead but sinister shadows, vast declivities and darknesses, inhospitable immensities, cold, wild, and terrible things.[32]

8

Complications of Imperialism

The myth of adventure furnished Edwardian writers with a stock
of plots, settings, and types of heroism, and from these, the
heightened and formalized realities of two hundred years of
European exploration in outlying lands, they constructed a series
of fictions emptying the landscapes of native populations and
providing ample room for heroic action. Unless writers were unusually sheltered from the controversies of their time, however,
like Stacpoole on his South Pacific island or Hichens mooning
about the garden of Allah, they had sooner or later to look up
from the myth and, like Bennett viewing London as though it
were a foreign city, view "for the first time" the real, contemporary world outside England. What they saw in these moments of
fresh looking was early twentieth-century imperialism. It was a
less satisfying and predictable sight than the vision the myth
gave them, and accordingly it was often translated into the cos-
metic terms of this myth or an even older one. Such was the pro-
cedure of Kipling making his dutiful colonial agents into "The
New Knighthood":

> Who lays on the sword?
> "I," said the Sun,
> "Before he has done,
> "I'll lay on the sword."
>
> Who fastens his belt?
> "I," said Short-Rations,
> "I know all the fashions
> "Of tightening a belt!"
>
> Who gives him his spur?
> "I," said his Chief,

Exacting and brief,
"I'll give him the spur."[1]

However ceremonialized, imperialism was an obvious fact in an era which respected facts, and it could not be ignored.

The pressure of imperialism on adventure fiction was the pressure of political infighting and historical event on memory and imagination, and it is best understood as a pressure which succeeded in altering the traditional patterns of memory and imagination, but not in sweeping them away. Adventure rituals and images continue to lie at the heart of novels about imperialism, even novels skeptical of imperialist morality, though on occasion they have to be not just prettied up, as in "The New Knighthood," but searchingly criticized. The figure of the courageous hero persists, fending off the darkness and dressing for dinner in the middle of the jungle, but now interest in him focuses on the passive heroism of suffering, or the pointlessness of his courage. Novels still shape themselves around plots crowded with exciting incident, but plot is revealed as an inadequate means of comprehending the significance of events. Discipline becomes ritual, allegiance sardonic self-consciousness—a pattern repeated a few years later in writing about the First World War, which expressed its beginning innocence in the images of patriotic chivalry and its subsequent disillusion in the same images made corrosively ironic.[2]

To begin with its most obvious effect, imperialism enormously complicated the adventure motive by substituting the work of possession for the deed of self-possession. Imperialists could never be adventurers in Zweig's sense; by definition they were responsible for others; they were heroes dedicated to an abstract cause or a geographical entity. Imperialism filled the theater of action with natives who would have to be variously pacified, exploited, educated, or enfranchised, and on the horizon it set competitors coming abroad quickly for their own share of the exploiting and educating. In Kipling's Indian stories, the competitors are the Russians just over the mountain passes of the

Northwest Frontier; in *Nostromo,* they are the aggressive Americans with money supporting the Gould Concession. The typical landscape of imperialism is crowded, and the conflicts enacted on it tend to be between men and men rather than men and elemental nature. Or the conflicts assume the even more complicated form of ideological struggle: militaristic, commercial imperialism against the ideal of bringing enlightenment to savage peoples; the idea of empire against the idea of commonwealth; the idea of common humanity against the idea of ever-more separate races (the polarity of East and West, the polarity of blackness and whiteness). Imperialism endowed adventure with economic consequences, which are hinted at in the metaphors of *Tono-Bungay,* but not spelled out there as they are in specialist studies like J. A. Hobson's *Imperialism* (1902) and Benjamin Kidd's *The Control of the Tropics* (1898), the latter a work cited approvingly in Wells's *A Modern Utopia,* or in fictional works willing to take a hard look at the most usual European motive for going abroad. In this respect Wells's *The First Men in the Moon,* for all its lunar setting, is a more realistic work than Masefield's *Multitude and Solitude,* and in turn Wells's allegorical fantasy is less realistic than those Edwardian books which insisted on the costs as well as the profits of imperial ventures—the costs in lost manpower, lost investment at home, and lost national confidence.

In the first decade of the century imperialism was a bitterly controversial topic seemingly incapable of compromise, and one response to the controversy was the reducing of arguments to articles of faith. Edwardians sought refuge in hardened ideological positions—Conservative against Liberal, Liberal Imperialist ("Limp") against Little Englander. Journals adopted ever more strident editorial policies as elections were fought on imperialist issues, among which the Edwardians included the essentially imperialist issue of Irish Home Rule. This trading of intellectual confusion for emotional certainty is reflected in the fiction of the period. For example, A. E. W. Mason's *The Broken Road* (1908), an untidy love story, is also a parable of men of different races failing to maintain friendship (like *A Passage to India*) and a compendium of attitudes toward British imperialism in India. For the hard-headed, misogynist colonial officer Luffe, the Raj is a test of his organizational ability ("Men figured in his thoughts as instruments of policy; their women-folk as so many hindrances or aids to the fulfilment of their allotted tasks"), while his countryman Hatch, an adventurer-spy in the mold of Lawrence of Arabia or Lurgan Sahib in *Kim*, dramatizes empire as a vast theater wherein he may play his dangerous game of passing for a native. The commissioner Ralston, prosaic and mildly cynical, finds an imperial symbol in a bullock-drawn waterwheel: "There's an emblem of the Indian administration. The wheels creak and groan, the bullock goes on round and round with a bandage over its eyes, and the little boy on its back cuts a fine important figure and looks as if he were doing ever so much, and somehow the water comes up—that's the great thing, the water is fetched up somehow and the land watered. When I am inclined to be despondent, I come and look at my water-wheel."[3] For Ralston, utility is everything.

All these attitudes pale beside the attitude which supplies the title and dominates the book: the empire as the expression of a fixed, hardened will. The Englishman Linforth has been killed attempting to push a road through the mountains on the frontier, and after Eton and Oxford his son, hearing "the call of the Road," accepts its continuance as a familial and patriotic obligation. The initiatory ordeal young Linforth would have to undergo as an adventure hero is here transformed into the duty that imperial heroes accept as their common fate, duty being a kind of endless, unceremonial ordeal which has no reference to the future, only to the present.

In Mason's novel little is said about the practical usefulness of the Road. It is simply a symbol of the imperial will to continue, to dominate, and to control. For Linforth's son it is an article of faith that the Road shall not remain broken; if he ceased to believe that, he would not know what he was doing in India and, by extension, what the English were doing there. The Road becomes his substitute for religion. As Chesterton claims in his *Autobiography*, writing from a stance of convinced anti-imperialism, men at the end of the nineteenth century "believed in the British Empire precisely because they had nothing else to believe in."[4]

In the Edwardian period there were three major challenges to the creed of imperialism: revelations about brutality in the Belgian Congo, the Boer War, and the Liberal Parliamentary victory of 1906. The lesson of the Congo was potentially the most subversive. A succession of writers, including E. D. Morel (*Affairs of West Africa*, 1903), Arthur Conan Doyle (*The Crime of the Congo*, 1909), and especially Roger Casement, who was consul at Kinshasa and wrote an influential 1904 report on Belgian colonial practices, supplied ample evidence of commercial greed, depopulation of villages, systematic maltreatment of African workers, and occasional atrocities. All this evidence struck directly at the fundamental hypocrisies of European imperialism. Casement showed how the Belgians took credit for abolishing the slave trade and then exacted forced labor in lieu of taxes from the natives; Doyle commented on the contrast between King Leopold's declared nobility and philanthropy and the actual practices of his agents, which included such measures as cutting off the hands of natives in order to frighten others into producing more rubber.[5] Thanks to these writers the Congo Free State became a byword for cruelty, as Joyce's *Ulysses* observes in its systematic gathering of the public topics of 1904:

> —That's how it's worked, says the citizen. Trade follows the flag.
> —Well, says J. J., if they're any worse than those Belgians in the Congo Free State they must be bad. Did you read that report by a man what's this his name is?
> —Casement, says the citizen. He's an Irishman.
> —Yes, that's the man, says J. J. Raping the women and the girls and flogging the natives on the belly to squeeze all the red rubber they can out of them.[6]

Casement had met a Captain Korzeniowski at Matadi in the summer of 1890, and after publishing his report, he wrote to the captain-turned-writer asking for help in stirring up public opinion. Conrad, indulging in gloom, replied that he was only a "wretched novelist" and could not help.[7] The truth was that Conrad had already put his black memories of the Congo and his moral imagination fully to work in "An Outpost of Progress" and *Heart of Darkness*. Any public opinion these two tales were capable of stirring up could not have been of much practical usefulness to Casement's cause, because they pertain to more than the greed of one set of European traders in one part of Africa, and thus they preclude the narrowly focused anger which practical world politics, as opposed to literature, required. One of the dangers of the Congo question for Englishmen was that it could stimulate too narrow an anger and make the English themselves feel morally superior to the Belgians.

The Congo also lacked a single, highly visible event to which public attention might have been directed, with the result that it became a wearily familiar Liberal cause, a history of abuses by all means to be condemned, but condemned without urgency or a sense that English issues were immediately at stake. With the exception of Conrad's two tales, Edwardian fiction found little to stimulate its imagination directly in the Congo: Wells mentions the maltreatment of children there savagely but briefly in *New Worlds for Old*—a gesture of near-automatic concern— and the transparent deceptions of Belgian colonialism probably underlie in a more general way the shallow anti-imperialist satire in Hilaire Belloc's *Emmanuel Burden* (1904) and Conrad and Ford's *The Inheritors* (1901). In the former the "M'Korio Delta Development" is a trap for a naive investor, while in the latter, which is much more the product of Ford than Conrad, the target is the Duc de Mersch's "Pan European Railway, Exploration, and Civilisation Company," an enterprise aiming to "let in light in dark places." The Duc projects a Trans-Greenland Railway Scheme as the first step in forming an international society for the preservation of Polar freedom, thus substituting, in an obvious reversal, the heart of whiteness for the heart of darkness; but the scheme is eventually revealed as a hypocritical fraud.[8]

The Congo presented a moral challenge to imperialists, first to see through the rhetoric of their public statements on enlightenment and progress, and then to see the costs of real imperialism in violence, illegality, and wasted human effort. The challenge of the Boer War was of a somewhat different kind, as it was directed at the practicality of imperialism. Even without regard to its outcome, the war was a plain demonstration that coercion would be needed to keep the British Empire together and "natives" less docile than the Congolese blacks in line; but the outcome was more troubling than that. In the fighting a small and backward "nation" of farmers and guerrilla fighters was pitted against the greatest imperial power in the world, and for two years at least the farmers more than held their own. The Boers ruined a few British military reputations, forced a drastic revision of tactics and a greatly increased expenditure of money and troops, and finally were paid *de facto* reparations for the destruction of crops and houses which in the end had been the only way to defeat them, with the result that the soldierly Edwardian mind might well wonder what the point of the whole war had been—especially when politicians at the peace negotiations seemed to give the Boers everything they asked for.

There was a simple and fairly reassuring way to react to all this: to think of the war as a lesson in tactics, pure and simple; a war that might have been more efficiently won with better management. This is the line taken by Kipling in work immediately after the war. All of his reactions to the war, which are gathered chiefly in the poems of *The Five Nations* (1903) and the stories of *Traffics and Discoveries*, reveal a pattern of narrow judgments slowly opening outward into general worries. At first, as in the grandiosely titled poem "The Lesson (1899-1902)," he acknowledges merely that mounted men are tactically superior to infantry, relying on technicality, as he often did, to prevent more subversive thoughts about men. There is a more complicated evasion in the short story "A Sahib's War." In this unpleasant tale a

Sikh servant sees his beloved English master killed by Boer treachery and exacts revenge by having the Boers taken prisoner and their house burned down. The Sikh's hatred, which is almost clinically scrutinized, is perhaps the real subject of the tale, but the ostensible theme is that Indian troops should have been permitted to fight in the war. Not only would their fierceness have been efficient but, as the Sikh notes, every part of the empire is involved with every other part: "It is for Hind that the Sahibs are fighting this war."[9] This sentiment was widely expressed at the time, often with the explicit inclusion of Ireland in "the Empire." Bonar Law, Asquith's successor as Prime Minister, said in 1921, using a significant cliché, that Ulster "held the pass for Empire." Casement, coming at the Irish question from the opposite point of view, claimed often that it was his knowledge of Irish history which enabled him to understand what was happening in the Congo.[10]

Judgments about cavalry methods and troop deployment were no more than momentarily satisfying to Kipling, and he cast about for other possible explanations of the wartime weakness, such as general mismanagement at the top, among the brass hats. In the wish-fulfilling "Army of a Dream" that mismanagement is obviated forever by a new military system of near-universal conscription, constant active maneuvers in England and abroad, war drill taught in all the schools, and competition among units. Or perhaps the British fighting man in South Africa was slack. That explanation is briefly entertained, then dismissed in "The Comprehension of Private Copper," a pro-Tommy story which asserts that the British fighting man, insulted as ever for his alleged stupidity, was actually more than ready for the enemy in a tight spot. Unable finally to explain the war in military terms, Kipling has no other explanation to offer but a crisis in the national spirit. The insufferably 'cute American narrator of "The Captive" first makes the diagnosis: the British are "brainy men languishing under an effete system which, when you take good holt of it, is England—just all England."[11] "Just all England" implies that military shortcomings were only a symptom of a widespread national malaise, that the English as a race were grown too complacent or corrupt or ridden with doubt to manage the empire their fathers had earned.

Kipling's implications grow shrilly certain in the bitter poem "The Islanders," which is about the lack of a will to fight. The poem questions the adequacy of The Game as a metaphor for responsible governance of an empire and brings the worry about spiritual preparedness home from Africa to England:

> Fenced by your careful fathers, ringed by your leaden seas,
> Long did ye wake in quiet and long lie down at ease;
> Till ye said of Strife, "What is it?" of the Sword, "It is far from our ken";
> Till ye made a sport of your shrunken hosts and a toy of your armed men.

The English depended on "younger nations" for "men who would shoot and ride," Kipling says, and then the English went home lessonless:

> Then ye returned to your trinkets; then ye contented your Souls
> With the flannelled fools at the wicket or the muddied oafs at the goals.[12]

The source of this once controversial poem is fear, fear that the nation has forgotten how to be imperial, fear which replaced turn-of-the-century optimism, jingoist or idealist, as the dominant national mood. "This mood of optimism did not survive the South African War. It received its death-blow at [the defeats of] Colenso and Magersfontein, and within a few years fear had definitely taken the place of ambition as the mainspring of the movement to national and imperial consolidation."[13] Thus writes the Liberal theorist L. T. Hobhouse in 1911. He regarded the South African lesson with complacency, as did the even more anti-imperialist Chesterton, who regarded all military and imperial power as fraudulent, and who was capable of dealing with the most worrisome national emergency by encapsulating it epigrammatically in historical process: "It may be said with rough accuracy that there are three stages in the life of a strong people. First, it is a small power, and fights small powers. Then it is a great power, and fights great powers. Then it is a great power, and fights small powers, but pretends they are great powers, in order to rekindle the ashes of its ancient emotion and vanity. After that, the next step is to become a small power itself."[14] In this scheme the English are the great power, the Boers are the small power magnified into a great power out of English vanity, and the emotion that drives them is pride or willfulness.

In the general election of 1906 cartoons were distributed showing the ghosts of British soldiers killed in the Boer War pointing to the fenced compounds where Chinese laborers, who had subsequently been imported to work in the South African goldfields, were lodged and asking, "Did we die for this?" "Pigtail" became an electioneering slogan, and working-class audiences were told that the Tories, if they stayed in power, would import Chinese labor into England.[15] Partly as a result of these tactics, the Liberals won an enormous victory, but their party was itself so badly split over the issue of imperialism and Ireland that once in office, it did nothing to dismantle or reshape the empire. The election victory presented, therefore, only an ideological threat to imperialists, yet the threat was substantial. Those who feared a lapse in the national spirit of greatness, like Kipling, now had the evidence of millions of votes to show them what they feared to see—doubts, moral scruples, careful accountings of the cost of overseas enterprise. The Little Englanders seemed in the ascendancy, if not actually in positions of power, and after 1906 it was time for the imperialists to take stock and strike back. Some of the striking back was crude, as in Kipling's "Little Foxes." This story vilifies the Little Englanders in the person of an interfering, anti-imperialist Member of Parliament, Lethabie Groombride. After the election, in which "Forces, Activities, and Movements sprang into being, agitated themselves, coalesced, and, in one political avalanche, overwhelmed a bewildered, and not in the least intending it, England," Groombride goes to Ethiopia to investigate charges of cruelty.[16] He is humiliated by the fox-hunting colonial officers there and laughed at by the natives, until finally he beats his native servant in vexation and is subsequently blackmailed into silence. "Little Foxes" shows Kipling nearly at his worst: vindictive, stupidly antagonistic to advanced ideas, and unwilling to allow a political opponent integrity or even a dignified name.

There was a more thoughtful imperialist response to 1906, from a likely writer in an unlikely form. John Buchan had published *The Watcher from the Shadows* in 1902, and in 1910 he would bring out the even more prototypically adventurous *Prester John*; in between, in the year of the election, came the very different work *A Lodge in the Wilderness*. This is a country-house discussion novel, like Goldsworthy Lowes Dickinson's *A Modern Symposium* (1905), but it is set in Africa, not on the North Downs, and unlike *A Modern Symposium*, it carries no whiff of Cambridge and higher thought. Mr. Francis Carey, "an intelligent Millionaire" residing in shooting-boxes and cottages scattered over the empire—this is a portrait of Cecil Rhodes with a touch of Lord Milner and his "kindergarten" of empire-building disciples—has called an informal conference at his great house "Musuru," where in the midst of a park of thousands of acres he lives "as Prester John may have lived in his Abyssinian palace." In a setting of delicate furniture and "all the trappings of a high civilisation," yet "looking out over the primeval wilds" where savage beasts roam a mile off "in that untamed heart of the continent," Carey sets his guests to talking. They are Tory statesmen out of office, friends, businessmen, artists; and their starting-point is the recent electoral defeat: "some little while ago the creed which is commonly called Imperialism was tossed down into the arena of politics to be wrangled over by parties and grossly mauled in the quarrel. With the fall of the Government which had sanctioned such tactics there came one of those waves of reaction which now and then break in upon our national steadfastness. The name of 'Empire' stank in the nostrils of the electorate."[17] For the moment England is insular again, Carey admits. Its past three centuries have been forgotten, and the task

109

before them is to rekindle the ashes of ancient emotion and vanity by understanding what they mean by imperialism, and then making that understanding public.

Imperialism is a form of romance, one debater ventures, "an enlarged sense of the beauty and mystery of the world"; or more prosaically, it is the connection under one crown of autonomous nations of one blood, "who can spare something of their vitality for the administration of vast tracts inhabited by lower races." For a clarifying metaphor one guest goes back to Plato: "Suppose a small tribe lived in a cave and never saw the daylight. One day the barriers at the door fall down, and they look out on a blue sky and meadows and a river, and are free to go out to them." That freedom is the essence of imperialism. Another guest, an artist, speaks of a "creative imperialism" which rejects the esoteric, the limited, and the merely aesthetic in life and embraces art as the conquest of new worlds for the mind. Lest she suffer the fate of the later Roman poets, for whom the outer empire was a metaphor or jest, the English artist must absorb into her work "the enlarged material basis of life." These approximations meet with no general approval, whereupon a visit to a gathering of native chiefs in the vicinity clarifies the racial principle to be borne in mind in all tropical ventures. The native, says Carey, using a Biblical figure nineteenth-century novelists like Dickens and Gaskell had used for the divided nations of rich and poor, "represents the first stage of humanity . . . Between his mind at its highest and ours at its lowest there is a great gulf fixed, which is not to be crossed by taking thought." The white man's duty is to inculcate the elements of citizenship and Christian morality in the benighted representatives of the first stage of humanity.[18]

In this and other expeditions the energy of the group is dissipated, so that in the end they reach no definition of imperialism and are forced to conclude lamely that "ours is still a cryptic faith, unformulated and incoherent. Our task is to bring its meaning to light." In spite of their ample leisure, congenial surroundings, and reputed political wisdom, the group at Musuru signally fail to do what they set out to do, having broken down in indecision and vague hopefulness—the same fate as that which greeted Edwardian Liberalism when it attempted to define its aims and put them into an effective political program. The fecklessness often attributed to a Liberal figure like the pessimistic, doubting C. F. G. Masterman belongs also to the superficially decisive circles of Edwardian imperialism, the "robust and practical" minds. The unintentional implication of *A Lodge in the Wilderness* is that imperialism can define itself neither in word nor in deed, for when Buchan's disputants seek action as an antidote to confusion, their exploring and lion-killing seem artificial and bathetic, especially after the high-toned advance billing they receive ("there is no satisfaction so intense as victory over some one of the savage forces of nature"). But then Buchan's book is full of inadvertent bathos. After much heady talk of the explorer, "the electric force in civilisation," the ladies and gentlemen go off on "a walking expedition," as though they were in Kensington rather than "Equatoria"; and after all the rhetoric about passionate selflessness and destiny, the grandest imperial vision one lady can achieve, when she thinks of an Africa settled by white men, is curiously suburban: "What a delightful society it would be! I can picture country-houses—simple places, not palaces like Musuru,—and pretty gardens, and packs of hounds, and—oh, all that makes England nice, without any of the things that bore us."[19] Allowance must be made for Buchan's misogyny, but his own vision of settlement is no different from this one in essentials; his vision of imperialism in practice falls short. In proselytizing empire, *A Lodge in the Wilderness* only demonstrates the fallibility of the creed.

9

The Black Panther

It cannot be argued that Edwardian fiction was dramatically affected by any of these events—the Congo, the Boer War, or the election of 1906—that there was a consensus about imperialism among novelists, or even that novelists aligned themselves neatly in opposed camps, imperialist versus Little Englander. The certainty of a Buchan and a Chesterton was exceptional. A sense of vague disquiet, as in Wells's admission that when the Boer War came along, "something happened to quite a lot of us," was typical.[1] In a few cases the disquiet, whatever its source, produced something one can only call a bad conscience about imperialism, and the bad conscience in turn produced imaginative reactions—fictions which in altered or symbolic form admit guilt, reveal atrocities, express doubts, and in general issue warnings about empire-building and the adventuring spirit which lay behind it. A pattern for this imaginative process is to hand in an actual occurrence of 1904. In that year an Anglo-Irishman named Samuel Chenevix Trench came to stay with two Irishmen in a Martello tower at Sandycove, near Dublin. Trench, an Oxonian, was an enthusiastic supporter of the Irish revival and had recently canoed through miles of Irish waterways, but canoeing was apparently not the source of a nightmare he had one September night. This nightmare featured a black panther, and Trench was frightened enough by it to fire some shots from his revolver at the fireplace. More shots followed later, and the end result was to drive one of Trench's tower-mates out into the rain and eventual exile from his homeland.[2]

No one would now know of this contretemps if it had not been translated by the exile, James Joyce, into a remembered episode

112

at the start of *Ulysses*, where Trench becomes "Haines" and the black panther is retained for its symbolic color. In 1904, in the consciousness of the real Trench, the animal suggests other meanings. Why a black panther at all? Why is the jungle imported into Ireland? This crude adventure drama of man versus beast seems to express an uneasy conscience about being an adventurer, an intruder, in a subject nation. (The Martello tower, the British Empire's fortification against the French Empire, would be a suitable place for fantasies of invasion and defense.) Just as other imperialists moved through the jungle or the bush, defending themselves stoutly against dark threats, so Trench, in spite of his assumed Irishness, could have seen himself as moving through Ireland, ostensibly absolving and secretly condemning himself for the Irish mess. If Ulster held the pass for empire, as Bonar Law was to claim, then the empire might well furnish a nightmarish symbol for misadventure in Ireland. In any case the black panther typifies the exotic dangers that the English habitually imagined, as if to punish themselves for being abroad as a nation at all, and abroad with guns in their hands. The black panther had to be shot in guilty acknowledgement that the empire, for all its high-mindedness, was ultimately based on violence or the threat of violence.

The black panther or his equivalents keep appearing in Edwardian fiction. Consider the strange experiences of Graves in John Buchan's story "No-man's Land" (*The Watcher by the Threshold*). He is a don, more expert on Celtic matters than Trench or Haines, who stumbles by accident into an isolated Highland region of Scotland ("the Scarts o' the Muneraw") and is captured by a fierce, primitive race of beast-men, remnants of the ancient Picts. Escape and flight follow, but like a man who cannot escape a recurrent dream, Graves eventually returns to the Scarts, is caught again, then rescued again. The tale is crowded with thrills, but it is also crowded with dark hints that the beast-men ought to have been left alone. There is something presumptuous or impious in the book-learned Graves' invasion of their retreat. The Picts, like the underground Morlocks in Wells's *The Time*

Machine, are rightly hidden away from rational civilization, and the penalty for encountering them—that is, for encountering the savageness at the extreme limits of human evolution—is mental anguish and isolation, in addition to whatever physical danger is involved. No one believes the adventurer when he returns with his news of the black panther and obscure sense of guilt; no one believes Graves' revelations about the Picts: he is laughed at and dies a failure.

The most recklessly imaginative Edwardian romancer, M. P. Shiel, was not content with mere Highland journeyings and isolation in the form of disbelief. His novel *The Purple Cloud* (1901), like *The Lord of the Sea,* exaggerates everything it is possible to exaggerate, including the charge of impiety laid against exploring. Shiel's adventurers sail to the Arctic in pursuit of a multi-million-dollar prize for the first man to reach the North Pole. They are as driven by greed as any Belgian colonialist, and as unscrupulous. Along the way they turn against each other viciously, scheming and cutting throats, so that only a remnant actually forces its way through "the great uncongenial ice," which is "a nightmare, and a blasphemy, and a madness, and the realm of the Power of Darkness," and reaches the Pole with its mysterious circular lake, "the Sanctity of Sanctities, the old eternal inner secret of the Life of this Earth, which it was a most burning shame for a man to see."[3] A pillar of ice engraved in unreadable characters is at the center of the lake. This is the *omphalos* indeed, and it is death to behold: the purple cloud of the title streams forth from the violated sanctuary and kills all human beings on earth except one survivor of the expedition and a young woman hidden in the dungeons of Constantinople. They eventually come together to share yet another Edwardian Eden, and after anxious debate, they decide to repopulate the earth.

The most interesting specter in Edwardian fiction is not very frightening in comparison with Picts and sacred pillars, but it is much more firmly tied to contemporary attitudes to imperialism and more obviously a projection of guilt. Toward the end of

114

Tono-Bungay there is a voyage of exploitation. Ponderevo's great empire is about to collapse and can be saved only by a massive coup—by sailing in stealth to Mordet Island, the possession of another colonial power, and seizing a valuable mineral deposit, the "quap" they have been told about. George Ponderevo leads the expedition, welcoming the chance to do something adventurous in his beloved's eyes; but there is nothing very adventurous about the stormy voyage to the coast of West Africa or the work undertaken when he and the crew reach the island. Ponderevo drives his men hard as they shovel up the radioactive ore and pile it into the ship's hold: "I understand now the heart of the sweater, of the harsh employer, of the nigger-driver. I had brought these men into a danger they didn't understand, I was fiercely resolved to overcome their oppositions and bend and use them for my purpose, and I hated the men. But I hated all humanity during the time that the quap was near me."[4]

This, the first stage of Ponderevo's education, leads him to comprehend the same obsessiveness that drives Linforth to complete his father's task in *The Broken Road* and Charles Gould to make profitable his father's Sulacan concession in *Nostromo*. For these characters and Ponderevo, imperialism is the fixed will. Later, when Ponderevo goes into the jungle to get away from the quap and the laborers, he makes a more unsettling discovery about himself. The emptiness of the landscape soothes him, but before he has time to savor his Eden fully, a black man materializes on the forest trail ahead of him, as suddenly as if he had been summoned up by Ponderevo's guilty imagination. Trench's tower had a black panther, Crusoe's island had a footprint not made by himself, Prospero's isle had a Caliban, Graves' Highland had a race of cavemen—and now Mordet Island has an aboriginal: a man with greater theoretic right to the quap than Ponderevo or the colonial power from whom Ponderevo is stealing it, and at least with the right to survival. But as the native turns and runs away, Ponderevo unhesitatingly shoots him in the back, killing him with a single shot. He destroys innocent strangeness. He cannot understand why he has done this and hurriedly buries the body out of sight, hoping it will take with it his sense of the deed's "pointlessness, its incompatibility with any of the neat and definite theories people hold about life and the meaning of the world."[5] But the confusion and the conviction of guilt remain with him until he leaves the island with the quap, the radioactivity of which sickens Ponderevo and his crew and makes their boat's timbers rot. After these punishments the boat sinks, carrying its illicit cargo to the bottom.

The clumsiness in Wells's handling of this episode extends to more than the silly name he invented for his priceless mineral. He supplies facile and unconvincing "scientific" explanations for events that should have remained inexplicable elements of a symbolic fable; he devotes too much time to the voyage out and not enough to the stay on the island; he contrives a patly symbolic connection between the radioactivity of quap ("a real disease of matter") and the decaying traditions of English society; and finally, in the sinking of the boat he drops the whole business with indecent haste, hurrying back to the story of Tono-Bungay proper.[6] Its setting and melodramatic antirealism make the quap episode alien to everything else in the book, and in a half-hearted apology for its extraneousness Ponderevo talks endlessly about the oddity of the journey: it is a mere episode in the pattern of his life, having no connection with what went before or after. However Ponderevo tries to explain it away, the quap episode remains an awkward addition to the novel. It is something that forces its way into Wells's scheme, regardless of the consequences, just as the gratuitous killing of the native forces its way into the episode as a whole; the quap business expresses a bad conscience which had to find relief. Wells could not rationally have felt guilt for killing a native; the guilt was simply in the atmosphere in which Wells and other Edwardians worked. They knew, in spite of the efforts of the Romance and Adventure Agency to tell them otherwise, that Eden was unavailable, and that in the populated landscapes where their heroes would have to act, heroism was less likely than inexplicable cruelty.

Wells's attitude toward empire was not so simply damning as

Tono-Bungay would lead one to think. That novel was written by a thoughtful and troubled man at the end of the decade; earlier, Wells had argued keenly for imperialism in meetings of the Coefficients.[7] While Wells was among the Fabians, he shared the Fabian respect for tough-mindedness and efficiency; he admired the "energetic young men of the more responsible classes" who so often entered imperial service. But just as he both idealized science and feared its powers, so he idealized and feared the personal powers of the subaltern caste, and in *First and Last Things* (1908) he noted their tendency to be harshly constructive and unscrupulous, to slip readily into a Kiplingesque brutality.[8] Wells worried even more about the cause to which they were dedicated, or sacrificed. *In the Days of the Comet* makes the British Empire no more than a thing adrift and aimless, which eats and drinks and sleeps and bears arms, and is inordinately proud of itself.[9] This mindless and devouring empire is one of the problems swept away by the comet's prophylactic vapor.

The starting-point of doubt appears in the 1901 scientific romance *The First Men in the Moon*, which on the surface conveys Wells's anxiety that moderns are grossly unprepared for the scientific discoveries about to be handed them. Equally on the surface is a mild satire directed against contemporary overspecialization. That is what Arnold Bennett saw in the book.[10] But beneath the surface—a metaphor the book itself makes great use of—other ideas are brooded upon. The real theme of *The First Men in the Moon*, never discussed openly but only figured in action and dialogue, is the destruction of innocence and the corruption by greed intimately associated with European colonialism, especially in Africa.

The novel begins with the arrival of Bedford, the narrator, in the neighborhood of Romney Marsh. There he is to work on a play, but he evades his desk for visits among the local people, one of whom is a scientist named Cavor, a "water-drinker, a vegetarian, and all those logical disciplinary things," but also a brilliant experimenter who has invented an antigravity substance and named it Cavorite after himself. They join forces, and

immediately commercial possibilities occur to Bedford, who like
Teddy Ponderevo dreams on a grandiose scale. He sees the mul-
tiplication of antigravity companies until one vast Cavorite
Company shall rule the world. Meanwhile Cavor's own ambitions are more than worldly. He has fashioned Cavorite into a
hollow, air-tight sphere and is ready to be lifted on a voyage of
cosmic exploration. This Bedford automatically interprets as a
voyage of exploitation promising "planetary rights of pre-
emption" and recalling the old Spanish monopoly in American
gold. "This is tremendous!" he cries. "This is Imperial!" Their
destination is the moon, and what they find when they arrive is
astonishingly like Africa, like the Congo. The surface of the
moon is covered with a dense growth of rapidly growing fleshy
plants: "About us the dream-like jungle, with the silent bayonet
leaves darting overhead, and the silent, vivid, sun-splashed li-
chens under our hands and knees, waving with the vigour of
their growth as a carpet waves when the wind gets beneath it.
Ever and again one of the bladder fungi, bulging and distending
under the sun, loomed upon us. Ever and again some novel
shape in vivid colour obtruded . . . the blood flowed through
one's ears in a throbbing tide—thud, thud, thud, thud."[11]

In this lunar version of a tropical landscape, complete to
threatening plants and throbbing sound-effects, Bedford is ob-
sessed by thoughts of empire-building. "We must annex this
moon," he declares, growing first bold and then thick-tongued
under the influence of some intoxicating fungi he has eaten.
"There must be no shilly-shally. This is part of the White Man's
Burthen. Cavor—we are—hic—Satap—mean Satraps! Nem-
pire Caesar never dreamt." Bedford is quickly sobered when
native inhabitants, the Selenites, appear. Though Bedford thinks
them contemptible, more like ants than human beings, they
make the imperial scheme dubious. For a moment Bedford is admirably conscientious, questioning what right he and Cavor
have to come to the moon and disturb the Selenites' society,
until he discovers that beneath the surface of the moon, in vast
caverns, gold is unbelievably plentiful, and immediately he

knows he must have it. Down he and Cavor go, into the sublunarian darkness. The lower they go, the more they feel trapped and oppressed. Eventually the explorers part company. Cavor, an idealist like Kurtz in *Heart of Darkness*, wants to stay and discover more; he thinks that he can get over the oppressiveness of the darkness and that the Selenites may come to understand him, that is, receive the benefits of civilization. Bedford merely wants to get away with all the gold he can carry. There is confused fighting between the Selenites and earthlings, and finally Cavor, who is injured, has to be left behind. He manages to get a note to his departing comrade, however, which ends: "And though I am wounded and helpless here, their appearance still gives me hope . . . They have not shot at me or attempted . . . injury. I intend . . ." At that point there comes "the sudden streak of the pencil across the paper, and on the back and edges— blood!"[12] This is a version of the "Exterminate all the brutes!" scrawled at the margin of Kurtz's highmindedness, and if Cavor is Kurtz, in this vulgarization of Conrad's tale, then Bedford is a corrupted and shallow Marlow. He must carry the message back to listeners on earth.

Having gotten thus far, Wells abruptly loses interest in the theme of exploitation and also in his plot; the book ends with awkward, scattered ironies and a return to the facetious tone of the opening. The Cavorite sphere is lost, and Bedford publishes a serial account of his journey. Meanwhile Cavor begins a series of wireless messages from the interior of the moon, describing a highly specialized, antlike society; but he makes the mistake of telling the "Grand Lunar" about the violence typical on earth and is not allowed to broadcast further.

It is impossible to say definitely whether *The First Men in the Moon* is responding to Wells's half-articulated intuitions about "rights of pre-emption" or to *Heart of Darkness*, from which it obviously borrows its machinery, but in effect it is an allegory of the dangers of imperialism. It illustrates what happens when civilized people discover a darkness to be illuminated and treasure to be had: they kill, they destroy. They fail to notice what

Wells himself notices, the strange beauty of alien life. They descend within themselves and find a frightening savageness. They contaminate everything they touch. Eventually, they go home with profits and nothing else, if they are lucky and insensitive. If they are unlucky or sensitive, like Cavor and Kurtz, they stay behind to be lost. Imperialism is condemned for what it does, impartially and inexorably, to victim and victimizer.

The same judgment is issued by another Edwardian romance, W. H. Hudson's *Green Mansions* (1904), though Hudson never uses the word "imperialism" and disguises his meanings, even more than Wells, in scene-painting and a mannered style; Hudson's literary indulgence was luxuriant melancholy, as Wells's was facetiousness. By the end of *Green Mansions* it is difficult to distinguish between victim and victimizer. The nominal victimizer is the narrator, Abel, who has fled political troubles in Venezuela and gone into the jungle. There he encounters fever and Indians, who treat him well but whom he still regards as "beasts of prey." He seeks gold, then abandons the search because he has become fascinated by something more elusive, a melodious call in a language he cannot understand, Rima's call. Rima is an Eve for Abel, and in incongruously Miltonic terms their meeting-place is established as an Eden: "I dropped on my knees and kissed the stony ground, then casting up my eyes, thanked the Author of my being for the gift of that wild forest, those green mansions where I found so great a happiness!"[13] A coral snake intrudes into this Eden and, when attacked, retaliates by biting Abel, demonstrating on a small-scale what the whole novel teaches, that innocence is best left alone. Abel recovers in the hut of Rima's grandfather and learns there the secret of her parentage: her mother was the survivor of a different race, living in distant mountains, and to these mountains Rima convinces Abel that she must go, to find her people, the speakers of her language. They journey there, dangerously and perhaps impiously, and when Abel forces Rima to realize that her people no longer exist, they separate for the return journey, as if Rima wishes to dramatize her perilous isolation in the world. She is, in fact, murdered by a band of marauding Indians, on whom Abel takes revenge by inciting an enemy tribe to kill them. Afterward he lives in the forest, worshiping Rima's memory, hunting while feeling guilt about it because Rima was pained by the death of any living creature, and passing through a period of near madness. He is finally comforted by a vision of Rima making him a promise: if he will forgive himself, Heaven will not oppose their being united. Abel, it is apparent, is to be Rima's Intended.

This plot summary shows why *Green Mansions* was a success: it allowed readers to indulge themselves in a satisfying sadness and then be consoled. Nevertheless, behind the sentimentalism, behind the Rackhamesque figure of Rima, who is half spirit of nature and half Peter Pan, was hidden an unconsoling conception of man's place in exotic nature.[14] Abel, an educated white man, carries greed, anger, and violence into the green mansions, and these evils not even Rima's innocence can cure. They are as inherent in him as in the murdering Indians, who merely dramatize, like the blacks in *Heart of Darkness*, a general human savageness. Abel and the Indians destroy Rima in the same inadvertent way that Ponderevo shoots the black man he encounters in the jungle, and then they destroy each other in reactions of revenge and guilt, for whatever his hopes for the future, Abel is a hollow man when he finishes his tale. Hudson's book is not about imperialism *per se* but about the motive on which it was based, the wish to enlighten, to control, and to possess. The movement of its plot parallels the movement of more overtly political fables, from civilization to the jungle, and from idealism to dark self-knowledge and even self-destruction.

Political interpretations of romance inevitably seem ponderous, because they impose a sententiousness on fictional structures not meant to bear the weight. Rima and the Selenites as oppressed colonial peoples, Bedford and Abel as oppressors, the Congolese jungle extended to South America and the moon— there is something schematic about these equations, and something unprovable, because they imply motives hidden from the authors' conscious minds. But authorial intention is only one factor to be considered in analysis, and the works themselves point insistently enough in the direction of doubt about imperial ventures. Over and over again the pattern of violence and disillusion appears, an Edwardian nightmare. A knowledge of what was happening routinely in Africa and elsewhere took on disguises and asserted itself, even in books which attempted to get away from Africa and the whole contemporary world.

This is not to argue that all Edwardian dreamers were troubled with the black panther. The proponents of imperialism, such as Buchan and Kipling, also had their symbolic fictions, and in these violence appears without disillusion, being accepted as a sign of efficiency or a historical necessity or the cost of civilization or perhaps just the result of an adventuring spirit which has no regard for the morality of its actions. A combination of these attitudes is at work in Kipling's story "The Knights of the Joyous Venture," one of the *Puck of Pook's Hill* lessons in Englishness. The Saxon Hugh and the Norman Sir Richard Dalyngrydge, grown old in a settled England, decide to make a last Ulyssean voyage. In the company of Witta the Dane, ethnic complicity being a strong motive of the *Puck* stories, they sail off to Africa in pursuit of gold. Penetrating inland, they kill "devils" (gorillas) which come at them from the jungle and in return are given ivory and gold by the grateful natives. The story is a parable of successful economic imperialism which only a child could believe—it is the least adult story in the collection—and the child who hears it, Dan, significantly compares it to R. M. Ballantyne's *The Gorilla Hunters* (1861), a continuation of *Coral Island* (1858).

Buchan's *Prester John* (1910), with its secret caves and hidden mountain paradise, is less believable still, but believability is the last quality it needs as an adventure romance. In its own terms *Prester John* is a nearly perfect work, so there is again something puritanical about digging beneath its satisfying surface to find the unpleasant assumption that a white man has every right to gain the ancient treasure of the blacks and then transform the veld into a fertile agricultural district. This deeply buried, confident assumption is less in control of Buchan's creative imagination than the suspicion of imperialist greed is in control of Wells's, which means that *Prester John* is a more shapely fiction than either *Tono-Bungay* or *The First Men in the Moon*, though it is also less ambitious and less ultimately satisfying. *Prester John* is an attractive lie. It dreams of a world in which enlightenment means something. In the Rooirand caves the hero Crawfurd undertakes a dark voyage like that of Graves in "No-man's Land," but there is nothing impious in his attempt, and beyond the heart of darkness he finds light: "Before me was the shallow vale with its bracken and sweet grass, and the shining links of the stream, and the loch still grey in the shadow of the beleaguering hills. Here was a fresh, clean land, a land for homesteads and orchards and children. All of a sudden I realized that at last I had come out of savagery . . . Behind me was the black night, and the horrid secrets of darkness. Before me was my own country, for that loch and that bracken might have been on a Scotch moor."[15] For Buchan and his hero, as long as they can keep the black panther out of sight and mind, settling Africa means possessing what they have always had.

10

Conrad and Adventure

There is nothing incidental about adventure in the work of Joseph Conrad from *The Nigger of the "Narcissus"* in 1897 to *Nostromo* seven years later. The ambitions driving men abroad and the actions taken once there form the substance of his novels and tales. These fictions comprise not a series of closed episodes capable of dramatizing and dispelling a bad conscience, as in the case of Wells's story of quap and Hudson's story of Rima, but a single ongoing disillusionment with the political structure in which the real adventurous action of his day was confined. That is, Conrad's disillusionment was with imperialism.[1] Characteristically, though, he shied away from the term and the strident controversy surrounding it. He analyzed imperialism neither as a great power fighting small powers and so convincing itself of its lost pride, nor as "the electric force in civilization." Conrad would have remained glumly silent in the discussions at Musuru, or responded to them, as he responded to Casement, that he was only a wretched novelist and could not help. The wretchedness consisted, among other things, of seeing too deeply into the lives of people in service abroad to comment on them with abstract simplicity.

The hero of *Lord Jim*, when questioned in an abstract, cut-and-dried way by the Court of Inquiry investigating the abandonment of the "Patna," has little to say. His sullenness suggests how pointless it would be to try to extract a formal "position" on imperialism from Conrad. For both Conrad and Jim, imposed verdicts are irrelevant, and the only investigations of their attitudes likely to have value must proceed at a slow pace, with due regard for the significance of evasion and extenuation, and without impatient probing for facts. For both men, meaning lies not inside, like a kernel, but outside, in the whole process of memory and imagination. A long process of remembering and sympathetic listening finally brings Jim to the point of being able to tell Marlow that he left the "Patna," when it seemed on the point of sinking, along with the rest of the crew. "I had jumped—it seems" is the plainest confession he can manage. A similarly banal statement in *Nostromo,* the phrase "material interests" on the lips of Emilia Gould, constitutes the plainest judgment on imperialism Conrad could manage, but even that judgment can be understood only in the context of the whole novel and the rest of Conrad's Edwardian fiction.

Romance, the adventure story written in collaboration with Ford Madox Ford, is not pure Conrad. But as David Thorburn has shown, it was taken seriously by Conrad, and contains enough of his own writing to be grouped thematically with his other works.[2] Published in 1903, after *Lord Jim* and *Heart of Darkness, Romance* does not develop ideas of the earlier books. There is no obvious chronological development in Conrad's attitude toward adventure and empire, only a shifting emphasis on one aspect or another of his subject—the nature of heroism, freedom of action versus social and moral constraints, ordeals of initiation and redemption, the corruption of greed, the politics of exploitation and nationalism. For reasons now impossible to recover, but probably involving its modest fictional aims, *Romance* is the least political of all Conrad's adventure tales. It says nothing about the relations between the governing and the governed or about colonial practices in Jamaica, where the hero John Kemp is briefly a plantation overseer, and though the Irish pirate Juez O'Brien explains often in lurid terms that he is moved by a hatred of England, no connection is drawn between Ireland's colonial status and Jamaica's or Cuba's. Conrad and Ford refused to impose a moral conscientiousness on the historical period of their romance, for they had another purpose in hand.

In title and substance *Romance* is abstractly, self-consciously devoted to the adventuring spirit. The work detaches romance as a quality from the experience of Kemp and holds it up for special admiration, as a piece of the True Cross might be held up cynically for the veneration of pious worshipers. Conrad and Ford treat romance as the relic of an antiquated belief. It is kept at some distance from the narrative present of Kemp, who in the style of Marlow in "Youth" constantly remarks how many years have passed between the time of the tale and the time of the telling. Kemp relates, for example, how he was snatched away from England to the West Indies by the dashing Carlos Riego, his first mentor in the adventurous life. Looking back, Kemp can best explain Riego as "an aristocratic scapegrace, a corsair—it was the Byronic period then." Later Kemp compares himself saving his beloved Seraphina with a knight rescuing a princess from an enchanted castle. Kemp's naively dated terms enable Conrad and Ford to be sophisticated, to make their tale both simply and ironically romantic, an adventure story that is also an Adventure Story. The authors draw on the freshness of the adventuring spirit, on the fictional energy of an action-filled plot and colorful characters, while simultaneously revealing their own knowingness. They are not above laughing at their characters. Tomas Castro, the retainer first of Riego and then of Kemp, has a sharpened blade at the end of his artificial arm, but when this wicked prosthesis goes into action for the first time, it only impales a cockroach. That is a small-scale deflation to accompany the large-scale deflation of Kemp himself, who announces the defining formula of all adventure fiction, "My mental anguish was excessive; action alone could relieve it," but then fails to be conspicuously active. Throughout the book, which has episodes of smuggling, two escapes to sea, boardings by pirates, a shipwreck, a near starvation, and much bloodshed, Kemp plays a curiously passive role, as though he had been made too small for the part thrust on him, or as though the full exercise of heroism would be impossible because incomprehensible to those around him. That seems to be the point of his reception on board the British ship "Lion," to which he, Tomas, and Seraphina flee in a small boat, with O'Brien's pirates right behind them. The wife of the ship's master, he is told, is troubled less by piracy than by propriety: "Mrs. Williams thinks it's irregular . . . you and your young lady being alone—in an open boat at night, and that sort of thing. It isn't what they approve of at Bristol."[3] No more can Mrs. MacWhirr in the drawing-room of her forty-pound house in *Typhoon* understand the stolid heroics of her husband aboard the "Nan-Shan," but Conrad's satire is much more pointed in *Typhoon* than in *Romance*, where the comedy of Mrs. Williams is diffuse and casually at odds with the whole basis of the fiction.

The truth is that *Romance* is a work at the end of an adventure tradition reaching back to Stevenson, Anthony Hope, and Marryat. The proper costumes are displayed, but so treated as to seem, in Henry James's phrase, both ready-made and sadly the worse for wear. The rhetoric rings hollowly, the action is greeted with puzzlement. The passing of the tradition is wittily saluted but cannot otherwise be contested, and the final impression *Romance* makes is summarized in the description of Seraphina's Cuban *casa*: "The general effect of the place was of vitality exhausted, of a body calcined, of romance turned into stone. The still air, the hot sunshine, the white beach curving around the deserted sheet of water, the sombre green of the hills, had the motionlessness of things petrified, the vividness of things painted, the sadness of things abandoned, desecrated."[4]

Conrad's reading and his experience in the world told him that adventure was never available in pure form, even purely abandoned or desecrated form, but was beset with complications, and that from these complications he might create fiction vastly more interesting than that formulated by Stevenson's heirs. Escape in the manner of *Romance* would always be possible, and at the end of his career Conrad would return to its rich simplicities in *Victory* (1915) and *The Rover* (1923), which are his contributions to the Adventure and Romance Agency. But for several years after the turn of the century, in company with other Edwardian novelists, Conrad sought deliberately to expand his subject-matter with the facts of experience. He rejected a weary tradition by overstating it in *Romance*, then went inward to his personal history and outward to the world to find substantiation for a fiction of reversals. That fiction would be about the failure of action to relieve mental anguish, the devastating isolation of the hero, the corruption of heroism for political purposes, and the puniness of human action when set against the mindless immensity of nature. These are the postulates of *Lord Jim*, *Heart of Darkness*, and *Nostromo*.

That Lord Jim is a romantic links him to Kemp, but throughout the book knowledge of his romanticism is kept from him, along with every other possible typification of his nature, so that he never knows that what has happened to him has happened to others before. Not being privy to Captain Brierly's doubts about courage or the French lieutenant's evaded memory of a failure in the past ("I, who am speaking to you, once . . ."), Jim thinks that his cowardice in abandoning the "Patna" could happen only once in the history of mankind. Later he thinks that the post in Patusan given him by the trader Stein represents a unique chance for salvation. After "failing" there, after allowing Gentleman Brown's raiders to slip away and kill his friend Dain Waris, Jim goes to his last meeting with Dain Waris' father in naive self-deception, not knowing he is making a romantic gesture. In spite of the course of light holiday reading which urges him to sea in the first place, and his boyish observation that what he is doing in Patusan is like something "you read of in books," Jim is an unbookish hero. His conspicuously unformulaic career suggests, as *Romance* never does, that a literary character is moving at some distance from literature, in a real world where disasters happen and are talked about later, on a verandah after dinner. The sea-captain Marlow and his fellow commentator Stein, who on that verandah or elsewhere contemplate Jim from the outside, carry all the weariness of the novel. It is from them that the reader learns what label to attach to Jim's troubles. He is a romantic, Stein says, and then, with the uncertainty of one who has been through the experience so long ago that he cannot decide how to value it, he adds, "And that is very bad—very bad . . . Very good, too."[5]

In the action of *Lord Jim* it is easier to see the badness of romance than the goodness. Romance fills Jim's mind with images of himself acting heroically, which leads to a false confidence that not even the episode of the training ship, when he nervously holds back from participating in a rescue, can quite shake. Once the habit of imagining things is indulged in, it cannot be dropped, so Jim cannot stop imagining what will happen when the rusty bulkhead on the "Patna" gives way. He lacks the saving ignorance of a MacWhirr, who sticks with his ship because he cannot imagine what might happen to it. Furthermore, Jim lacks the clear field of action on which heroes of romance are allowed to move. His field of action is cluttered with eight hundred Mecca-bound passengers, the men and women who, no less than their sleeping babies, are the unconscious pilgrims of an exacting belief. Their unconsciousness is in Jim's hands, and in this sense he has an infinitely harder task than any set for Kemp, who at most has Seraphina to care for. Whether Jim realizes it or not, he has a social responsibility—a "racial responsibility," the anonymous recipient of Marlow's letter would say. He is placed at the periphery of empire and charged with carrying out the empire's purposes. Kipling would have allowed him diversions—a comrade, a tale to tell, a game to play—and perhaps let him succeed; Conrad surrounds him with the rest of the "Patna's" rascally crew and makes him fail. The cowardice of the others does not excuse Jim's jumping from the ship and abandoning his responsibility to the sleeping pilgrims, but the others unquestionably clutter his field of action and contaminate him with their hatred for responsibility.

For all these reasons Jim's initiation is ruined; he fails the test which would prove him a hero, a team-player. There follows a period in which the chief problem, more pressing even than what to do with him, is what to make of him. Both Captain Brierly and Marlow worry that Jim's subtle unsoundness may subvert, one by one, the signs of reliability they depend on: the frank aspect, the artless smile, the youthful seriousness, possibly even the white uniform of men in the Eastern service. You would trust your deck to Jim on the strength of a single glance, Marlow says, and you would not be safe (fourteen years after *Lord Jim*, in *The Good Soldier*, Ford adopted almost exactly this language for the deceptive gentlemanliness of Edward Ashburnam; Ford learned from Conrad). By every test of appearance Jim should belong to the right sort, should be "one of us," and because he does not, he forces Brierly to suicide and Marlow, the braver of the two, to a long series of questions. The Court of Inquiry asks its own questions and decides that Jim is not to be counted among the certifiably decent—the "good, stupid" kind, as Marlow says, who pass initiations and survive inquiries with ease. Jim is nothing like the seaman who eventually rescues the "Patna," the French lieutenant with his matter-of-fact courage, as habitual as the glass of wine taken with meals; or the young Stein, single-minded rather than stupid, who fought off enemies and collected rare butterflies at the same time, never letting the splendid opportunity of his dream escape. But neither is Jim to be classed with the rapacious failures of the book: the German captain of the "Patna," Chester, Chester's senile partner Holy-Terror Robinson, Jewel's detestable father Cornelius, or Gentleman Brown. These have no romantic ideas to betray them (Chester boasts of never taking anything to heart) and are still more detached from the real world than Jim, being wholly occupied within their private realms of hallucination, envy, triumph, and revenge (a guano island transported miraculously to Queensland, Patusan pillaged and burnt). They suggest a deformed imperialism with no pretensions to ideals or discipline, merely the reckless will to rip an island apart for what it holds or ransack a jungle village where a white man keeps by him a fabulously valuable Jewel. Yet Marlow does not claim a perfect selflessness for the more attractive imperialism of Stein, which promises enlightenment as well as trade. Marlow's cynicism urges him to look for the profit motive at the bottom of all romantic ventures, however genuine their coloring of romance:

> I have no doubt [Stein] had been [in Patusan], either in his butterfly-hunting days or later on, when he tried in his in-

corrigible way to season with a pinch of romance the fattening dishes of his commercial kitchen. There were very few places in the Archipelago he had not seen in the original dusk of their being, before light (and even electric light) had been carried into them for the sake of better morality and—and—well—the greater profit too.

To us, their less tried successors, [the first explorers of Patusan] appear magnified, not as agents of trade but as instruments of a recorded destiny, pushing out into the unknown in obedience to an inward voice, to an impulse beating in the blood, to a dream of the future. They were wonderful; and it must be owned they were ready for the wonderful. They recorded it complacently in their sufferings, in the aspect of the seas, in the customs of strange nations, in the glory of splendid rulers.

In Patusan they had found lots of pepper.[6]

Jim's isolation from both the "good, stupid" kind and the failures, from both the decorous and the savage imperialists, no longer matters when Stein sends him off as the protector of Patusan, because there isolation is taken for granted. He will simply have to be lonely. Marlow remembers Jim as a white speck shining against the darkness, a figure standing "on the brink of a vast obscurity . . . by the shore of a sombre and hopeless ocean."[7] This image of Jim abandoned in a dark world is Conrad's chief device for acknowledging the cost of Jim's becoming Tuan Jim, an imperial servant, a sahib. He is left for good among a people not his own, in a land more impervious to his efforts than he realizes. He has no support and yet no real freedom to act for himself; the villagers crowd around him as thickly as the "Patna" pilgrims. Still, Patusan represents a chance for redemption. In the unpromising decrepitude of the trading post Stein has recognized the destructive element to which Jim must resubmit himself, the dream that he must set himself to follow—*ewig—usque ad finem;* Stein's romantic metaphors are burnished and presented for Marlow's inspection like so many prize butterflies. In an adventure story more conventionally romantic than *Lord Jim* the redemption of the hero would succeed, as for example it does in A. E. W. Mason's *The Four Feathers* (1902). Here also cowardice is to be rehabilitated: Harry Feversham breaks under the threat of battle, for the same reason that ruins Jim ("That was my trouble always. I foresaw. Any peril to be encountered, any risk to be run—I foresaw them"), and he is given four white feathers as a token of cowardice. A confessional scene between Feversham and an older, wiser lieutenant mimics the long colloquy between Marlow and Jim, but afterward the novels part company, as Feversham goes forth to the wars and in the course of time redeems himself, returning the feathers one by one.[8]

In Patusan, Jim repels attacks, protects his people, and begins to believe himself redeemed. Although his bravery is scarcely recognized, let alone ceremonialized like Feversham's, he can survive the world's indifference, along with the loneliness of his outpost, the native politics, and the enforced closeness to Cornelius. These are merely the ordinary working conditions of the prosaic heroism he has chosen—the heroism of dozens of Kipling's subalterns and colonial agents. What Jim cannot survive is a fatal ignorance about himself. All through the novel this is his problem. He has no terms, "romantic" or otherwise, for his personality. After the inquiry, he seeks confirmation of his true identity, the one that the inquiry could not reveal, and he does so by talking to Marlow. The novel's epigraph explains why he needs the older man: "It is certain my Conviction gains infinitely, the moment another soul will believe in it." And though Jim is evasive even with Marlow, circling around and around the naked fact which has cut him off from the rest of his fellows, that is not just because he finds it hard to admit cowardice openly. It is because he is genuinely ignorant about his cowardice. It takes him hours of circumstantial description to come to even an incomplete understanding of what he is. He cannot detach himself from his emotions to get a clear view. Feversham, in contrast, tells the sympathetic lieutenant "the whole truth, without exaggeration or omission, forcing himself to a slow, careful, matter-of-fact speech, so that in the end [the lieutenant] almost fell into the illusion that it was just the story of a stranger which Feversham was recounting merely to pass the time."⁹ Jim depends on others for his sense of himself, and thus he is at the opposite pole from Kemp as well as from Feversham. At the end of *Romance* Kemp acquits himself of a charge of piracy by triumphantly establishing his real identity. In Patusan Jim allows his emerging self-knowledge to be undermined. Believing, or refusing to examine, the bogus claim of moral kinship Brown insinuates, that he and Jim are alike under the skin, Jim lets Brown and his men slip away as though he wished to be reminded of having slipped away once himself, and he causes the catastrophe of Dain Waris' death. Deciding no one will ever understand, Jim finally gives up his attempt to write and dies, with his hands over his lips, preferring not to express himself. The tableau symbolizes the final cost of Jim's becoming Tuan Jim: he has accepted a role in lieu of an identity. Rather than explain himself, he dies a tight-lipped sahib.

Although Marlow thinks Jim inscrutable at heart, he clearly understands Jim's motives; Marlow's real ignorance is of the value of the sacrifice. At a venture he attaches the word "tragic" to Jim, but "tragic" is as ambivalent as Stein's "romantic," and leaves Marlow sadly dubious, sure of nothing but his need to share his doubts with others. The ambivalence of *Lord Jim*, unlike that of *Romance*, is sincere rather than contrived, and it results from understanding that the romantic dream, figured by Stein as "the destructive element," may lead to a specific and literal destruction.

Heart of Darkness, begun a few months after Conrad had started work on the 20,000-word sketch that became *Lord Jim*, was worked on hurriedly "for the sake of the shekels" and finished more than a year before the novel.¹⁰ But *Heart of Darkness* gives the impression of beginning where *Lord Jim* stops. In the tale the failure of individuals is a foregone conclusion, regeneration in the form Jim hopes for it an impossibility. Conrad's attention shifts to institutionalized adventurism—that is, to a political system, imperialism in the Belgian Congo—allowing him to develop in a systematic way those ironies about the profitability of electric light in the jungle which *Lord Jim* only touches on. *Heart of Darkness* argues that institutionalizing adventurism inevitably makes it greedy. Marlow, acting as narrator once more, expresses disdain for individual dramas ("I don't want to bother you much with what happened to me personally") and emphasizes the broader figurative meanings of his voyage up the Congo River to rescue the trader Kurtz ("It was the farthest point of navigation and the culminating point of my experience").[11] He thus saves his tale from being either an anti-imperialist tract or an adventure story—a white man rescued, an attack repulsed, a perilous journey triumphantly carried out—and implies that Kurtz's fate throws light on "everything."

Heart of Darkness is made portentous by the reckless expenditure of style on a mere hundred pages of novella: accumulating images of darkness, reiterated unspeakabilities, implacable forces piled up broodingly on inscrutable intentions. It is made allusive, a different matter, by coinciding personal and historical experience. Conrad wrote the tale ten years after he had taken a steamer up the Congo, retrieved from the interior one Georges Antoine Klein, a trader who became the model for Kurtz, and gone through a profoundly disturbing period of sickness and mental depression; and three years after he had excoriated colonial stupidities in "An Outpost of Progress" (*Tales of Unrest*, 1898), which gave him the chance to rehearse the themes and also to write the heavy-handed ironies out of his system. Conrad's memories needed years to sort themselves out and find the right expression in fiction. The narration of *Heart of Darkness*, delivered by Marlow to a small group on the cruising yacht "Nellie" in the Thames while they wait for the ebb of the tide, belongs, with the narrations of *Lord Jim* and "Youth," to a period of fascination with storytelling that would also need years to develop, as Conrad grew slowly skeptical about this simplest of all interchanges of experience between men, and then slowly nostalgic. One of the ambitions of the tale is to preserve storytelling in literary prose while implying reasons for its decline in contemporary life. Historical experience enriches the tale with information about the Congo, thanks to Casement and others the most notorious of European colonies in Africa, and with a vaguer sense that the idea of empire was itself in decline and that institutionalized adventurism, which was in the process of harming both Europeans and natives alike, would accomplish nothing permanent.

This fin-de-siècle disillusion was reinforced by thoughts of the historical parallel between Roman and contemporary imperialism. The parallel was not necessarily ominous. Outsiders particularly could view it with detached complacency, as in *The Golden Bowl:*

> The Prince had always liked his London, when it had come to him; he was one of the modern Romans who find by the Thames a more convincing image of the truth of the ancient state than any they have left by the Tiber. Brought up on the legend of the City to which the world paid tribute, he recognised in the present London much more than in contemporary Rome the real dimensions of such a case. If it was a question of an *Imperium*, he said to himself, and if one wished, as a Roman, to recover a little the sense of that, the place to do so was on London Bridge, or even, on a fine afternoon in May, at Hyde Park Corner.[12]

But as Samuel Hynes has noted, Edwardian Englishmen were deeply worried by the memory of Rome's physical and moral degeneracy. Could the same thing be happening to Rome's heirs?[13] Kipling's Romano-Britons Parnesius and Pertinax offered the momentary reassurance of an imperialism strong in its traditions, disciplined at the frontier, and pious in defense of its secular creed, but fictional heroism from Kipling or anyone else could not obscure awareness that the Roman Empire had in the end grown corrupt and fallen. The bitterest thought of all was that Roman grandeur and Roman corruption had alike passed away into oblivion, leaving nothing behind but melancholy ruins. Parnesius and Pertinax were by the twentieth century ashes under Uricon. The narrator of Wells's *The First Men in the Moon*, who might seem immune to sentiment of this sort, gazes down on Watling Street and feels the Ozymandias mood painfully: "I used to stand on the hill and think of it all, the galleys and legions, the captives and officials, the women and traders, the speculators like myself, all the swarm and tumult that came clanking in and out of the harbour. And now just a few lumps of rubble on a grassy slope, and a sheep or two—and me!"[14] Sardonic disenchantment was standard in Edwardian poems about Rome's Empire, such as Ford's "The Proconsuls" (1907):

> But Rome's a ruin, all her standards down,
> See the Proconsuls come to London Town.
> Where are the emblems? What the tokens shown
> Of pomp imperial, where the banners thrown
> In sign of rule o'er hill and dale and flood?
> Why here's no emblem! Through the London mud
> Under the sleety sky our consuls come.
> Shall not old ghosts laugh amid ruin'd Rome?[15]

Conrad's allusion to Rome elaborates and sharpens the parallel. In *Heart of Darkness* one of Marlow's listeners meditates on the Thames as a pageant of the great exploratory spirit of the past: adventurers and settlers, "hunters for gold or pursuers of fame," had all gone out on that stream, "bearing the sword, and often the torch, messengers of the might within the land, bearers of a spark from the sacred fire." As if contemptuous of these well-worn metaphors, Marlow announces that the Thames also has been one of the dark places of the earth, and his subsequent speculations on the Roman colonization of Britain ironically reverse the geography of the story. While waiting with the others for the outgoing tide, he visualizes a tide carrying other men *in* to an ancient Britain, even as in the tale proper men will go out once again for the European invasion of Africa. Marlow's boat seems the only still point in a restless movement from colonizing to being colonized and back again. But Marlow's historical musings have more than an ironic appropriateness. They admit the essential rapaciousness of imperialism. Adventurers have always gone out bearing swords and torches, the latter for burning as well as lighting, and the Roman adventure in Britain was no exception, "just robbery with violence, aggravated murder on a great scale, and men going at it blind." Marlow's bluntness reveals what will later appear in the Congo, but also forestalls any facile condemnation of the colonists there, who are to be considered not aberrations but heirs of a long tradition. Marlow's imagination is stimulated even more by inward than by outward violence—the "mysterious life of the wilderness" closing round some Roman soldier or decent citizen in a toga, plunging him into darkness and cold and savagery, into the incomprehensible which is also the detestable.[16] Clearly, Marlow is pulled in two directions, toward condemning the "evils" of imperialism and toward sympathizing with the evils done to imperialists. As much as W. H. Hudson, he blurs the distinction between victim and victimizer.

The task given Marlow is to captain a river steamer; the tasks he eventually sets for himself are to recognize Kurtz's differences from the other ivory hunters and colonialists, to save Kurtz from the dark interior of Africa and what it has apparently done to him, to understand the lesson of Kurtz's death, and finally to carry a report back to Europe—to the woman waiting patiently for Kurtz in Brussels, Kurtz's "Intended." The task implicit in all of these is to observe imperialism at work, and when Marlow first glimpses it, he sees only an ineffectual scratching on the surface of a vast and unaffected darkness. The ship taking him to Africa passes a man-of-war shelling the coast: "Pop, would go one of the eight-inch guns; a small flame would dart and vanish, a little white smoke would disappear, a tiny projectile would give a feeble screech—and nothing happened." So much for military control of the dark continent. At the coastal station a railway is being built: "a heavy and dull detonation shook the ground, a puff of smoke came out of the cliff, and that was all. No change appeared on the face of the rock." So much for the railway. Marlow's rickety boat creeps up the Congo "like a sluggish beetle crawling on the floor of a lofty portico." Two of the Belgians struggle up a hill "leaning forward side by side . . . tugging painfully uphill their two ridiculous shadows of unequal length, that trailed behind them slowly over the tall grass without bending a single blade."[17] Africa is too grandly amorphous for man to dominate, inhabit, or comprehend.

If imperialism is to be judged by its success in building railways, pacifying the countryside, or even making bricks, it is a grotesque failure. But failure, Marlow discovers, is not a laughing matter. The black victims of the railway-building and ivory-gathering clamor for his attention. They suffer because their colonial masters, with all the freedom to act of heroes of adventure, can yet accomplish nothing; their freedom has nothing to express itself in but cruelty. Conrad expresses their cruelty in elaborate allegories, such as the Grove of Death with its echoes of Dante ("the gloomy circle of some inferno") and insistently symbolic "bit of white thread from beyond the seas" tied around the neck of a dying black. Marlow's commentary is simpler: "The glimpse of the steamboat had for some reason filled those savages with unrestrained grief."[18] Savage though the blacks may be, and they are never sentimentalized, they have learned enough to fear the mere sight of civilization, whether it is coming to take away their god Kurtz or set them in search of ivory. One function of *Heart of Darkness* is to make such cruelties known and to deprive the Belgians' "high and just proceedings" of their spurious idealism. Marlow strips away layer after layer of hypocrisy until he gets to the essential hollowness, in the process becoming an accessory to the ruthless anatomizing carried out by Africa itself. The Congo is full of dead men's bones, as Marlow sees when he looks at the emaciated body of Kurtz and the skeleton of Fresleven, his predecessor as captain of the steamer:

> [Kurtz's] covering had fallen off, and his body emerged from it pitiful and appalling as from a winding-sheet. I could see the cage of his ribs all astir, the bones of his arm waving. It was as though an animated image of death carved out of old ivory had been shaking its hand with menaces at a motionless crowd of men made of dark and glittering bronze.

... when an opportunity offered at last to meet my predecessor, the grass growing through his ribs was tall enough to hide his bones. They were all there. The supernatural being had not been touched after he fell. And the village was deserted, the huts gaped black, rotting, all askew within the fallen enclosures.[19]

Fresleven was killed after beating one of the blacks. The white man and the native village rot indistinguishably together. This is the defining emblem of imperialism.

The better-advised colonialists take steps to avoid Fresleven's fate, protecting themselves from anger or corruption by routines of discipline, the equivalent of dressing for dinner in the jungle. Hence the accountant's starched collars, the station manager's political intrigues, and the general worship of ivory as a god to be propitiated with human sacrifice. In singleness of intention, in the fixity of will setting a limited aim, the "pilgrims" maintain their hold on Africa and inadvertently show Marlow the way he may preserve himself. The discipline of work—riveting his boat together and then keeping his eyes on the surface of the water while he steams upriver—keeps Marlow out of the depths of the destructive element, which here consists of imagination, depression, moral sickness.

The Harlequin is a disciple Kurtz has made but not fully educated. When he spoke of his master, Marlow tells his listeners, "he nodded a nod full of mystery and wisdom. 'I tell you,' he cried, 'this man has enlarged my mind.' He opened his arms wide, staring at me with his little blue eyes that were perfectly round."[20] The gulf between Kurtz and the other colonialists in the Congo, enemies or disciples, is never so apparent as at this moment. The Harlequin's little blue eyes look up from the battered copy of Towson's Manual of Navigation—that is his protective discipline—and show no sign whatsoever of an enlarged mind. As his costume suggests, he is merely a holy fool licensed to wander harmlessly in the wilderness. He and the others are immune to Kurtz's discoveries because they have never had

Kurtz's substance; emptiness is their permanent condition, not a killing affliction as it is with Kurtz. Kurtz came to Africa with what, according to Marlow, is the only thing that can redeem empire, "an unselfish belief in the idea," perhaps also with a "firm conviction in the truth of ideas racially our own," as *Lord Jim* puts it, and certainly with all the achievements of a refined culture.[21] Kurtz paints, writes, might have been a great musician. All Europe has contributed to his making, but it requires only a few hundred miles of jungle isolation to unmake him. Changes take place "inside," the old doctor warns Marlow. The unselfish idea of imperialism is worthless in the abstract if in practice it depends on fallible human exponents. Kurtz is corrupted by the limitless power he works over his native tribes, by the employment of violence, and by the conversion of all his reforming energy not merely into a debilitating cynicism, which might have preserved him, but into a radically simplified will for ivory. Everything belongs to Kurtz, he claims—"My Intended, my ivory, my station, my river"—but the powers of darkness have claimed him for their own. Meanwhile the remnants of his culture lie haphazardly about in the form of paintings and unfinished reports, like the decaying traces of European material culture that Marlow has seen at the coast—the boiler wallowing in the grass and the railway truck lying on its back. As for Kurtz's report for the International Society for the Suppression of Savage Customs, it receives from Kurtz a last-minute addendum: "Exterminate all the brutes!" The sequence in which Lord Jim moves from a wordiness with Marlow to the plain admission "I had jumped" and then to silence is here paralleled by the sequence from Kurtz's eloquence in the report to the addendum and then to his dying remark "The horror! The horror!" These statements, though extreme, are not emotionally untruthful, as their brevity alone shows, for among Conrad's characters, except for Marlow, plainspokenness is a validation of the truth. Cries like "The horror!" are a form of victory when set against all the wordy ignorance of men.

Kurtz is a more finished victim than Jim. Like Brierly, he is ruined by what Jim never manages to get, knowledge of himself. Put another way, he is ruined by not being able to stop at a partial knowledge of himself, which Marlow suggests is a wise precaution for old-stagers in the tropics, a kind of inoculation against infectious despair: "if you were man enough you would admit to yourself that there was in you just the faintest trace of a response to the terrible frankness of that noise [the native villagers beating their drums], a dim suspicion of there being a meaning in it which you—you so remote from the night of first ages—could comprehend."[22] Marlow and Kurtz have both looked at the inhumanity of the savages and found there a familiar humanity. Up to, but no further than, the edge of the abyss Marlow follows Kurtz. He looks into Kurtz's mind, as he dares to look into no other aspect of his sojourn in the Congo, and sees why Kurtz wished to die when he discovered his closeness to "the night of first ages." Later Marlow brings Kurtz's story to the outside world, an ancient mariner expiating someone else's guilt and fending off his loneliness by spinning a tale for a group of friends. The solidarity with another person is Marlow's reaction to not being able to believe in anything else: when all abstract ideals are lost, the notions of "one of us," of "the craft," or of personal loyalty persist.

Marlow also lies for Kurtz, in spite of his professed detestation of lying. It is necessary to tell Kurtz's Intended that his last words were her name, furnishing her with a conventional adventure story rather than the truth. Marlow's great and saving illusion is thus the inspiration-from-afar ethos of *Multitude and Solitude, The Broken Road, The Riddle of the Sands, The Garden of Allah,* and every other Edwardian book in which love triumphs over despair. Marlow in fact needs the Intended's carefully preserved innocence to compensate for his own cynicism. He relies on the illusion of human connectedness as much as she does, since Kurtz is now lost, and since the darkness has so deepened that it fills all Brussels and the Intended's room, until finally only her forehead remains illuminated by the unextinguishable light of belief and love. The familiar Conradian image of light versus darkness is here deprived of heroic meaning and made a conscious fiction, the token of a white lie. The Intended's faith in love depends on Marlow's fictional words. That is the only form in which *Heart of Darkness* preserves love, idealism, and the significance of human endeavor, and they are preserved only while Marlow speaks. When he ceases, they are as lost to the men in the boat as the first of the ebb, as the possibility of sailing down the Thames to the ends of the earth and the heart of an immense darkness.

Nostromo, Conrad's largest canvas and his most complicated, forgoes the black-and-white duality of *Heart of Darkness* for a confused struggle among Costaguanans and foreigners, conservatives and revolutionaries, masters and servants. The Englishman Charles Gould inherits from his father the great silver mine of San Tomé—an analogue of Mason's Broken Road—a cause to which Gould dedicates his life. The mine is made to function with the aid of foreign capital and the exertions of Nostromo; silver is amassed. Meanwhile the soldier Montero declares that the national honor has been sold to foreigners; the rabble-rousers on the plaza call out for revenge on the local gentry, the "Goths and paralytics" of the Amarilla Club; and the revolution in Sulaco is born. Even Gould's caged parrot shrieks *"Viva Costaguana!"* ruffling his feathers and assuming an air of puffed-up somnolence behind the wires (such is Conrad's view of rhetorical patriotism). The revolution is contested with strange alliances, such as that between Gould, the master of the mine, and Hernandez, the bandit chieftain of the campo, or between Nostromo and Decoud, bosun and boulevardier, who together spirit a barge-load of silver to safety, hiding it on an island in the gulf. After Decoud dies, Nostromo continues fighting on the side of Gould and Mitchell, the captain of the steamship line, but the hiding place of the silver remains his secret. When the revolution is defeated and a new republic established, its declaration of independence written out on stationery of the San Tomé mine, Nostromo ceases to serve his masters and enriches himself slowly on their stolen silver.

In this thickened fictional texture of manipulation and betrayal few absolutes are available; *Nostromo* keeps its readers in the position of old Giorgio Viola averting his eyes from the "white dome of Higuerota, whose cool purity seemed to hold itself aloof from a hot earth" and examining instead the random struggle of men fighting on the plain:

> Knots of men ran headlong; others made a stand; and the irregular rattle of firearms came rippling to his ears in the fiery, still air. Single figures on foot raced desperately. Horsemen galloped toward each other, wheeled round together, separated at speed. Giorgio saw one fall, rider and horse disappearing as if they had galloped into a chasm, and the movements of the animated scene were like the peripeties of a violent game played upon the plain by dwarfs mounted and on foot, yelling with tiny throats, under the mountain that seemed a colossal embodiment of silence.[23]

Conradian cynicism makes only the landscape absolute, lumping all human pretensions together as a farce in the literal sense of the word, as "scene" and "peripeties" suggest.

Nevertheless, *Nostromo* is also a novel of narrowed approaches and interests. It is a more specific work than *Heart of Darkness* or *Lord Jim*, analytic rather than speculative, and its tendency is to neglect the suggestiveness of "the destructive element" or "the darkness" for a detailed investigation of economic imperialism in Sulaco, the way in which Gould's mine produces wealth and dominates lives. More is made known about the extended working methods of the fictional San Tomé than of ivory-gathering in the real Congo; and because the mine's methods are so successful, they lead into every corner of Costaguanan society. Everyone in *Nostromo* sooner or later becomes the agent of the imperium in imperio, which is no less monolithic than Higuerota, and no less aloof from the human dwarfs who serve it.

The fact is that *Nostromo* is a novel in conflict with itself. On one hand, it upbraids the mine for specific acts of political corruption, but on the other, it does not charge it with outright brutality; nor does it suggest, as would a straightforwardly anti-imperialist document, that the country would be better off if the foreigners were expelled and the silver diverted to "the people." National honor, the right of self-determination, economic independence—these are matters swallowed up in Conrad's gloom, matters for the dwarfs scurrying back and forth under the disdainful gaze of Higuerota. In the long run does it matter if the new republic is manipulated by Gould, if General Barrios is purchased by foreign gold, or if Captain Mitchell is allowed to parade his complacency through the picturesque harbor gate and past the Sulaco National Bank? There is no reconciling these questions with the simple anger of doctrinaire anti-imperialism. Yet the novel needs a direction of some kind if it is not to end in mere negativism. Conrad finally supplies what is necessary in a shift from results to processes. Much more comprehensively here than in *Lord Jim* and *Heart of Darkness,* Conrad deplores the subjection of the imperialist to the routine amorality of his task. The mine is a huge machine gathering men to it—workers, hangers-on, engineers, soldiers—and forcing them to do its will. It does not permit lawlessness or violence or adventure; that is not the way silver is mined and profits made. It uses the individual braveries of men and then discards them. It victimizes those who think they are in control of it. Consider a figure on the periphery of the mine and yet controlled by it, the bandit Hernandez. At the beginning of the novel he is a dreaded and unpredictable freebooter, but in the course of time his fierce energy dwindles as it is put to work. He becomes a guerrilla leader on Gould's side, then a general, and finally a devoted worshiper kneeling before the cathedral steps. He ends as a fully accepted member of the establishment, and doubtless it will be only a short time before he is voted in to the exclusive Amarilla Club, where he will be able to have some of that excellent coffee and reminisce—"Ah, youth! Pass the bottle"—about the exciting days in Costaguana. There is a dreadful bathos in Hernandez' history.

144

Doctor Monygham, the most intelligent moralist of the book, makes a general point about victimization:

> There is no peace and no rest in the development of material interests. They have their law and their justice. But it is founded on expediency, and is inhuman; it is without rectitude, without the continuity and the force that can be found only in a moral principle . . . the time approaches when all that the Gould Concession stands for shall weigh as heavily upon the people as the barbarism, cruelty, and misrule of a few years back . . . It'll weigh as heavily, and provoke resentment, bloodshed, and vengeance, because the men have grown different.[24]

Monygham's reference to men who have "grown different" means the townsmen, who now chafe under the rule of the mine, but his words apply with even more force to Gould and Nostromo, who have grown different in having lost their inducements to action—altruism in Gould's case, honor in Nostromo's.

In Gould's case, the San Tomé mine originally expressed an idealism more private but also more genuine than anything promulgated on behalf of the Belgian Congo. Working the mine successfully would have permitted Gould's father to witness a rift in the darkness of Costaguana, and after he fails, his son and daughter-in-law choose to rehabilitate his cause and transform his metaphorical hope into specific accomplishments: law, good faith, order. Wealth is a means to these ends; "material interests" is a shorthand phrase for the will to provide a profit-making security that will be shared with the oppressed people ("A better justice will come afterwards"). The security is in fact shared with them, and the promised material improvements do appear. This is no superficial Congolese imperialism littering the landscape with broken-backed machinery and grabbing all the ivory it can get, but a powerful economic system which accomplishes all it sets out to do. The only problem is that the idea of justice recedes indefinitely into the future as Gould is forced to maneuver and bribe. He acquiesces in the Sulacan sense of material interests ("we shall grow rich, one and all, like so many Englishmen, because it is money that saves a country"), all the time acting as if "the immense and powerful prosperity of the mine had been founded on methods of probity" and on the principle of usefulness.[25] Gould is thus corrupting himself as he corrupts the Sulacans, and shrinking more and more within the role of the Señor Administrador. According to Edward Said, Gould is to Costaguana as Prospero is to his island, the "commanding executive spirit." But "just as Prospero has sacrificed his own dukedom for the scholar's robes, so conversely has Gould sacrificed his proper estate, his humanity, for the mine."[26] Gould's choices are predicated first on the mine's survival, then on his personal will that the mine survive; it becomes crucial to him that the San Tomé, if it must perish, be blown up at his direction. Like Jim and Kurtz, Gould the administrator assumes an identity so complete that it obviates any need for self-discovery. He loses his freedom to act in proportion to his growing power over others. He is a modern version of the Assyrian conqueror noticed by Herbert Spencer on a bas-relief, who is depicted as leading his captive by a cord but is in fact bound with that cord himself.[27]

Having formed his identity on that of his father, Gould nourishes his intelligence on facts and avoids emotion ("his mind preserved its steady poise as if sheltered in the passionless stability of private and public decencies").[28] Efficient, he is yet no stolid MacWhirr in whom efficiency is the only conceivable virtue. Possibilities of love and imagination in Gould are called out briefly by his marriage, then lost in his work. The cost of his Sulacan victory is the destruction of his wife's happiness. She is first different from her husband, then estranged from him, and finally abandoned.

Conrad singles out Emilia Gould, as Marlow singled out Kurtz's Intended, as a source of light. At the ground-breaking ceremony for the new railway her dress is the only festive note in the somber gathering of black coats behind the president-dictator. Later she is said to have "the vividness of a figure seen in the clear patches of sun that chequer the gloom of open shades in the woods." Yet her distinctiveness takes the particular form of a self-effacing compassion, a knowledge of how people about her are suffering. Highly gifted "in the art of human intercourse, which consists in delicate shades of self-forgetfulness and in the suggestion of universal comprehension," Emilia looks at the peasants of Sulaco and sees "the man under the silent, sad-eyed beast of burden." When she looks at the silver of the mine, she endows that lump of metal, "by her imaginative estimate of its power . . . with a justificative conception, as though it were not a mere fact, but something far-reaching and impalpable, like the true expression of an emotion or the emergency of a principle." In her, not her husband, idealism is preserved, as in her water-color sketch the memory of a waterfall with fernery, "like a hanging garden above the rocks of the gorge," is preserved, though the waterfall itself has become a trench half filled with the refuse of excavations and tailings.[29]

In making Emilia distinctively virtuous, Conrad puts her on a pedestal. *Nostromo* ceremonializes Emilia with condescension (she feeds her "woman's love for excitement on events whose significance was purified to her by the fire of her imaginative purpose") and insistent symbolism (the "wall of silver-bricks, erected by the silent work of evil spirits, between her and her husband"). Emilia's portrayal with "little head and shining coils of hair, sitting in a cloud of muslin and lace before a slender mahogany table . . . a fairy posed lightly before dainty philtres dispensed out of vessels of silver and porcelain" is crudely shattered by her knowledge of the history of the San Tomé mine, which was worked "in the early days mostly by means of lashes on the backs of slaves."[30] Here Conrad's sense of grim political reality blunders into his idealization of woman's purity. Taken in isolation, the view of Emilia as a fairy sitting on a cloud puts her in the same category as Jewel in *Lord Jim* and the savage princess in *Heart of Darkness,* who are strained typifications of femaleness rather than women. But in fact *Nostromo* does not present Emilia as a fairy. She is the victim of a subtle conjugal infidelity, and in that infidelity Conrad found the occasion for a comparably subtle technique, as he did not in presenting the situation of the aloof and austere Antonia whom Decoud worships from afar. Antonia is merely an elaborated "Intended," whereas Emilia, off her stylistic pedestal and acting in dramatized scenes, attests to a new sympathy in Conrad's fiction.[31]

"I thought you had understood me perfectly from the first," Emilia's husband says to her. "I thought we had said all there was to say a long time ago. There is nothing to say now."[32] The distance between them has grown too wide to need the figuration of silver bricks. They have parted company over the issue of the proper object of love: Emilia feels for the suffering of people, Gould feels for the suffering of a mine, the desolation of which appeals to him "like the sight of human misery." They live apart in different moral regions, which Conrad indicates in a domestic scene both understated and declamatory. After a year in Europe Emilia and her husband have returned to a once again prosperous Sulaco. The servant comes to Emilia with a message that her husband has much work to do and will spend the night at the mine, then goes off with his child on his shoulder, leaving Emilia alone in her garden. For a second her face becomes set and rigid, as if to receive without flinching a great wave of loneliness. With the words, "Had anybody asked of her what she was thinking," Conrad begins a profoundly sympathetic examination of her innermost thoughts, the point being that there is no one around her to inquire into her opinions or the cause of her loneliness. Conrad's sympathy has to suffice. Emilia will never again have her husband to herself. She imagines the mine possessing, consuming, burning up the life of the last of the Costaguana Goulds—she and her husband will not have children—and she foresees in the fullest detail that her loneliness will continue indefinitely into the future. Conrad finishes the scene with a wrenching stylistic contrast, the only device capable of saving it from a sympathy grown sentimental:

> An immense desolation, the dread of her own continued
> life, descended upon the first lady of Sulaco. With a pro-
> phetic vision she saw herself surviving alone the degrada-

tion of her young ideal of life, of love, of work—all alone in the Treasure House of the World. The profound, blind, suffering expression of a painful dream settled on her face with its closed eyes. In the indistinct voice of an unlucky sleeper, lying passive in the toils of a merciless nightmare, she stammered out aimlessly the words—

"Material interests."[33]

The effect of this crass phrase is much like that of "Look at dese cattle" following the sympathetic description of pilgrims boarding the "Patna" in *Lord Jim*, or of similarly flat words following an examination of Winnie Verloc in *The Secret Agent:*

> With eyes whose pupils were extremely dilated she stared at the vision of her husband and poor Stevie walking up Brett Street side by side away from the shop. It was the last scene of an existence created by Mrs. Verloc's genius; an existence foreign to all grace and charm, without beauty and almost without decency, but admirable in the continuity of feeling and tenacity of purpose. And this last vision has [sic] such plastic relief, such nearness of form, such a fidelity of suggestive detail, that it wrung from Mrs. Verloc an anguished and faint murmur that died out on her blanched lips.
>
> "Might have been father and son."[34]

In all three passages vision is juxtaposed against banality, but in the views of Emilia and Winnie, two women linked by their common loneliness and childlessness, vision and banality are contained within the same personality. Emilia and Winnie are pathetically inarticulate; their moral consciousness far exceeds their ability to speak. Conrad therefore speaks for them, as he speaks for Lord Jim, another character with too few truthful words at his disposal: "One sunny morning in the commonplace surroundings of an Eastern roadstead, I saw his form pass by—appealing—significant—under a cloud—perfectly silent. Which is as it should be. It was for me, with all the sympathy with which I was capable, to seek fit words for his meaning."[35] In *Nostromo, The Secret Agent,* and *Lord Jim* eloquence is the recompense Conrad has to offer to those who might in different circumstances have expressed their visions instead of remaining mute and suffering. Eloquence so conceived is a moral duty, literature an imaginative generosity.

One major figure remains to be considered. Nostromo himself moves more freely in his world than either Gould or Emilia, yet he is bound by the requirements of his usefulness to the *hombres finos.* He is a retainer to everyone. Giorgio Viola regards him as a son and then a son-in-law, Teresa Viola invokes him as a saint, Captain Mitchell counts on him as "our fellow," Doctor Monygham expects him to carry an important message to the troops at Cayta. It seems a shameful diminution of the man that his energies should thus be controlled and limited, and especially that his quality should have to be transmitted through the genial and uncomprehending medium of Mitchell's condescension. Nostromo himself resents the role forced on him, and to assert his independence he indulges in the reckless gestures of liberality and the burning desire to be admired of an antique hero. By sheer effort of will Nostromo seeks to convince himself that he is an adventurer rather than a good fellow. Hence his pathetically repeated comment on the escape with the silver: "I am resolved to make this the most desperate affair I was ever engaged on in my whole life."[36] The affair *is* desperate, with all the conventional heightenings of romantic escape fiction. It takes place on a dark night in circumstances of the utmost secrecy and suspense, it involves strenuous physical and mental exertions, it has an agonizingly close brush with death, it features a terrified stowaway and a young dilettante who has to prove his courage to himself. The affair implies that adventure has not, after all, passed away from the earth, and at its end Nostromo glories in his moment of greatest innocence and greatest freedom. But then he abruptly remembers his tangled mess of obligations and loses his freedom. His animal magnificence is suddenly devalued. Sulaco has been glad to use him but has no way to honor him, and for Nostromo the antique adventurer, a deed has no meaning unless it contributes visibly to his honor. Therefore the secret affair of the silver has no meaning, and everything he has done before also has no meaning. A "revulsion of subjectiveness" drains his adventure of its value. All he can do is to mutter resentfully about not being properly paid, which makes him a grousing Caliban to the Prospero of all the *hombres finos* in Costaguana: "You taught me language, and my profit on't / Is, I know how to curse." Nostromo's profit from having to think is confusion and superstition. He would have been happier as an animal.

As for the second great affair Nostromo undertakes on behalf of Sulaco, the escape to Cayta to fetch troops, Conrad arranges the narrative so that the episode is never directly described. It comes to light much later, in piecemeal fashion, from Captain Mitchell, whose pompous account deprives the deed of its exciting and romantic qualities. There is no suspense, no breathless participation in Nostromo's heroics, and no escaping historical realities. Nostromo makes his dash to Cayta in order that Captain Mitchell may one day bore travelers with anecdotes of revolution. There could hardly be a more effective deflating of the new Sulaco, a city where adventure has been entirely replaced by material interests.

In reaction to his doubts about honor, Nostromo passively accepts the silver everyone thinks lost and with it the new role of secret thief, isolating himself from those who have never valued him properly and eventually turning himself into the victim of an obsession. The whole point of his life, like Gould's, becomes the digging up of silver; nor is it just in this symbolic coincidence that Nostromo resembles the Englishman. After a point, neither man is able to distinguish clearly between lying to others and lying to himself, and neither has anything to show for his loss of integrity but a phrase: "material interests" and "I must grow rich very slowly." Nostromo's phrase is the expression of that other soul which, in a lurid Conradian conceit, is said to have crept into his untenanted body at the moment he knew the silver was his to take. Perhaps it is also this other soul which remains silent when Nostromo is asked to name his beloved. But later, when Nostromo is dying and tells Viola's daughter Giselle that he came back to the island for love of her, it is impossible to know who is speaking: the old Nostromo, preening himself chival-rously before a woman; "Captain Fidanza," keeping his guilty secret to the last; or Nostromo the lover, confusing one of his passions for the other. His passing is as ambiguous as Jim's. Nos-tromo's failure, however, makes the plain point that there is no longer a place for adventurism in the world. Neither the mine nor the revolutionary comrades have a use for it. Adventurism is no longer a good and a bad thing, as in *Lord Jim,* nor a corrupti-ble energy, as in *Heart of Darkness,* nor an opportunity for lit-erary artifice, as in *Romance.* It is simply a thing of the past.

PART THREE

Coming Home

Walking along the wreck of the dykes, watching the
   work of the seas!
These were the dykes our fathers made to our great
   profit and ease.
But the peace is gone and the profit is gone, with
   the old sure days withdrawn . . .
That our own houses show as strange when we
   come back in the dawn!

                  —Kipling, "The Dykes"

Take of English earth as much
As either hand may rightly clutch . . .
It shall sweeten and make whole
Fevered breath and festered soul.
It shall mightily restrain
Over-busied hand and brain.

                  —Kipling, "A Charm"

11

The Theme of Recessional

In several ways 1897 marks a more appropriate beginning point for Edwardian fiction than 1901. Thomas Hardy last published as a novelist in 1897, and in the same year H. G. Wells had a great success with *The Invisible Man*, which inaugurated an era of new fictional possibilities. The majority of these possibilities were less astounding than invisibility, time travel, extraterrestrial invasion, lunar exploration, and the other inventions of Wells's scientific fantasy, but no less stimulating to the artistic imagination in the long run. Invisibility, the Edwardians discovered, might be deemed the symbolic state of millions of the London poor, who were leading hidden, silent, and inexplicable lives far out of reach of the older novelists' comprehension—lives more literally obscure than any led by Hardy's Jude, and only partially revealed by such late Victorian tales of mean streets as Arthur Morrison's *A Child of the Jago* (1898), Israel Zangwill's *Children of the Ghetto* (1895), and Somerset Maugham's *Liza of Lambeth*, his fictional debut of 1897.

Symbolic invisibility was not the only discovery the new era made. In 1897 the Webbs published *Industrial Democracy*, and Havelock Ellis brought out the first volume of *Studies in the Psychology of Sex*. In the same year Conrad published *The Nigger of the "Narcissus"*, including a preface written for the same half-apologetic, half-iconoclastic motives that had led Wordsworth to compose a preface for the second edition of *Lyrical Ballads:* the newly ambitious writers were attempting to shape an audience for their methods. In December 1897 Arnold Bennett read the conclusion of *The Nigger* in the *New Review* and commented in his journal that he had a mind to go on with his Staffordshire

novel, *Anna of the Five Towns*, "treating it in the Conrad manner, which after all is my own, on a grander scale." But he had
been more prophetic about his own manner when three months
earlier he described in the journal "the grim and original beauty
of certain aspects of the Potteries," which had fully revealed
itself to him for the first time in 1897. Burslem "is *not* beautiful in
detail, but the smoke transforms its ugliness into a beauty tran-
scending the work of architects and of time . . . it thrills and
reverberates with the romance of machinery and manufacture,
the romance of our fight against nature, of the gradual taming of
the earth's secret forces."[1] In spite of later sophistications, Bennett never lost his admiration for the romance of manufacture,
or his provincial pride in Staffordshire, and from these emotions, working with and sometimes against his sophistications,
came his best fiction in the following decade. In 1897, finally,
Henry James signed the lease for Lamb House in Rye, commit-
ting himself to a new "embeddedness" and facilitating the
method of dictation to a typist that would help to produce the
late Jamesian style. In spite of his doubts and excitements about
settling down, 1897 had been a distinguished year for James's
work; it saw the publication of *The Spoils of Poynton* and *What
Maisie Knew*.

1897 was the year of the Queen's Jubilee and of the poem Kipling wrote in response to it, "Recessional," the most splendidly
received and influential piece of *vers d'occasion* ever penned.
The tumult and the shouting of the Jubilee celebrations had died
down, the captains and the kings had departed; it was the morning after a great national expression of pride and pomp when
Kipling published in the *Times*, as if on stone tablets carried
down from the mountain or on theses nailed to the cathedral
door, a solemn call for national humility and contrition. "Recessional" is openly Old Testamental and prophetic in insisting on
the verities of the law and in carrying through resolutely the
identification of the English as God's chosen people in modern
times. The recurrent call of the poem is to memory. The English,
the breed within the law, are never to forget that the origin of

their exalted destiny lies in the will of the Lord God of Hosts, not the reeking tube and iron shard. Kipling is as covenant-minded as Jeremiah or Isaiah.

But Kipling's poem carries an unscriptural burden. It is a statement of age, even of weariness. Kipling's phrases—"known of old," "ancient sacrifice," "our pomp of yesterday"—look backward. They fail signally to incite enthusiasm, even a moral, self-scrutinizing enthusiasm, or to invoke the future. The English dominion over palm and pine is cast into history and made one with the empire-building of Nineveh and Tyre. The fire is sinking; the navies are melting away; dust is building on dust. This same elegiac or sunset mood is inadvertently captured in another period piece, William Watson's "Ode on the Day of the Coronation of King Edward VII":

> And winds have plotted with us—and behold,
> Kingdom in kingdom, sway in oversway,
> Dominion fold in fold . . .
> So great we are, and old.[2]

The English have grown old in imperial service, and they have nothing to show for it but the continuing need for sacrifice and the blustering of a jubilee or coronation.

"Recessional" implies a still more troubling question: is an era of English history about to close? The poem marks a turning point not in public policy or in historical understanding, but rather in Kipling's personal loyalty, which was representative as well as generative of the national emotions underlying both policy and historical understanding. Before "Recessional" is buoyant expansionism and confidence in the heroic national purpose which produced the far-flung battle lines and far-called navies cited in its lines. After the poem is worry about what England would become in the future. This worry the immediately succeeding years refined into questions of identity and inheritance: What was the nature and condition of the English land itself? Who would own it, cultivate it, and perhaps keep it from being one with Nineveh and Tyre?

Almost certainly Kipling was unaware of these implications in "Recessional," the surface meaning of which is hortatory, not valedictory. But neither Kipling's expressed intentions nor his later endorsements of English imperialism can change the poem's implications. Kipling was always saying more than he meant to say. In "A Deal in Cotton" Kipling no doubt intended to champion the morally energetic imperialism of his young hero, Strickland; but the occasion for the story is a forced retreat from Africa. Strickland is home in England on sick leave. His duties have taken their toll. The listeners to his tale sit in the dusk, talking about their past lives in India across a table decorated with "cemetery" marigolds ("marigolds to us mean hot weather, discomfort, parting, and death").[3] The tale is a memorial service for the whole imperial enterprise. The organ playing of Strickland's mother supplies its accompaniment, but even more suitable music might be heard in the tolling ("Shoal! 'Ware Shoal!") of Kipling's "The Bell Buoy," an 1896 poem collected in *The Five Nations*. When Kipling sent this volume to the publisher in 1903, it marked "the end of an epoch for him as for the Empire."[4] Not that the tolling in the poem is explicitly funerary; "The Bell Buoy" shares in the general mood of "A Deal in Cotton" and "Recessional" only because it derives from a knowledge of the human cost of empire. Imperialists like Strickland come home broken from their posts. The solution, in lieu of utopian Aerial Boards of Control, is to "man" England's outer defenses with the tireless, the indestructible, and the perfectly dependable—that is, with the mechanical. For all its indulgence in pathetic fallacy ("At the careless end of night/ I thrill to the nearing screw"), the poem celebrates the buoy because it lacks human emotions and human fallibility.[5] The buoy improves on and replaces imperial agents like Strickland. In another sense, it inspires the Stricklands to yet more stoical devotion to duty.

In Kipling's works after the turn of the century it is impossible to miss a sense of withdrawal, of retreat, of recessional from more than a jubilee. Like all those Edwardians troubled by the parallel between Rome and Britain, he wishes to fall back behind inner defenses before the barbarians gather their strength to strike. He dreams about standing fast behind the bell buoys, or behind the Dykes, as in another poem from *The Five Nations.* He returns to home truths. There are reasons for this reversal in Kipling's life. He believed in the brotherhood of the Anglo-Saxon peoples, the English and the Americans. Racial solidarity was for him a significant moral fact. But when he went to Vermont in 1892 to live with his American wife and quarreled bitterly and ludicrously with his brother-in-law Beatty Balestier, he grew less certain that blood was thicker than water. After the death of his daughter Josephine in New York in 1899, Kipling decided to make his permanent home in England. In the stories and poems written after 1900, largely in England, Kipling turned his hand to celebrating the more narrowly English virtues. He relied on tighter fellowships. He neglected the idea of racial solidarity for the idea of a close companionship between soldiers in an idealized Roman Britain, as in the Hadrian's Wall stories of *Puck of Pook's Hill,* or for its civilian analogue, the bond between master and man who are both servants of the same patch of English soil, as in "The Land." Regrettably, he turned also to the melding of three or four individuals into a tight little commando for practical joking, as in "The Bonds of Discipline," "Their Lawful Occasions," and "Steam Tactics." Practical joking is perhaps Kipling's delayed revenge on Vermont and his brother-in-law; the fascination with small groups seems to derive from a suspicion that only those closest to one may really be trusted. Later, after the disillusionments and losses of the First World War, Kipling would imagine with yet more longing conspiracies of another sort, the closed societies of the Freemasons and the Janeites.

The Kiplings settled first at Rottingdean and then in 1902 at Bateman's, Burwash, which was inland in Sussex and years behind Rottingdean in development. Bateman's was a house steeped in the past, but not unpleasantly haunted like "Holmescroft" in "The House Surgeon" (*Actions and Reactions*). Kipling said of it, "We went through every room and found no shadow of ancient regrets, stifled miseries, nor any menace, though the 'new' end of her was three hundred years old."[6] He roamed the countryside in his steam motor-car and explored his own thirty-three acres on foot. In moving to Bateman's, he wrote in a 1902 letter to Charles Eliot Norton in America, "we discovered England which we had never done before . . . and went to live in it. England is a wonderful land. It is the most marvellous of all foreign countries that I have ever been in."[7] The last sentence is one version of that artificial perception of foreignness which is a constant of the period. Yet only one Kipling, the author of "Sussex" and the *Puck* stories, thought England a wonderful land. In another mood entirely he wrote to Cecil Rhodes that England was "a stuffy little place, mentally, morally, and physically."[8] From 1900 to 1907 he acted out his ambivalence and looked after his family's health by spending the winter in Cape Town, in a house given to them by Rhodes himself.

If his homeland struck Kipling the world traveler and bestselling author as a stuffy little place, that might be an inducement to do something about the stuffiness, namely to awaken the nation to a sense of purpose by educating her in the lessons of the past. "Recessional" had hinted that imperial history was burdensome; but now other histories were to be discovered. The fiction of the years of Kipling's English settlement holds the English past up didactically to the present and reassures the present that a few truths never change, that the continuities of English life are its essential meaning. The cat and mouse in "Below the Mill Dam" (*Traffics and Discoveries*), whose Liberal fecklessness is revealed in their cynical, Mandarin style of discourse, are surprised when the old mill in which they live is given additional water-power and modified for the generation of electricity. They have stupidly assumed that the past is decrepit; the mill itself adjusts stoutly to its new task and so demonstrates the theme of continuity in change. Teddy Ponderevo in *Tono-Bungay* is much taken with this fable. He praises it to his nephew and explains how it has taught him "to hang together, George—run the show. Join up with the old order like that mill-wheel of Kipling's."[9]

As Kipling explored the land around Bateman's, investigating local superstitions and talking with Sussex peasants (hedgers, poachers, well-diggers), he discovered more and more ways of joining up with the old order, until finally he had a complete English history ready to transmit to the young. The stories of *Puck of Pook's Hill* and *Rewards and Fairies* teach only slightly less directly than "Below the Mill Dam" that England's future lies in repossessing her past. In "Weland's Sword" the two children Dan and Una are acting *A Midsummer Night's Dream* in the meadow when Puck himself appears to announce that the fairies, the People of the Hills, have gone, but if the children care to "take seizin" from him, he will show them "something out of the common here on Human Earth." They go through the ceremony of taking seizin with a transfer of clods: "Now are you two lawfully seized and possessed of all Old England." The first lesson the children learn is that the word "fairies" is wrong. The People of the Hills "don't care to be confused with that painty-winged, wand-waving, sugar-and-shake-your-head set of imposters" whom they have just been reading about in Shakespeare.[10] Also intended, no doubt, is a slap at the saccharine fairydom of J. M. Barrie, then much in fashion. Kipling's People of the Hills are made of sterner stuff, and the history Puck conveys to Dan and Una teaches lessons from which adults might profit. There is much about the strong man who conquers disorder by sheer will power, the cold iron of slavery, and military discipline. The history in the two collections takes its meaning from individual acts of heroism—by Parnesius and Pertinax in Roman times, by Saxon knight and Norman overlord in the medieval period, and by the two gallants who sail against the Spanish at Queen Bess's command, never to return, sacrificial victims to imperial duty ("Gloriana"). These gallants are proto-Stricklands representing the price of overseas enterprise, while the buccaneering and indestructible Hugh and Sir Richard Dalyngrydge represent its tangible rewards ("Knights of the Joyous Venture").

Kipling remarks of the tales in *Rewards and Fairies* that they

> had to be read by children, before people realised that they were meant for grown-ups; and since they had to be a sort of balance to, as well as a seal upon, some aspects of my "Imperialistic" output in the past, I worked the material in three or four overlaid tints and textures, which might or might not reveal themselves according to the shifting light of sex, youth, and experience. It was like working lacquer and mother o' pearl, a natural combination, into the same scheme as niello and grisaille, and trying not to let the joins show.
> So I loaded the book up with allegories and allusions, and verified references until my old Chief [of the newspaper on which Kipling worked in India] would have been almost pleased with me.[11]

In other words, Kipling's stories are only ostensibly addressed to children. They match in subtlety of literary texture those Indian or South African stories belonging to the previous stage of his career. Here Kipling openly declares that the English stories "put a seal upon" the imperialistic fiction, which is the closest he comes to acknowledging that the theme of recessional has superseded the theme of expansion.

Kipling's ambitions for the two story collections are only partly realized. In the simplest stories—"Knights of the Joyous Venture," "Simple Simon," and "Brother Square-Toes," the last with its poetic sequel "If"—history is "loaded up" with moral purpose rather than with the alleged allegories and allusions. The characters summoned for the children's enlightenment wear the right costumes and say the right things, but all seem to be versions of Robert Baden-Powell. In stories like "Cold Iron" and "The Wrong Thing," however, there is less lecturing. The continuity between past and present is revealed in the narrative frame. Consider the description in "The Knife and the Naked

Chalk" of a farmer, a sheep dog, and Dan and Una returning from the hillside where the children have just heard a tale about prehistoric shepherds on the chalk downs: "the sheep knew where their fold was, so Young Jim [the sheep dog] came back to his master, and they all four strolled home, the scabious-heads swishing about their ankles, and their shadows streaking behind them like the shadows of giants." In learning about the heroic past, the children are magnified by it—though only in metaphor, and not in such a way as to violate the naturalism of the scene. Elsewhere in the stories the past is artfully confused with the present. In "The Wrong Thing" Dan is making a model boat in the workshop of old Springett the builder while listening to Sir Harry Dawes's tale of working under the architect Torrigiano in the reign of Henry VII. Springett never quite realizes that the tale is ancient. To it he keeps adding confirmations from his own technical experience. Builder speaks to builder across the centuries. In "A Doctor of Medicine," the physician Nicolas Culpeper talks of having rescued a village from plague by noting—in the midst of much astrological hocus-pocus—the connection between rats and the disease. "Where did we put the plague-stone?" Dan asks at the end. "I'd like to have seen it." " 'Then look at it now,' said Puck, and pointed to the chickens' drinking-trough where they had set their bicycle lamps."[12] The point here is not the decay of a tradition but the presentness of a tradition unpretentiously available in the furnishings of ordinary life. "The Old Things of our Valley glided into every aspect of our outdoor works," Kipling reports in *Something of Myself*.[13] The world he dwelt in and the world he imagined are alike constructed of old things.

Kipling's stories of movement from present to past and back again might have supplied Henry James with the *donnée* of "The Third Person" (*The Soft Side*), in which the elderly Misses Frush must learn for themselves how to lay the ghost of a male ancestor hanged for smuggling. In the process, the sisters make a larger discovery of the past and the land within which the past has been accomplished:

They had, each for herself, re-discovered the country; only Miss Amy, emergent from Bloomsbury lodgings, spoke of it as primroses and sunsets, and Miss Susan, rebounding from the Arno and the Reuss, called it, with a shy, synthetic pride, simply England . . . The country . . . was in the objects and relics that they handled together and wondered over, finding in them a ground for much inferred importance and invoked romance, stuffing large stories into very small openings and pulling every faded bell-rope that might jingle rustily into the past.[14]

"Synthetic pride" is an excellent phrase for the Edwardian rediscovery of England. There had to be a certain self-consciousness in the act, a certain willfulness, a certain artificiality ("stuffing large stories into very small openings"). The redirecting of energies after the turn of the century called for the finding of much inferred importance and much attendant publicity. *To Colonise England*, a 1907 collection of essays by C. F. G. Masterman, W. B. Hodgson, A. G. Gardiner, and others, was an effort in that cause. One essay urges the improvement of British agriculture: "We must colonise the countryside . . . What is the reason of the continuous desertion of the land, until, like a new Columbus, Sir Henry Campbell-Bannerman is able to rediscover it as a colony of great and fruitful promise for the British people?"[15] This is Liberal social criticism taking its cue and adapting its rhetoric from the Tory Kipling, whose works could be read as a directive to enlist formerly imperial ambitions in a large-scale return to the soil.

The apprehensiveness of Kipling—his retreating, withdrawing side—is apparent not just in James but in other novelists who seem utterly different from Kipling, like E. M. Forster. The large-scale movement of Forster's Edwardian fiction is from Cadsbury Rings and a Florentine room with a view to the narrowing circles of the field outside Howards End and, finally, to the darkened room where the former master of telegrams and anger, Henry Wilcox, takes refuge from his hay fever. All through the decade the Adventure and Romance Agency had serious competition from Forster and others, who were fascinated by what could be seen when men came home from their adventures abroad. They were as strongly drawn to insularity as John Buchan, John Masefield, and company were drawn to adventure. They were part of what Asa Briggs has called Edwardian Britain's demand for its own islands.[16]

Insularity had both narrow and broad expressions. The smugness of Little Englandism was at the narrow extreme; the enthusiasm of novelists discovering new fictional territory was at the other. Much of Edwardian fiction followed the interests of the English Kipling: the idea of refuge or retreat, the substitution of small-group loyalty for the larger allegiances of racial solidarity or patriotism, and the new interest in English traditions. The idea of refuge was at bottom a desire for the greatest possible exercise of human control. The vision of freedom promised by adventure fiction gave way to the realistic objective of orderly management. The empty landscape, the clear field of action, were replaced by the delineated English countryside, the garden, the house, the room. In these spaces, increasingly limited in extent and defined in function, there could be few unforeseen threats, few opportunities for bewilderment or meaningless violence, few involvements in large-scale immorality, and few visions of futility. On the contrary, there could be safety, control, security, and the confident certainty that the space around one was subject to one's needs and desires—was metaphorically an extension of one's identity. The secular monastery of James's short story "The Great Good Place" (*The Soft Side*), to which the overworked George Dane retreats, is soothing because it is null ("an abyss of negatives," "an absence of everything," "all beautified with omissions"), but also because it is a reflection of Dane's mind. Dane's interlocutor gives him back his own image. In *Howards End* the Schlegel home on Wickham Place, a backwater or estuary offering shelter from the beating London waves outside, keeps the Schlegels happy because it keeps them being Schlegels. The room of his own that Edwin Clayhanger resorts to in Arnold Bennett's novel invests him with a proper sense of identity. In that room, fully in control of his furnishings, Edwin can dream fondly that he is emancipated from all the things of English provincial life and, more realistically, that he is going to be freed from his father's influence. His room teaches Edwin that someday he "would utterly belong to himself."[17]

Edwardian fiction was not uniformly generous in the provision of refuges. It withheld them for satiric or tragic purposes, as in the series of Ponderevo retreats in *Tono-Bungay*, none of which is capable of containing Teddy's energies or holding off his creditors, and most subtly, in the spatial imagination of James's Kate Croy. In *The Wings of the Dove* Kate thinks of her involvement with Densher as "a particular performance":

> She had observed a ladder against a garden wall, and had trusted herself so to climb it as to be able to see over into the probable garden on the other side. On reaching the top she had found herself face to face with a gentleman engaged in a like calculation at the same moment, and the two inquirers had remained confronted on their ladders. The great point was that for the rest of that evening they had been perched—they had not climbed down; and indeed, during the time that followed, Kate at least had had the perched feeling—it was if she were there aloft without a retreat.[18]

The garden Kate would like to enter is a walled refuge from the miserable dodges of her father and her own subjection to Maud Lowder. But she will never be able to move about in its moral serenity, for Densher and all the entanglements he brings with him stand in the way. *The Wings of the Dove* is a study of the way refuges become traps.

As yet another response to the complications of life, Edwardians imagined a retreat into small groups. In such groups novelists set characters to licking wounds, finding out their identities, exercising intimate virtues, or even preparing for apocalypse, as in the strange shifting conspiracies of G. K. Chesterton's *The Man Who Was Thursday*. But always characters were interested in the act of exclusion implicit in the forming of groups. The period provides alliances of the tightly defined few against the vaguely defined many: anarchists against police, police against politicians, and doers against talkers in Conrad's *The Secret Agent*, a novel patently about small-group loyalties and treacheries; the Forsytes against all non-Forsytes in the Galsworthy novels; artists against philistines in James's "Broken Wings"; Grub Streeters against the *haut monde* in his "The Papers" (*The Better Sort*); father and daughter against worldly corruption in *The Golden Bowl*, or against innocence in *The Wings of the Dove*. There is, finally, that loyalty in Conrad, temporary but significant, exchanged among the teller and the listeners of a given narrative, as in *Heart of Darkness*, "Youth," and *Lord Jim*. In *Lord Jim* Marlow's unnamed friend, the one who receives from him the packet of papers finishing Jim's story, is a spokesman for national and racial solidarity. But his opinionizing is much less convincing than the personal bond that ties him to Marlow and Marlow's uncompleted tale. The fellowship of moral investigation is stronger than any other fellowship in the book.

Finally, the Edwardian fascination for English tradition, like the longing for physical refuge, was a desire to find channels directing the flow of energy and thought. Personal action became significant when aligned with time-honored practices of cultivation, settlement, recreation, or culture. Hence the Edwardian poems about Sussex, supposedly the locale of particularly English values. Hence the reviews of English history and topography in novels, and the revival of landscapism as it had been practiced by George Borrow and Richard Jefferies.[19] Hence the fictional confrontations between foreignness and Englishness, usually to the advantage of Englishness. Hence the occasional Edwardian attempts to comprehend all of some English thing in a single book, as in Walter de la Mare's *Henry Brocken* (1904), where the narrator rides out on his uncle's mare Rosinante to meet, in succession, the characters of English literature: Lucy Gray (with whom he has a Wordsworthian encounter), Jane Eyre and Mr. Rochester, Nick Bottom, Lemuel Gulliver, Sleep and Death from Keats, the Physician from *Macbeth*, and la Belle

Dame sans Merci. This investigation of Englishness via fiction was roughly comparable to researches going on in other intellectual fields—in Edwardian music, for example. The Folk Song Society was founded in 1898, and Ralph Vaughan Williams himself collected folk tunes, composed pieces based on themes by Purcell and Tallis, and published *The English Hymnal* in 1906. The greatest figure of English folk music, Cecil Sharp, collected in 1903 the first of his thousands of songs from a vicar's gardener named, in an almost too significant symbolism, John England.[20]

Literal returns to the heart of England accompanied the discovery of Englishness as a theme. Sheila Kaye-Smith and Hilaire Belloc ("The South Country") were as drawn to the ancient continuities of Sussex as was Kipling, or Israel Zangwill, the romancer of the London ghettos, who settled in Sussex in a house named "Far End." But no Edwardian writer quite so immersed himself in the rural life as Maurice Hewlett. Having been "almost an Italian" as a young man, Hewlett returned to England when the success of his fiction gave him the means to be a country gentleman. He "took long solitary walks among the downs in a solitary cloak, and put the soil in the forefront of his meditations, displacing naughty ladies and tapestry. He talked of entering Parliament as the champion of the farm labourer and worked feverishly on an epic poem of English tillage called *The Hodgiad*, which he feverishly completed. It was a noble project but did not quite come off."[21]

Hewlett's rustication was a case of literary success buying its way into established society. It was paralleled again and again in an era rich with literary successes. After *The Broad Highway* Jeffrey Farnol returned from America to settle in comfort in Kent, and after *She* (1887) and *King Solomon's Mines* (1885) Rider Haggard made himself a Norfolk country gentleman. He had returned from the Transvaal in 1881, well before "Recessional," but his later, Edwardian works of nonfiction—*A Farmer's Year* (1899), *Rural England* (1902), *A Gardener's Year* (1905), and *The Poor and the Land* (1905)—imply a major involvement in the effort to colonize England. In James's purchase of Lamb House there was nothing agricultural, but there was more than a touch of Hewlett's and Farnol's motives. James had been envious of the palatial residences of best-selling novelists and had wanted to be established himself; accordingly, he husbanded his resources, published as much as he could, and by deliberate effort gained for himself the "little unsophisticated town . . . perched picturesquely on its pedestal of rock and overlooking the wide sheep-studded greenness of Romney Marsh." The "red-roofed and clustered Old World town" of Rye, which James had discovered in 1896, staying first in rented homes, "was in a manner a small and homely *family.*" It was therefore a place to assuage the essential loneliness of his life, though it also represented the serious risk, Leon Edel has argued, of breaking James's connections with London and making him an anchorite. Much of his fiction of this period displays ill-concealed doubts about the wisdom of the move, and barely concealed transferences, such as the similarity between Lamb House and the Suffolk home of Mr. Longdon in *The Awkward Age* (1899). The frontispiece to the New York Edition of that novel even uses a photograph of Lamb House.[22]

But almost from the start of his life in Rye James's fears of losing London were balanced by a pleasure in controlling his surroundings. In Rye James had his privacy well protected. In a letter of 1898 he comments, "After so many years of London flats and other fearsome fragilities, I feel quite housed in a feudal fortress." The playful alliteration here saves James from a too frank avowal of his feelings. There is a similar stylistic protectiveness, involving arch capital letters, fussy punctuation, and the pronoun "one," in a later comment about belonging to the society of Rye and having neighbors to tea: "What will you have? The Squire—! One's 'people' . . . one feels with one's brass knocker and one's garden-patch, quite like a country-gentleman, with his 'people' and his church-monuments." The language is so loaded with irony that it becomes inadvertently revealing. Lamb House gave James the man a pride in belonging to a domestic tradition, and James the writer a detachment from issues, such as imperialism, not immediately involved with that tradition. In February

1899, with the Spanish-American War much on his mind, James wrote approvingly of English imperialism: "To live in England is, inevitably, to feel the 'Imperial' question, in a different way . . . Expansion has so made the English what they are—for good or ill, but on the whole for good—that one doesn't quite feel one's way to say for one's country 'No—I'll have *none* of it!' It has educated the English." But in a subsequent letter James admitted that living deep in the English countryside made the imperial question uninteresting; he wanted only to "curl up more closely in this little old-world corner," where he could "successfully beg such questions. They become a spectacle merely."[23] Here James sounds much like the Schlegels of *Howards End*, who would at times dismiss the whole British Empire with a puzzled if reverent sigh.

Relatively close to James in Rye were Conrad at Pent Farm, Ford at Aldington (until 1904), Stephen Crane briefly at Brede, and Wells on the coast at Sandgate, in Spade House, which he had occupied since December 1900. Wells's books of the next eight years were written there, some of them, above all *The Sea Lady*, drawing on the Sandgate scenery, and all of them benefiting from the social confidence that came with building and settling. As early as 1898 James had advised Wells that a beach cottage, "though a trifle gritty," might suggest "views"—and views might suggest something else. Later, congratulating Wells on his moving-in, and not forgetting to remind the new householder that he *was* new, James commented, "There are (I say it as a country gentleman of slightly longer standing,) stages *more* exquisite, shades of sensation—depth within depth, wheel within wheel, to come; but nothing really so ingenuous as the first delirum of occupation."[24] Spade House was visible evidence that Wells had escaped from his below-stairs past. He was no longer confined in a basement room looking up at the boots of prosperous passers-by, a Dickensian memory turned to political account in *The Misery of Boots* (1907); he was a man of letters with an establishment of his own. Still, establishment meant having an identity fixed in certain respects, and a house meant a system of walls impinging on Wells's freedom. The restlessness in Wells put him in two minds about the confining structures that men foolishly build up around them. In 1910 he sold Spade House deliberately, because he felt that otherwise it would become the final setting of his life.[25] In *The New Machiavelli*, written at the time of this departure, Wells sends his second self Dick Remington away from the great world which has rejected him. In a safe retreat Remington rises superior to defeat and, consciously patterning himself on his great Italian predecessor, contemplates the uses of tactical withdrawal. Remington hates the idea of a final retirement.

Henry Ryecroft, on the contrary, who is the second self of George Gissing, takes the Edwardian theme of retirement to an extreme of unassertiveness. In the words of Wells, who was a close friend, Gissing "was made to be hunted by Fate. He never turned and fought. He always hid or fled."[26] *The Private Papers of Henry Ryecroft* (1903) shows Gissing fleeing to a contented autumnal retrospection. The book is as un-Balfourian a work as the decade produced; it belongs to the moment when the artistic impulse of the Victorian century had flagged, "when the energy of a great time was all but exhausted."[27]

Gissing sentimentalizes himself as a struggling writer who escapes from Grub Street by coming into a life annuity and buying an isolated cottage in Devon. There, keeping a journal, he broods on remembered scenes from his London career. Like other elderly gentlemen in Edwardian novels, Ryecroft thinks fondly of a second-hand bookshop in London, and plans someday to revisit both the shop and all the places where he housed in his time of poverty. His papers are retrospective, reflecting the period's interest in autobiographical writing—like Yeats's *Reveries over Childhood*, Gosse's *Father and Son*, Butler's *The Way of All Flesh*, Forster's *The Longest Journey*, Joyce's *Stephen Hero* and *Portrait of the Artist*. The difference between the other works and Gissing's is that they narrate a triumphant escape from confinement, cultural or parental, while Gissing values confinement as a means to self-knowledge. Ryecroft knows he is never going to become other than what he is, so he directs his efforts to cultivating that identity and keeping the world at a distance. There is, after all, plenty to observe in the natural surroundings of Devon, his own homely name is "Ryecroft," and he knows his traveling days are over: "whatever temptation comes to me in mellow autumn, when I think of the grape and the olive . . . what remains to me of life and energy is far too little for the enjoyment of all I know, and all I wish to know, of this dear island." In cruder form, Ryecroft voices James's isolationism: "What is it to me if nations fall a-slaughtering each other? Let the fools go to it!" After reading *The Tempest*, he decides that it was the poet's "last work, that he wrote it in his home in Stratford, walking day by day in the fields which had taught his boyhood to love rural England."[28] Here, with a vengeance, are the mood of withdrawal and the pattern of authorial return. *The Private Papers of Henry Ryecroft* captures in a particularly clear form the curiosities and longings felt not just by this one unhappy man, but by all the writers—happy, unhappy, indifferent—who formed the Edwardian recessional parade.

12

Continental Rescues and Autumnal Affairs

One trouble with the Continent as a place for adventure was that it gave too little scope for imagination and movement. It was too well known. When the hero of Henry Harland's *My Friend Prospero* (1904) is encountered in an Italian castle and complimented on having remained so English, he responds modestly that he must not be given too much credit: "to be English nowadays is so ingloriously easy—since foreign lands have become merely the wider suburbs of London."[1]

This is the initial impression Italy makes on the traveling English of Forster's *A Room with a View* and *Where Angels Fear to Tread.* In the first novel Lucy Honeychurch and Charlotte Bartlett are disappointed to find a Cockney *signora* waiting for them at the Pension Bertolini in Florence ("It might be London," Lucy says), not to mention a table full of English visitors sitting under portraits of the late Queen and late Poet Laureate and a notice for the English Church. In *Where Angels Fear to Tread* Philip Herriton, who is better read than Lucy and consequently has more illusions to lose, is dismayed to discover that the province of romance has been invaded by realism. Lilia, the Englishwoman he has come to Monteriano to rescue, has married a banal Italian, the son of a dentist: "A dentist! A dentist at Monteriano. A dentist in fairyland! False teeth and laughing gas and the tilting chair at a place which knew the Etruscan League, and the Pax Romana, and Alaric himself; and the Countess Matilda, and the Middle Ages, all fighting and holiness, and the Renaissance, all fighting and beauty! He thought of Lilia no longer. He was anxious for himself: he feared that Romance might die."[2] Philip's impressions are false but not ludicrous. Romance of a

173

certain kind has indeed died in Forster's Italy, to be replaced by something unbookish and unpredictable, something that turns adventure inward, into the undeveloped hearts of the English. The irony Forster insists on in both books, though much more sadly in *Where Angels Fear to Tread*, is that this Italian something will prove too much for the Honeychurches and Herritons. They go to Italy looking for the kind of romance that can be extracted from Baedeker or Ruskin, and they leave the Italians with an uneasy and incomplete knowledge of genuine strangeness and genuine romance, their hearts awakened but not enlightened. This is a favorite Edwardian theme: hearts half-awakened, spirits partially enlarged, were congenial to a decade which believed equally in the longing for and the resistance to human happiness.

Forster's ironies—appreciating the muddles to which innocent decisions lead—stem from the differentness of the choices his characters are given.[3] Not just *Howards End* with its prose and passion but all his novels are constructed from polarities, sometimes comically extreme, sometimes subtly merging. *A Room with a View*, the first-started though second-published (1908) of the two Italian novels, frankly explains how to define polarities. The contest lies not between love and duty, the overdramatized terms of the romances Forster's Miss Lavish composes, with their pages soaked in local color and their scenes of Antonio kissing Leonora ("Perhaps there never is such a contest," Forster comments), but between "the real and the pretended." In this one master contention are implied all the contrasts of the book— the ongoing contrast between Miss Lavish as a writer and Forster as a writer, the opening contest between the English ladies and the Emersons over who will have the room with a view, the genteel battle between Charlotte's proprieties and George Emerson's emotional courage, the juxtaposition of merely scenic Florence with the Florence able "to evoke passions, good and bad, and to bring them speedily to a fulfilment." Sometimes one term of a contention must be inferred. Mrs. Honeychurch praises the eligible young man Cecil Vyse to her daughter Lucy: "I know his mother; he's good, he's clever, he's rich, he's well connected—oh, you needn't kick the piano! He's well connected—I'll say it again if you like: he's well connected."[4] Everything in the second half of the novel resists Mrs. Honeychurch, successfully, but there is no single idea for the Emersons or anyone else to put up against her "well connected," which affirms social distinctions. The single idea had to wait for the motto on the title page of *Howards End*, "only connect," which is a plea to reconcile differences.

The contest between George and Cecil for Lucy's love turns in part on the two men's attitudes to marriage—Cecil's being feudal ("that of protector and protected"), and George's being advanced, even Fabian ("This desire to govern a woman—it lies very deep, and men and women must fight it together before they shall enter the Garden"). George wins by offering Lucy "the comradeship after which the girl's soul yearned," a marriage in which wife and husband are connected, not subordinated one to the other. But Lucy also allows herself to be connected with the son because she is fascinated by the father, whose gospel preaches Life and pagan joy ("Let yourself go. Pull out from the depths those thoughts that you do not understand, and spread them out in the sunlight and know the meaning of them"). Old Mr. Emerson manages to bring some of Florence home to England, its emotional frankness and personal courage. With his help, Lucy is able to spread her thoughts out in the sunlight and know their meaning, namely that she loves George. Meanwhile, on her own, she makes herself receptive to Florentine lessons by translating Italy into familiar terms: "Ah, how beautiful the Weald looked! The hills stood out above its radiance, as Fiesole stands above the Tuscan plain, and the South Downs, if one chose, were the mountains of Carrara. She might be forgetting her Italy, but she was noticing more things in her England. One could play a new game with the view, and try to find in its innumerable folds some town or village that would do for Florence."[5] Forster is not inclined to laugh at Lucy's aestheticism; it takes a deliberate act of will ("if one chose") to be aesthetic in

England. But neither is he inclined to overvalue this "new game with the view." To take Italy as a view is to take it only partly, to take it without the strangeness and violence natural to it. The English lose something in coming home. Knifings in Florence are replaced by nude bathings in a pond, the Weald domesticates Fiesole, ecstasy is recollected in tranquillity, and no one character of the novel, not even old Mr. Emerson, quite succeeds in proving himself an *inglese italianato*. Lucy and George are to be wed, not changed by passion into something else.

These ironies become sharper in *Where Angels Fear to Tread* (1905). That novel declines to provide a love scene between Philip Herriton and Caroline Abbott and finally denies the hope that English hearts can be fully opened to joy or that the English town of Sawston can be transformed by memories of Italy. Philip, believing Italy to purify and ennoble all who visit her, optimistically expects the Italian Gino to transfigure Lilia. The same happened to the Goths. Dentistry in Monteriano dashes these hopes, and Lilia is discouraged and defeated by her marriage. But another chance for transfiguration arises in the Italian journey of Caroline, on which she is enlightened about Sawston's idleness, stupidity, respectability, and petty unselfishness. From the Italians she begins to learn how to enjoy herself, how to pay homage to the complexities of life. The comfortable sense of virtue leaves her, to be replaced by "something greater than right or wrong." "Anger, cynicism, stubborn morality"—all those qualities the English carry to Italy, along with their baggage—end in feelings of good will toward the city which has received them.[6] For a moment Forster allows his novel to rescue Philip's confidence in Italy as a place for ennoblement, that confidence having been just as much endangered as Lilia in this many-layered rescue novel (its first, tentative title was in fact *Rescue*).[7]

The death of Lilia's baby reawakens the English sense of morality: Italians are careless and irresponsible; they make accidents happen. But well before the catastrophe Forster has made the notion of transfiguration problematical. Some Sawston visitors, above all Philip's sister Harriet, are unmoved by Monteriano, and even Caroline remains narrow, pathetically so because her narrowness is joined with an emerging consciousness of wider things. The pathos of Caroline's situation, loving Gino but fearing that love, is recorded in the tableau Philip sees: Caroline holding the baby with Gino looking proudly on. She can enact an Italian scene and yet cannot take from it the happiness she needs. Meanwhile Philip's own form of narrowness is revealed in his distancing of emotions. He turns the living tableau into a "painting" of Virgin and Child with Donor. This is the Italy of Baedeker reasserting itself. At the end of the novel Philip goes home with his aestheticism and intellectualism intact. Able to understand everyone else's motives ("You are the only one of us who has a general view of the muddle," Caroline says), he is unable to press his own feelings for Caroline to some outcome or even a declaration.[8] He is left with nothing but his rescued admiration for Italy and the choice, to be made after the novel ends, between renunciation or recrimination. The Sawston to which he returns will get along very nicely without Italianate views.

Two years before *Where Angels Fear to Tread* Henry James had published a rescue novel with a plot strikingly like Forster's. In *The Ambassadors* Lambert Strether goes to Paris to rescue Chad Newsome from his entanglement with Madame de Vionnet, is seduced by the sense of place and tone of time he finds there, and shortly is in need of rescuing himself. The intransigent role played by Harriet Herriton in Forster's novel is played here by Sarah Pocock; Mrs. Herriton in Sawston resembles the equally redoubtable Mrs. Newsome in Woollett; Caroline is something like Maria Gostrey, at least in her potentially loving relation to the middle-aged male of her story. Even the Woollett view of Madame de Vionnet as wickedly French is like Sawston's view of Gino as treacherously Italian.

More generally, Forster's theme is about the limitations of the English, whereas James's is about the limitations of belated knowledge. Strether is Forster's Philip Herriton grown into mid-

177

dle age and into a sharper awareness of opportunities missed. At fifty-five Strether regards his personal past as having been crowded but pointless; his present is empty. His name on the cover of the literary review he edits for Mrs. Newsome seems to define him adequately. At the start of his European mission, when he encounters Maria Gostrey at Chester, he pretends to feel in his overcoat for something he has forgotten, so as to "gain time before speaking with her." Time is indeed what he has little left of. If he is ever going to succeed in making up late for what he failed to have early, he will have to make time serve his purposes, which means eventually that he will have to engage in delaying tactics against Mrs. Newsome and the Pococks. That is, he will have to oppose their "sacred rage" to bring Chad home with the *vieille sagesse* he learns from Paris. In this novel the culturally old do battle with the culturally young on behalf of the sexually young, although Strether himself understands only that Chad, for all his gray hairs, and Madame de Vionnet, for all her marriageable daughter, are "young enough . . . they're mine. Yes, they're my youth, since somehow, at the right time, nothing else ever was."⁹ *Vieille sagesse* is paradoxically the means to become young again, if only by proxy.

What first moves Strether to regain time is his awareness that Chad is not Chad; sharp ruptures of an identity, the equivalents of Forster's transfiguration, seem possible. Chad has been made over by his *éducation sentimentale* at the hands of Madame de Vionnet, and it occurs to Strether that he may be made over too. For a while he resists the parallel between himself and the young man because such a parallel would lead to painful self-examination. But Paris works against these inhibitions. Retreating to Notre Dame in search of safety and simplification—his "private concession to cowardice"—and finding there no altar for his worship or direct voice for his soul, Strether nevertheless confesses to the feeling of being a plain tired man taking the holiday he has earned. In a passage remarkable for its simplicity James allows the plain tired man to grow more and more under the spell of the monument, until finally he seems "a student under the charm of a museum—which was exactly what, in a foreign town, in the afternoon of life, he would have liked to be free to be." Paris has elicited from Strether his secret wish. Even earlier, the pavilion in Gloriani's garden has served as a secular confessional. Gloriani's is thronged with ghosts, which forces Strether to think of his past. That in turn forces him to urge the present on the youthful Little Bilham: "It's not too late for *you* . . . keep an eye on the fleeting hour . . . Live all you can; it's a mistake not to." The fiction of this speech is that the older man is purely regretful about his metaphoric missed train ("Now I hear its faint, receding whistle miles and miles down the line"), whereas in fact he is giving himself hope in the only way he can, by speaking to himself under cover of speaking to Little Bilham. He may lack the memory of the illusion of freedom, as he tells the younger man, but the illusion of freedom is exactly what Paris gives him at this hour. And Strether is learning how to believe the illusion. Much later he gives advice about living to Waymarsh, in phrases reminiscent of Forster's Mr. Emerson ("*Let* yourself, on the contrary, go—in all agreeable directions. These are precious hours—at our age they mayn't recur"), and this time he sounds like a man who has savored the letting go of which he speaks.[10]

At the end, Strether is unwilling to let go of his old sense of himself, and he turns toward Massachusetts if not toward marriage with Mrs. Newsome. There have been crucial failures in his progress toward transfiguration: chiefly his realization that Chad is unworthy. The model for being "made over" turns out to be a Chad ready to finish his affair and go home. Strether must transfer his allegiance to Madame de Vionnet, who now seems pitiable rather than admirable. There are also failures in Strether's courage. When the onlooker Miss Barrace makes him the hero of the drama they all are enacting, he comments that the hero has taken refuge in a corner; he shrinks from his part. He certainly shrinks in the final passages with Maria Gostrey, where Strether, confessing none of his own feelings, allows her to sigh her feelings for him "all comically, all tragically, away." Instead of admitting love for Maria, he decides to "be right"—the old

sacred rage asserting itself at last—and to enjoy a virtuous renunciation ("That, you see, is my only logic. Not, out of the
whole affair, to have got anything for myself"). He defers the
troubling future by refusing to budge beyond a comfortably
enigmatic present. "Then there we are!" is the last sentence of the
novel.[11]

Still, the moment in Gloriani's garden is relatively untouched
by this scene with Maria. Strether has had his vision, as he has
had just enough regeneration to make it regrettable he cannot
have more. Regret is the emotion to which the whole work,
through all its detours of Parisian finesse and Pocockian farce,
has been tending. The regret is scarcely judgmental. The characters of the novel are led to feel the conflicting claims of fine
understanding and moral decisiveness; if Strether's renuncia-
tions cannot be accepted at quite the value he gives them, neither
are they simply cowardly. The reader of *The Ambassadors* is left
not knowing what, if anything, has really been rescued in the
book; only that the premise of the rescue novel—the moral certainty that the innocent need rescuing from the wicked—has
itself been made doubtful.

The same claim can be made for Forster's two books, but not
for a rescue novel coming at the end of the period, Hugh Walpole's *Maradick at Forty* (1910). Walpole's novel is superficially
Jamesian in its outline and details. The characters have read the
Master ("I'm perfectly lovely to-night, and it isn't the least use
telling me it's only vanity, because I know perfectly well I'm the
real right thing, as Henry James would say if he saw me"), and
Walpole writes like him: "He looked so perfectly charming as he
stood there, recognising, with a kind of sure confidence, the
'touch' that was necessary to carry the situation through. He
could see, of course, that it *was* a situation . . . They were all
needing the most delicate handling, and, in fact, from this
moment onwards the 'fat' was most hopelessly in the fire and the
whole business was rolling 'tub-wise' down ever so many sharp
and precipitous hills."[12] Maradick is fifteen years younger than
Strether and married unhappily, but he is otherwise like James's

ambassador, a man conscious of disillusion and regret. At the seaside resort of Treliss Lady Gale entrusts him with the oversight of her son Tony, who is impressionable, innocent, and in the process of falling in love with the daughter of a mysterious local. Maradick is much taken with the youthful pair; the stirring Cornish landscapes have their effect; and a novelist who is a fellow guest urges him toward pagan joy ("we are obviously pushing back to Greek simplicity, and, if it isn't too bold a thing to say, Greek morals"). In short order Maradick begins to flirt with Mrs. Lester, the wife of the novelist, declaring himself to her in a simplified version of Strether's pronouncement to Little Bilham: "I'd never seen what life was before. These last weeks, you and other things have shown me. I thought it was life just going on in any office, making money, dining at home, sleeping. Rot! That's not life. But now! now! I know. I was forty. I thought life was over. Rot! Life's beginning. I don't care what happens, I'm going to take it. I'm not going to miss it again. Do you see? I'm not going to miss it again. A man's a fool if he misses it twice."[13] Mrs. Lester is eager for his attentions but too shallow to value them properly, and eventually Maradick realizes he is in love with romance rather than with her. He breaks off the affair and rescues the young couple from various evil influences, feeling sharply jealous of the girl as he does so: "He saw now a thousand little things that Tony had done, ways that Tony had stood, things that Tony had said, little tricks that he had; and now he had gone away." These longings for the youth quite possibly represent what Walpole thought James's longings were for him; the novel is among other things a record of the two novelists' passionate friendship. In any case, the Maradick of the novel virtuously forgoes Tony and Mrs. Lester alike, seeking contentment, like Strether, in a moral victory. Renunciation gives him "something very precious to keep—his *vie sacré*, as it were."[14] In fact Maradick samples the pleasures of both renunciation and regeneration, since his marriage is greatly improved by the salutary shock the affair with Mrs. Lester gives his wife. As a reward for savoring the exquisite, bittersweet sadness of being excluded from life, he is granted the bracing happiness of greeting life afresh. The novel provides a happy ending for all, finishing with letters from all the major characters detailing their varieties of domestic bliss.

Maradick at Forty, though formula fiction, captures effectively the decade's mood of autumnal longing. The hero's belated discovery that life is in the process of passing him by is one with Strether's regrets, with the Indian summer melancholy of Galsworthy's Mrs. Pendyce in *The Country House* (1907), with the middle-aged discontents of his Hilary Dallison in *Fraternity* (1909), with the strange gloominess of Arthur Lawford in Walter de la Mare's *The Return*, and with Gabriel Conroy's loss of the present to the past in Joyce's "The Dead," a story written in 1907 though not published, with the rest of *Dubliners*, until 1914. All these characters and others from the period are attuned to the sense of the past, to use a phrase that became a James title. They become sharply conscious of having lived long in years without having lived long in experience. Introspection is therefore an ordeal ("he came and went, mainly in the cold chamber of his own past endeavour, which looked even to himself as studios look when artists are dead and the public, in the arranged space, are admitted to stare").[15] But it is a necessary ordeal, because it may lead to regeneration, and regeneration is the secret hope of most of these melancholic, afternoon-of-life fictions. The hope of regeneration saves this belated decade's novels from being overwhelmed by an oppressive sense of belatedness.

Edwardian characters whose stories turn on the possibility of being transfigured, awakened, or rejuvenated may be placed on a scale running from absolute failure to almost absolute success. At the extreme of failure is John Marcher of James's "The Beast in the Jungle" (*The Better Sort*), who achieves nothing in his life but the thought of possibility. At the symbolically named "Weatherend," where everything is old, Marcher meets the even more symbolically named May Bartram, who reminds him of a confession made to her ten years earlier in Italy: Marcher felt then that something significant was to happen to him. But nothing significant has happened or does happen. Their acquaintance ripens over the years, never declaring itself as love. May discovers Marcher's nullity but dies without revealing her knowledge of it, protecting him to the last, and her death forces Marcher to an admission of his lifelong lovelessness. He is a Strether who never enjoys a moment of vision in Paris, who pays the price for not speaking freely to Maria Gostrey. All Marcher gains at the end of his belated introspection is a consciousness of death—the beast in the jungle poised to strike—and a *vie sacré* which helps him fend off that consciousness. He feels a certain comfort in going ritually to May's grave: "The plot of ground, the graven tablet, the tended flowers affected him so as belonging to him that he felt quite for the hour like a contented landlord reviewing a piece of property."[16] This sentimental egotism makes Marcher contemptible, whereas Herbert Dodd, the equally unregenerate protagonist of James's "The Bench of Desolation" (*The Finer Grain*), is merely pathetic. Dodd's life has been ruined by a scheming woman. She enters his life years later to repay the money taken from him and to declare her attachment, but the rescue comes too late. Sitting together on the bench of desolation on the marine parade, they can only commiserate together. The past overcomes them.

For all his dedication to the old Paris, Lambert Strether stands closer to his present than Dodd or Marcher do to theirs, and therefore closer to the opportunity for change. He at least knows what his transfiguration requires—the grasping of the present moment for all it is worth—and he knows how to value the experience that Paris and Madame de Vionnet provide, even if it falls short of full transfiguration. In his company appear Caroline Abbott and Philip Herriton of *Where Angels Fear to Tread*, George Moffat of Ford Madox Ford's *The Benefactor*, and Hilary Dallison of Galsworthy's *Fraternity*. Forster's Caroline and Philip, altered by Italy, are finally too English to commit themselves to Italian values or each other. Moffat falls in love with a young woman who loves him and gives him hope of redeeming his shattered life, but at the last moment is kept from taking her to Italy with him by a distorted sense of English gentlemanliness and by his craving for renunciation. "Self-sacrifice . . . Doesn't that ever end?" cries the young heroine bitterly at the end.[17] Dallison too would like to take a young woman away with him to the Continent, as a way of escaping his confused, stifling existence in London, but he is too indecisive to act. The young woman is also too venal to be a fit soul-mate for Dallison; her idea of regeneration is purely economic. These characters all fail to renew their lives, but their attempts to do so sufficiently distinguish them from Marcher.

The successfully redeemed are at the other end of the scale. In the desolate middle age of their careers James's Stuart Straith and Mrs. Harvey come together in love and artistic seriousness ("Broken Wings"). Alice Staverton saves Spencer Brydon from a dangerous fascination with the past, receives his love, and admits her love for him in return ("The Jolly Corner"). Both these stories are about rescue from premature age and release from the sterile pleasures of renunciation, and as such they follow an established pattern in Edwardian sentimental fiction. "The Jolly Corner" is a sophisticated version of Arnold Bennett's *Buried Alive* (1908) or Leonard Merrick's *Conrad in Quest of his Youth* (1903), the express moral of which is "a man is young as often as he falls in love."[18] Merrick's hero Conrad has spent years working overseas as a colonial official. On retiring, he returns first to the Latin Quarter of Paris, where he studied art as a youth, but finds it changed and sordid. He next goes to a favorite watering-place in England, "Sweetbay," site of his youthful love for Mary Page. Conrad's coming home is a personal version of withdrawal or recessional; on its tiny scale it matches the withdrawal or recessional going on in the national mood after 1897. The town is desolate, the rain falls relentlessly, and Mary Page turns out to be married, unsentimental, and grossly disappointing. England offers Conrad another chance, however, in the person of Rosalind, a well-to-do actress who has been trying to recapture her own youth. The actress and the former colonial official fall in love, triumphantly demonstrating what the present will provide once the past is forgotten.

Bennett's fantasia *Buried Alive,* less predictable in plot and less optimistic in tone, nevertheless teaches a similar lesson. Its hero Priam Farll, a famous artist, is painfully shy. A sudden chance allows him to drop the old burdensome identity, at which point he can move about more freely than ever before, enjoy reading his own obituaries, and eventually marry a good-hearted woman with money of her own and a comfortable home in Putney. Farll has much in common with the hero of Wells's *The History of Mr. Polly* (1910), who is "buried alive" in the sense that he wanders away from his dreadful shop and marriage and buries himself in the placid comfort of a country inn. Both Farll and Polly are passive victims of middle-aged life, and both manage to be just active enough to escape that life when the opportunity comes. They are not so much regenerated as miraculously removed from an intolerable personal past.

The most thoroughly rejuvenated characters of all are those most intimately and romantically linked with the young. Richard Remington in Wells's *The New Machiavelli* counts the old political world well lost when he chooses to love the young Isabel Rivers. Perhaps even Maradick's blunt confidence in a new start ("Rot! Life's beginning") derives from his having unconsciously fallen in love with the young Tony Gale. The heroes of E. V. Lucas' novels *Listener's Lure* (1906) and *Over Bemerton's* (1908) seem initially to belong in this category. Lynn Harberton and Kent Falconer are middle-aged men who, after delays and vicissitudes, win young women. Yet neither man is really regenerated or transfigured. Neither exchanges the past for the invigorating present. The Lucas novels, though not the most accomplished nor the most ambitious Edwardian autumnal fictions, are perhaps the most revealing of Edwardian complacencies. Lucas shows what general reassurances could be drawn from the theme of delayed romance.

Listener's Lure is much devoted to incidental observations about contemporary manners: the crowded anonymity of London, fashionable skepticism, the back-to-the-land movement, motoring ("So long as motorists rush in where men of temperament are meditating setting a tentative foot, so long will the spirit of *Lavengro* be mute. I cannot imagine Borrow setting out with his knapsack and stick today"). But there is a plot, which turns on the slowly developing love affair between Harberton, a Boswell scholar, and his ward and amanuensis Edith Graham. At the start their situation is roughly analogous to that of old Mr. Emerson and Lucy Honeychurch in *A Room with a View*, but in Lucas' novel there is no George Emerson in the role of *jeune premier*. Harberton must both fascinate and woo Edith. At first he sends her selflessly away to London, to see the "great world," while he takes himself to Algiers. But home and love draw the unwilling emigrant back, in comic contrast with his half-brother Sir Herbert Royce, an explorer who "talks of settling down in England now, but of course will not—the go-fever burns too fiercely in his bones."[19] In the end Harberton regains England and Edith together. The girl is eager to take him exactly as he is—middle-aged, bookish, fond of gardening—with the result that their marriage symbolizes the amicable joining of past and present, old England and new England. The moral is that the middle-aged do not need to be rejuvenated to be happy. They simply need to find the sympathetic young.

Over Bemerton's describes another revenant, Kent Falconer, who returns to London after thirty years' exile in Buenos Aires. The first movement of his story is an excited exploration of the city: "I roamed London from west to east, from south to north. I drifted wherever the impulse took me. I was intoxicated with humanity—bemused by people." Like Conrad in Merrick's novel, Falconer finds things altered almost beyond recognition: "It was too often not the London of my dreams. My dreams had taken no account of change. The Piccadilly I had visualised so long and so longingly was the Piccadilly of 1875—how different from this!"[20] Falconer notes the electrification of the Underground, the arrival of motor-buses, the scarcity of hansom cabs, and the speeded-up tempo of life. Following Arnold Bennett's counsel, he tries to see London afresh, as though it were a foreign city, but he cannot forget the London of his memories, which stands in the way and keeps him from being invigorated by the new facts on all sides.

The second movement of the novel is away from the new and back to the old. The "Bemerton's" of the title is a second-hand bookdealer's shop above which Falconer takes lodgings. He likes the well-spoken, genteel dealer, and "besides, think of the name —Bemerton—with the suggestion of holy Mr Herbert in it."[21] From the shelves of the shop he takes down two books, a *Chinese Biographical Dictionary* for himself and a copy of Walton's *Lives* ("with holy Mr Herbert of Bemerton shedding a gentle light over all") for Naomi, the daughter of his stepsister. The bookshop offers him refuge from the new city, soothes his spirits, and reassures him that the past has not been discarded. In it, like James's Herbert Dodd, the one-time owner of an old book-and-print shop, he can enjoy "his happiest collocations and contrasts and effects, his harmonies and varieties of toned and faded leather and cloth, his sought colour-notes and the high clearnesses, here and there, of his white and beautifully figured price-labels."[22]

Falconer leaves the bookshop long enough to become friendly with his stepsister's family, to travel with them to Venice, and eventually to fall in love with Naomi. She returns his feelings and, not content with a Lucy-Mr. Emerson relation (or a Nanda-Mr. Longdon relation, as in James's *The Awkward Age*), she decorously encourages his suit. But again, like Edith Graham in *Listener's Lure,* she does not want her lover to be rejuvenated. She likes Falconer specifically because he is middle-aged and steeped in the English past. Their coming together at the end suggests that England itself belongs neither to the past nor to the present, but equally to both. England offers her sons returning from abroad a certainty about life drawn equally from bookshops and family happiness, the gentle light of holy Mr. Herbert and the youthful spirit of Naomi.

Not all Edwardians, witnesses of the Balfourian age of doubts and challenges, would be convinced by Lucas' old-fashioned love story or sympathetic to his antiquarianism. Wells, for one, in the guise of Richard Remington, declared that "London is the most interesting, beautiful, and wonderful city in the world to me, delicate in her incidental and multitudinous littleness, and stupendous in her pregnant totality; I cannot bring myself to use her as a museum or an old bookshop."[23] For these youthful spirits there was always Leonard Merrick's faith in rejuvenation ("a man is young as often as he falls in love"). Other Edwardians read Lucas with pleasure, for he demonstrated that autumnal longings can be translated into September-May marriages, and that such marriages do not require radical personal change. Love does not insist that memories, sentiments, or antiquarian interests be discarded, nor old habits, nor old homes in the country, nor old bookshops in London, nor traditional English verities. For Lucas' heroes and for his readers, life is not always "beginning," in the hearty phrase of Walpole's Maradick; it is always continuing.

13

The Backward Hunt for the Homely

> Not to everyone is it given to take a wide view of things
> —to look over the far, pale streams, the purple heather,
> and moonlit pools of the wide marches, where reeds stand
> black against the sundown, and from long distance comes
> the cry of a curlew—nor to everyone to gaze from steep
> cliffs over the wine-dark, shadowy sea—or from high
> mountain-sides to see crowned chaos, smoking with mist,
> or gold-bright in the sun.
>   To most it is given to watch assiduously a row of houses,
> a back-yard, or, like Mrs. and Mr. Pendyce, the green
> fields, trim coverts, and Scotch garden of Worsted
> Skeynes.[1]

Worsted Skeynes, Robin Hill, Overdene, Hamlyn's Purlieu,
Flickerbridge, Mundham, Burbeck, Catchmore, Weatherend,
Newmarch, Matcham, Fawns, Mertle, Beccles, Holm Oaks,
Bladesover, Lady Grove, Crest Hill, Pendragon, Friars Pardon,
Violet Hill, Holmescroft, Hawkins' Old Farm, Baskerville Hall,
Windy Corner, Cadover, Oniton Grange, Howards End—these
are the country houses of Edwardian fiction, and even when
listed partially they suggest how heavily the imagination of the
decade was invested in landed property.[2] Novelists as disparate
as Forster and Kipling, Florence Barclay and John Galsworthy—
from whose *The Country House* (1907) the opening quotation is
taken—watched in their books the life of grand or modest
houses, and did so more voluntarily than Galsworthy's "it is
given" implies. Householders may have had to accept the limited
dimensions of places apportioned to them, but novelists actually
chose limited dimensions as being suitable to a fictional purpose.
And the choice was not a specialized one. Even romancers like

Anthony Hope came home on occasion from *Rupert of Hentzau* and *The Prisoner of Zenda* to *The Intrusions of Peggy* or *The Great Miss Driver*, woman-centered, house-centered novels hinting strongly that the most interesting things were going on in England, not abroad. For Galsworthy's "crowned chaos," Hope and others were glad to substitute the country house and its environs, which gave them an emblem of safe retreat, community, and tradition—the major expressions of Edwardian insularity. The country house was a definition of England itself. Country houses were microcosms, islands within the island of England; they were approximations to that idealized great house Sackville-West would call "Chevron" in *The Edwardians*.

Setting a novel in a country house, in a metaphorical island, did not necessarily mean "watching assiduously" rather than "taking a wide view of things." Edwardians made the country house a *locus* of Englishness when they took a deliberately wide view of its rituals, proportions, and control of space and time; they made it symbolic; they looked out into England from the aesthetic and psychological vantage point it offered, which meant they received from the country house the gift of security. They were absolutely in control of one small space. From that small space they moved outward into larger regions, occasionally with that sense of suddenly expanded moral responsibility characteristic of Victorian fiction. But more often the Edwardians looked out with a sense of complacency. The small space at the heart of a country house could itself contain, in a suspension of time and a concentration of space, the largeness of the world. Country-house novels of the period repeat images of space folded into space. All of England is implied in a house, all of a house is implied in a room, and all of a room is implied in a single character's individuality: "In darkness above and in darkness below the country house was still; all the little life of its day, its petty sounds, movements, comings, goings, its very breathing, seemed to have fallen into sleep. The forces of its life had gathered into that pool of life where George stood listening. The beating of his heart was the only sound; in that small sound was all the pulse of this great slumbering space."[3]

Here Galsworthy, not George Pendyce, who is going to inherit Worsted Skeynes automatically some day, is speculating on the intimate emotional connection between house and owner. The more self-conscious householders of Edwardian fiction scrutinize their inheritances, often because the inheritances are sudden rather than long expected, or because the householders come from afar into an unfamiliar England and so are forced to a consideration of Englishness. Houses are for them a means of repossessing the whole country. In a simple form this theme is observable in Conan Doyle's *The Hound of the Baskervilles* (1902). The young Sir Henry arrives from the Colonies with an uncouth accent and an impatient manner, but also with a willingness to restore Baskerville Hall to its former greatness. Doing so educates him in the responsibilities of his family and class. There is nothing passive about his slipping into the role of country squire. Still less is there anything passive about the repossessing instincts of Theodore Racksole, the multimillionaire hero of Bennett's *The Grand Babylon Hotel.* Though a conventional middle-aged American, Racksole was educated at Oxford (his father was a bedmaker there), and admires the Old World: "Yes, I shall transfer my securities to London. I shall build a house in Park Lane, and I shall buy some immemorial country seat with a history as long as the A. T. and S. railroad, and I shall calmly and gradually settle down."[4] Transferring his securities to London epitomizes the whole point of his vast wealth, which is its power to buy him a place in established society and therefore personal security. In becoming a man-about-town and a country squire, the bedmaker's son protects himself permanently against the past.

Henry Trojan in Hugh Walpole's *The Wooden Horse* (1909) belongs by right to landed society but has gone out into the world for a larger perspective on what he has left behind. After twenty years in New Zealand he returns to the ancestral home at

Pendragon, Cornwall—not as a wandering Odysseus come to claim hearth and wife, but rather as an invader who defeats by stratagem the stodgy defensive forces raised against him. Hence Walpole's title. Trojan longs for the old established ways but finds they have fallen into desuetude, his father moribund, his uncle a dilettante, his sister a snob, his son an aesthete. In the first part of the novel there is much throwing open of windows and letting fresh air in, much revealing of hitherto ignored vistas: "Isn't [the view] splendid . . . Oh! I don't suppose you notice it now, after having been here all this time; you want to go away for twenty years, then you'd know how much it's worth."[5] Trojan immerses himself in Cornish folkways, which the others despise, and by combining New World energy with Old World wisdom, he finally makes himself victorious, winning clear title to mastery of the house and family. Like Sir Henry Baskerville and Theodore Racksole, Trojan represents a sentimental heroism which has consciously decided to embrace the traditional verities of English life, not just accepted them feebly in the Pendyce manner. All three characters are the domestic equivalents of Buchan's Young Imperialists in *A Lodge in the Wilderness*, who assert the doctrine that inheritances not earned are unlikely to be permanent.

Kipling's "An Habitation Enforced" compresses the theme of repossession into a single short story, with a predictable loss of plausibility. Bennett thought the story the finest in *Actions and Reactions* but complained about its sentimentality, use of character types, and reliance on coincidence.[6] Clearly the work had fabular meaning for Kipling, who wrote it less as a transcript of reality than as a parable of faith. The lead story in *Actions and Reactions*, it demonstrates why he turned from his imperial settings to England. "An Habitation Enforced" is a composition of place ambitious of becoming a celebration of Englishness, and consequently it takes fictional chances that Kipling the realist did not allow himself in other stories. There are also personal reasons why the story is so intensely contrived: it compensates for Kipling's unhappy personal experience in America by postulating a happy experience of settlement in the other direction, that of an American in Sussex. In Kipling's imagination, if not in his life, different nationalities can meet in friendship—just as in "Young Men at the Manor" in *Puck* Norman and Saxon are brought together.

The settlers of the story are the American financier George Chapin and his wife Sophie. Having spent an indefinite term wandering about Europe as an invalid tourist, the situation of dozens of James's characters, Chapin finds no real health until he retires with his wife into the English countryside. There they purchase a deserted manor, Friars Pardon, which Chapin identifies with himself ("Looks as if it had had nervous prostration, too") and begins to bring back to life. They are, however, cautious about retouching its chaste proportions or disturbing its settled customs. Yankee instincts to modernize are corrected by the stubborn silences of Chapin's tenants, who get him to build in long-lasting oak, following age-old patterns. What is more, they make him as silent, patient, and "English" as themselves. They teach him traditions attached to the house without, apparently, doing more than asserting their rights to public pathways or showing how telephone lines must be carried around ancient trees.

As a reward for the Chapins' submissiveness, order is brought into their life. The slight unhappiness of their marriage is cleared up, Chapin's prostration is forgotten in the press of estate business, and his wife learns how to deal with neighbors and dependents. That is, she and her husband join a community with its own laws and routines. To crown all, they become parents of a son, whom the neighboring Lady Conant welcomes with a note hoping he will appreciate his native land now he has come to it. By that she means not only that Americans in general stem from England, but also that the baby specifically has come home, for by sheer coincidence the Chapins have returned to the place in England from which Sophie's ancestors set out for America. The quasi-miraculous point of the story is that the purpose of history is coming home.

Kipling summarizes this same lesson in the poem "The Recall," which follows "An Habitation Enforced" in *Actions and Reactions:*

> I am the land of their fathers.
> In me the virtue stays.
> I will bring back my children,
> After certain days.
> Under their feet in the grasses
> My clinging magic runs.
> They shall return as strangers,
> They shall remain as sons.[7]

Here the land speaks in the voice of the God of the Covenant, welcoming back the errant and the exiles to what, had they but known it, has always been theirs to recover: the healing discipline of a life ordered in traditional ways and therefore free of ambiguity and nervousness. Chapin cannot stand the freedom to travel his money buys for him, though he does not fully discover this fact until he has spent a great deal of money discarding American rootlessness for English roots. His predicament and salvation are exactly those of the Englishmen Henry Trojan and Henry Wilcox. It would be wrong, however, to think of Edwardian fictional houses as being so purely therapeutic as Kipling's poem suggests. The houses need the therapy of use their new owners bring to them. Howards End sits mortgaged until the Wilcox business acumen rescues it; Friars Pardon sits in its park gently decaying until the Chapins come along. There is a reciprocal act of healing in the deed of repossession.

Possession was not the same thing as repossession. The Edwardians were firmly and snobbishly skeptical about the likelihood of rank outsiders, however monied, being fully accepted into established society. The Chapins are finely sensitive to English virtues and besides have a family connection; they are "one of us" with an assurance denied another new owner in the story, a Brazilian named Sangres who spends too much money on the wrong things and whose skin is the wrong color. Sangres is that detested phenomenon, the interloper, like the Reuben Lichtenstein who eventually becomes the owner of Bladesover in *Tono-Bungay*, or the Abraham Brightman who purchases Mrs. Pendyce's family home in *The Country House*. The interlopers, it is implied, can never be good for the land because, never having had it in the past, they have never learned what the land is capable of sustaining. Sangres turns the four farms of his place, Violet Hill, into a park with deer, to the dismay of the natives. The hatred of interlopers rests on the incurable English xenophobia Conrad had observed on a much lower social level in "Amy Foster," and on anti-Semitism and racial arrogance besides. This is the least amiable aspect of Edwardian insularity, as also the most fear-ridden. The Lichtensteins and the Brightmans represented a restlessly acquisitive power which threatened to deny the very idea of Englishness as a single cultural tradition. They were not likely to find in the village church what Sophie Chapin does, a monument to her mother's family with its pious motto "Wayte awhyle." The new money was not willing to wait.

Sangres can be relegated to the prejudiced insecurity of the "bad" Kipling. The "good" Kipling was worrying about the idea of community in a far more subtle way. One year before he published "An Habitation Enforced," he published "They," and this story is as much a fable of separation and loss as "An Habitation" is a fable of repossession. In order to say what it does, "They" runs somewhat against its grain: it is a ghost story and so requires a belief that one spirit can reach to another spirit through the most forbidding of barriers, death. "The Return of the Children," the poem that precedes the tale in *Traffics and Discoveries*, presents this postulate of the genre in orthodox religious language: children in heaven wish to return home and are allowed to do so by the compassionate Virgin and Christ. But the tale proper is at odds with the poem and the convention. There is no assured commerce between the spirit world and the real world.

The narrator of "They" is the owner of a steam-car with which he explores the Sussex countryside. He loses his way, in the manner of a hero of romance, and discovers a remote Elizabethan house with a formal topiary garden and a beautiful blind owner. She mingles worldliness and unworldliness, being half *genius loci*, like Miss Avery in *Howards End,* and half competent landlady who keeps her accounts in perfect order using the ancient English system of tallies. In the shrubbery and windows of the house the narrator catches glimpses of young children, or he hears them moving about and laughing, but he can never keep them in sight for long. On a second visit he learns that those who have recently lost children go "walking in the woods" about the house. A third visit takes him inside, where he once again catches only glimpses of children: "In the failing light a door creaked cautiously. I heard the rustle of a frock and the patter of feet—quick feet through a room beyond."[8] The narrator finally realizes that the house is a place of return for the spirits of dead children, including his own dead daughter, whose hand he touches, and whom he will not be permitted to see again.[9] The revenants form a closed and out-of-time community presided over by the woman who herself cannot see them. They belong to the past, as the tallies, topiary figures, and other old-world ways indicate, and this past cannot be re-entered by the outsider with his steam-car and his freedom to explore. The story is about exclusion, which may have obliged Kipling to create his tale of successful repossession, "An Habitation Enforced."

At one point the manor in "They" is referred to as the House Beautiful—an accidental link between Kipling and James, who briefly considered that phrase as a title for *The Spoils of Poynton,* his 1897 novel of possession and inheritance.[10] James's interest in houses did not end with that work but was intensively cultivated in the novels and tales of the Edwardian decade. These reveal more points of contact with Kipling than a phrase. Take the theme of refuge or retreat. For George Chapin the retreat to Friars Pardon makes possible the expenditure of personal energy on the limited space of house and family. By contracting his world about him, he makes himself ready for a new beginning. An analogous contraction heals George Dane in James's "The

Great Good Place." The cloister to which Dane repairs in his state of exhausted unconsciousness ("the world was everywhere, without and within") has nothing to do with family life; it is rather "some mild Monte Cassino, some Grande Chartreuse more accessible," a retreat and remedy for the overworked of the great Protestant peoples. Yet it is appropriately compared to the country house because it has everything to do with leisure, understated ritual, an absence of demands, and easy communication between equals. The Great Good Place in fact resembles a country house where a particularly distinguished and placid weekend party is going on. There Dane is never importuned, as he was unceasingly in his London study, and he may return to that London life whenever he feels ready. He is in control of everything he sees, the Place being an extension of his dreaming mind, which means that he enjoys there a state of complete passivity.

In addition to everything else, the Great Good Place represents the triumph of art: in it "all the sweetness and serenity [are] created, calculated things."[11] The idea of control, whether belonging to the self or to the presiding spirit of a country house, could not long be entertained in James's mind without touching on the ideal of artistic control—the authority wielded over an author's characters and situations. Houses, in James, are demonstrations of the art of proportion, of background-foreground relations, of vista and perspective, of collection—heterogeneous objects brought together to express a single cultivated taste—and these arts are in turn the methods of James's own fiction. He celebrates his cherished ideal of form by making the structures he is writing about correspond to the "structures" he is writing. For example, in *The Outcry* (1911), the narrative version of a play written in 1909, James constantly poses his characters in open doorways and not infrequently has them deliver character-defining speeches from that position. The literal framing, appropriate in a plot about precious art, has the further effect of emphasizing how James's men and women are set apart from each other, made distinctive, surrounded with a suitably bland mar-

197

gin of random talk and movement—in short, "framed." Correspondences of this sort are at times so multiplied that they make James's fiction seem stifling. There is no getting away from the framing, the relentless snobbishness about taste, or the equally relentless language of aesthetic obsession ("This she beautifully showed that she beautifully saw").[12] But these are excesses of self-consciousness about method, not of method itself.

When James writes of houses, he is conscious that control of space gives control over time: "a field of polished pink marble . . . seemed to say that wherever in such a house there was space there was also, benignantly, time."[13] James's ample spaces keep the world away from some of his characters, and with the world away, they have all the leisure they need. At least that is Dane's experience. Other characters are less cosseted because they must deal with the practical problem of preserving the right sort of space for the right sort of people. James lacks Kipling's faith that the past is naturally handed on by a pious present to an appreciative future. In *The Outcry*, as in *The Spoils of Poynton* more than a decade earlier, James's whole subject is the troubled inheritance of beautiful things gathered in a house. Shall the Lawrence portrait of Lady Sandgate's great-grandmother remain at home or be sold to pay off gambling debts? The villain waiting in the wings—this is almost literally his position, the narrative betraying many signs of its origins as a play—is Breckenridge Bender, the American buyer of art treasures, whose featureless disk of a face is worn with the confidence of a "warning headlight or a glaring motor-lamp. The object, however one named it, showed you at least where he was, and most often that he was straight upon you."[14] Bender would not be a threat if Englishmen were not base. Through a dedicated connoisseur James expresses his disdain for the despoilers, who ship precious things out of the distracted country, thereby severing the connection between their rich past and their impoverished present. The solution of the dilemma, finally, is to give the Lawrence and other paintings to the National Gallery.

The curious story "Flickerbridge" (*The Better Sort*) is less decisive. Here the inheritance is the house itself, Flickerbridge, which a footloose American painter, Granger, visits after an illness: "He had been floated by the strangest of chances out of the rushing stream into a clear, still backwater—a deep and quiet pool in which objects were sharply mirrored." Granger naturally thinks about his refuge in these imaging and framing terms, but Flickerbridge has no particular use for his creative talents and gradually turns him into a connoisseur: "The scene was as rare as some fine old print with the best bits down in the corners. Old books and old pictures, allusions remembered and aspects conjectured, reappeared to him; he knew now what anxious islanders had been trying for in their backward hunt for the homely."[15] In the same way Paris has no use for Strether the man of letters and every use for Strether the appreciator of fine old things. At Flickerbridge, the fine old things belong to a Miss Wenham. Her cousin Addie, Granger's fiancée, is a bustling, publicity-minded journalist who will, Granger suspects, make a noisy fuss about Flickerbridge and ruin the place. Not wishing to witness that or to see the past despoiled, Granger decamps and simultaneously breaks his engagement; he may also be aware of his temptation to flirt with Miss Wenham and so obtain Flickerbridge for himself by intrigue. At the story's end there is no one in sight worthy of inheriting the house.

Oldness is inseparable from the moral value of James's houses. Without the tone of preserved time they become merely the setting for comedies of manners, if not for something worse, the exercise of dubious modern taste and corrupt modern behavior, the trapping of the unwary. In "The Two Faces" (*The Better Sort*), Burbeck is the place where Mrs. Grantham horribly overdresses an unwary young bride and so gains revenge on the man who jilted her. In "Mrs. Medwin" (*The Better Sort*) Catchmore— a wittily apt name—is the place where Mamie Cutter introduces a dubious woman into high society by bribing the lion-hunting hostess with the promise that she will also introduce her alluringly wicked half-brother. Though James is attracted by the sophistication and spaciousness of country-house life, he hardly regards these qualities as automatic virtues, which is the way they are regarded in run-of-the-mill novels of high life like Florence Barclay's *The Rosary* (1909) or Phyllis Bottome's *The Master Hope*. "She had passed from house-party to house-party all through the golden summers of her life, and nature had seemed a picturesque setting—a back-ground for well-dressed humanity."[16] The tone of that comment from *The Master Hope*, with its envy for the life of a pampered heroine, is utterly alien to James's fictions. He sits as an appreciative judge over the life of his country houses, condemning them when they hurt the innocent, praising them when their leisure fosters the humane art of social intercourse. Occasionally he overpraises them with ironic intent. He comments on Mundham in "Broken Wings": "Life was, indeed, well understood in these great conditions; the conditions constituted in their greatness a kind of fundamental facility, provided a general exemption, bathed the hour, whatever it was, in a universal blandness, that were all a happy solvent for awkward relations."[17] Surely this praise is feline. The truth about Mundham is that it solves awkward relations by trivializing human relations altogether. Its life is hypocritical and fashionable; and the painter and novelist who feel so ill at ease there are right to transfer their love and creative seriousness ("And now to work!") to other settings.

Neither James nor Kipling is as critical of the country house as John Galsworthy seems to be, or as openly ambitious of investigating its place in English society. The mere title of *The Country House* hints that Galsworthy wishes to be definitive, and the novel begins by breaking down country-house life into constituent parts: "its perfect cleanliness, its busy leisure, its combination of fresh air and scented warmth, its complete intellectual repose, its essential and professional aloofness from suffering of any kind—and its soup—emblematically and above all, its soup —made from the rich remains of pampered beasts."[18] But Galsworthy never probes deeper into the matter. His satire is wasted on trivial details and then lost entirely. The emblems stay half-facetious. The men of Worsted Skeynes are displayed in the full glory of their immemorial motto "Kings of our own dunghills," but they remain picturesque and are never connected in any significant way with the economic and social system that permits them their petty conceit. The promised definitiveness fails to appear.

The problem is that Galsworthy cannot decide about the country house. He laughs at it, he disapproves of it, he enjoys it, he admires it. Most of all, he knows it. Its rituals may be empty, but they are utterly familiar to him. Galsworthy is in the position of Sackville-West with regard to Chevron, a disillusioned insider who cannot bear to leave. In order to postpone the act of leaving—or its fictional equivalent, the disinterested examination of the country house as a contemporary social institution—Galsworthy savors indefinitely the autumnal mood the house offers, the china bowl on a table filled with dry rose leaves, the Indian summer sun. Galsworthy grows more and more attached to the expressive melancholy of his setting, especially to the pathos of Mrs. Pendyce, until he cannot resist bestowing on her an out-of-character virtuousness. She goes courageously to London, solving the problem at the center of the complicated plot, and the novel ends with the country house of its title still unassessed. Worsted Skeynes is drinking its soup and gathering the forces of life into a small space, but what Worsted Skeynes means is not clear.

One thing in the novel is clear: Mrs. Pendyce is spiritually limited by the complacencies of her house and must abandon them if she is to exercise her virtues. Her affinities are therefore with Mrs. Harvey in James's "Broken Wings," for whom Mundham is a trap, rather than with the characters she superficially resembles, Emilia Gould in *Nostromo* and Ruth Wilcox in *Howards End*, for whom the house is a sanctuary. Mrs. Gould and even more Mrs. Wilcox are aristocrats in the sense that they deal gracefully with people, value the past for its own sake, and find humane uses for the money their husbands earn. They belong to the aristocratic literary tradition Yeats ceremonializes in poems contemporary with these novels, such as "Upon a House Shaken by the Land Agitation" (*The Green Helmet*, 1910). Yeats found custom and ceremony in every aspect of Coole Park, sympathetic largesse in every gesture of Lady Gregory. Galsworthy the Liberal refused to declare himself openly for an aristocracy of this sort, or even for the suburban aristocracy celebrated in *Howards End. The Country House* is influenced by an alternative literary tradition, that of the house as the figurative expression of the character of its occupant. In Jane Austen this characterization of houses provides the opportunity for judgment. Elizabeth Bennet in *Pride and Prejudice* must revise her notions of Mr. Darcy when she witnesses the perfections of Pemberley, which correspond almost point by point with the tidy excellences of his mind. In Dickens, houses are large-scale metaphors for their inhabitants, whose every eccentricity or benevolence is writ large on the walls or in the structure. Chesney Wold in *Bleak House* is a subtle expression of the Dedlocks within; Mrs. Clennam's house in *Little Dorrit* is a more lurid demonstration of her spiritual paralysis and rickety sanity. In *The Country House*, the tradition has dwindled and become mildly satiric: the overbred Pendyce and his overbred spaniel have long narrow heads, and they sit in a long narrow study with long narrow windows and long narrow rows of books—"a fitting place for some long, narrow ideal to be worked out to its long and narrow ending."[19]

Galsworthy makes the country house in *The Man of Property* (1906) count for a good deal more, because it expresses not a physical peculiarity but the essence of Soames Forsyte, which is the will to control himself and others. Bosinney convinces Soames to build a country place at Robin Hill by engaging Soames's pride of property, his need to express his prosperity. Soames goes along passively with the plan, but in fact comes to covet the house, because it responds to his pressing need to get out of that great London which the Forsytes have conquered and in which they have become merged. In order to escape from London, Soames has been collecting paintings—landscapes with figures—but when Robin Hill is built, he will be yet more freed from the tall houses and interminable streets of the city, yet more distinctive, yet more advantageously presented in a composition of his own devising. Robin Hill will be a limited space he can control absolutely—a suitable place for his contest of wills with Irene. No doubt Soames, foreseeing victory from the start, thinks of Robin Hill as a place to show off Irene, once she has been tamed and has accepted her role as prize *objet* in the collection. Soames's attitude to his wife is paralleled by James Forsyte's conviction of power over Irene: "James looked at her sharply; he felt that now he had her in his own carriage, with his own horses and servants, he was really in command of the situation."[20] The catastrophe of the novel—Bosinney's suicide, Irene's broken-spirited return to Soames—prevents any portrayal of Robin Hill in operation as an expression of Soames's will, but this is not needed, so clear has been Galsworthy's exposition of the motives behind its planning. The idea of Robin Hill is far better defined than the idea of Worsted Skeynes, which is one reason *The Man of Property* is a better novel than *The Country House*.

An axiom of the Forsyte novel is that characters are defined by the human and domestic property they own: "All Forsytes, as is generally admitted, have shells . . . habitats, composed of circumstance, property, acquaintances, and wives, which seem to move along with them in their passage through a world composed of thousands of other Forsytes with their habitats. Without a habitat a Forsyte is inconceivable—he would be like a novel without a plot, which is well-known to be an anomaly."[21] What the idea of habitat most significantly suggests is Galsworthy's control over the characters and events of his fiction. If Soames is defined by his habitat, then an exact description of that habitat will lead to a sympathetic and comprehensive understanding of the man. Hence all the details of landscape paintings, carriages, clothes, and decorations. Galsworthy does not scruple to describe exactly what is eaten during a Forsyte dinner. In the end he owns his characters in the same way that Soames owns the things of his life. He orders their movements with fine manipulations of their surroundings, he enjoys his authorial sense of property. The country house in *The Man of Property* is a fitting symbol of the whole fictional structure Galsworthy himself builds up around his characters.

Houses in the work of H. G. Wells stand for the containing of human energies within limits, which in a few fictional situations are as beneficial as they were to Wells in real life. Limits control distraction, houses supply a refuge: "This fugitive impulse is an inevitable factor in the lives of us all, great or small, who have been drawn into these [social] activities . . . Our lives are threaded with this same, often quite desperate effort to disentangle ourselves, to get into a Great Good Place of our own, and work freely . . . I have built two houses and practically rebuilt a third to make that Great Good Place to work in."[22] The Jamesian phrase was important to Wells. He had used it on the opening page of *In the Days of the Comet*, where it introduces the narrative frame of the novel and perhaps acknowledges a literary debt. The narrator sees "a grey-haired man, a figure of hale age, sitting at a desk and writing." The figure, the tower room in which he works, and the surrounding landscape make the narrator think of "the Happy Future, or Utopia, or the Land of Simple Dreams; an errant note of memory, Henry James's phrase and story of 'The Great Good Place' twinkled across my mind."[23] The old man's manuscript becomes the novel proper, which in turn makes a Great Good Place of the entire earth by relating how it passes through a comet's tail and has its hatreds changed to love.

A tower room in which a fantastic memoir is composed is hardly a "house" in the usual sense, but the places that Wells celebrates in his fiction, which he views with unequivocal relief or pleasure, are never ordinary. They are always at one remove from the real places where people live. Sometimes they are inns rather than private homes, and therefore casually encountered places without associations or entanglements. Inns give shelter and demand nothing but coin in return. Such are the Menton Inn with its wisely ignorant landlady, a kind of lesser good place in

In the Days of the Comet, or the inn near Canterbury that Bedford happens upon in *The First Men in the Moon* ("bright with creepers, and the landlady was a clean old woman and took my eye"), or the most elaborately developed of all these hostelries, the Potwell Inn in *The History of Mr. Polly*, a riverside inn untouched by the twentieth century.[24] There Polly retreats when his life in Fishbourne falls to pieces, to remain forever content under the eye of the complaisant landlady. The anonymous comfort of inns is what Wells would like to have himself: a place to hide from responsibility. The landladies—always maternal, always comforting—obviate the need for any romantic involvement with women, and that too was something the constantly infatuated Wells must have longed for.

When Wells writes of real houses, such as Kipps's, Lewisham's, or the Ponderevos' house in Wimblehurst, he does so in a sharply different way. Gone is the dreamy serenity and out-of-time inviolability, replaced by a detailed awareness of limitation. Houses close in on their inhabitants. Domesticity becomes a trap. Marriage is identified with the cramped quarters in which, for people like Kipps and the Ponderevos, it must be conducted; Wells could never have written, as James did, of "the grand square forecourt of the palace of wedlock."[25] In *Love and Mr. Lewisham*, after the hero's marriage to the shallow Ethel, he tears into scraps the grandiose scheme for self-improvement made in earlier days and settles down, half-willingly, half-resentfully, into an ordinary house and an ordinary life full of gradual changes he cannot control. Lewisham will grow more and more estranged from Ethel, and therefore more and more subject to "the dull stress deepening to absolute wretchedness and pain, which is the colour of so much human life in London."[26]

Kipps takes a more cheerful view of domesticity, in that it grants its hero a wife complementary to his needs. Together they earn a domestic happiness of the Dickensian sort which features the exchange of dangerous riches for modest comfort, a cosy retreat, and the rapid production of offspring. But Kipps's previously rapid movement through class barriers makes this return to ordinariness seem not entirely satisfying. The Kipps who was once in love with another woman and desirous of making something of himself was often absurd, but he was also free in his imaginative movement through a world subject to his moods. He reached out into the world in appeal by touching his silk cravat and suddenly sensed that the world smelt of his rosebud. Resenting the loss of that freedom, the married Kipps feels claustrophobic and goes for long walks while worrying about his grandiose new house, that house the world so quickly takes from him. The married Kipps, indeed, eventually defends himself from the world by taking shelter within his bookshop. Or does the bookshop keep him? Wells's question acknowledges the effect that a small enclosed space may work over its inhabitant. In the story "Filmer" (*Twelve Stories and a Dream*, 1903) he had described an aspiring scientist whose inability to spell leads him to write of his laboratory as the "gaol" of his ambitions.[27] The bookshop is the gaol of Kipps's ambitions; it keeps him, it protects him, it imprisons him.

At the time of writing *Love and Mr. Lewisham* Wells did not consciously apply the hero's story to his own circumstances, but "down below the threshold of my consciousness the phobia must have been there."[28] The phobia was of monogamy. Though Wells wanted to be protected from change and to achieve a satisfying relationship with one woman, he wanted even more not to be fixed in one emotional state. Like D. H. Lawrence, he hated the smug privacy of ordinary monogamous love, and since houses were an expression of that sort of love, he lashed out at houses, especially in his romances, which do not respect the middle-class values preserved in a novel like *Kipps*. In *The Food of the Gods* Wells declares openly that houses are "prison cells." *In the Days of the Comet* is even more contemptuous of "the crowded squalor, the dark inclosure of life . . . the insensate smallness of the old-world way of living . . . the petty interests, the narrow prohibitions . . . the jealous prisons," where men and women "formed a secret secluded system of two . . . went apart into couples, into defensive little houses, like beasts into little pits, and in these 'homes' they sat down purposing to love, but really coming very soon to jealous watching of this extravagant mutual proprietorship."[29] After the comet's cleansing of the earth, proprietorship is forgotten. The narrator works out a free-love arrangement and lives happily, unjealously thereafter.

Ann Veronica, though not a romance, is just as resentful of enclosure. In order to live fully, Wells's heroine first escapes the deadening, antierotic forces around her; these are imaged as belonging to a house: "All the world about her seemed to be—how can one put it?—in wrappers, like a house when people leave it in the summer. The blinds were all drawn, the sunlight kept out, one could not tell what colours these grey swathings hid." She hates the thought of being "cooped up in one narrow little corner" like her repressed maiden aunt: "Was there anything at all in those locked rooms of her aunt's mind? Were they fully furnished and only a little dusty and cobwebby and in need of an airing, or were they stark vacancy except, perhaps, for a cockroach or so or the gnawing of a rat?" Romance is outside these dead spaces beckoning to Ann Veronica, "as if it were a voice shouting outside a house, shouting passionate verities in a hot sunlight, a voice that cries while people talk insincerely in a darkened room and pretend not to hear."[30] The darkened room has become the symbolic opposite of the country houses folding all English space within their rooms or proffering a great good place for healing.

Romance conveys Ann Veronica to London, to advanced ideas, to imprisonment for suffragist activism, and eventually to the Alps and her lover. No enclosed space can contain her once she learns to take pleasure in sexuality. Nor can any house express her as, say, Clarissa Dalloway is expressed by her house in Virginia Woolf's novel. That house provides Clarissa with spaces for hiding fears already hidden in the recesses of her memory and supplies drawing-rooms for the exercise of the collocative powers of her mind. Fears and collocative powers the romantic Ann Veronica does without. Wells's novel makes its case for open-air freedom more persuasively than *The History of Mr. Polly* makes its case for the cosiness of the Potwell Inn, which suggests that in the long run Wells preferred freedom with all its uncertainties to the thought of being imaginatively enclosed. He admitted as much in departing from Sandgate, the expression but also the gaol of his authorial ambitions. Of all the major Edwardians, Wells was the least attracted to the vision of an ordered, traditional England made up of happy, private domesticities. He was immune to sentimental villagism, as his caricature of Cheasing Eyebright in *The Food of the Gods* demonstrates: "The whole prospect had the curiously English quality of ripened cultivation—that look of still completeness—that apes perfection, under the sunset warmth . . . We live in an atmosphere of simple and permanent things [the Vicar comments], Birth and Toil, simple seed-time and simple harvest. The Uproar passes us by."[31]

Arnold Bennett, like Wells, was a split author—split in personal allegiance to the cosy or the exciting, to the provinces or the great world. Even more than Wells, he was split in the sense of writing radically different sorts of books, novels and romances or fantasias. In the first ten years of the century he alternated regularly between one sort and the other, keeping up a dialogue within himself more informative than any epistolary dialogue carried on with Wells.

Bennett the author of fantasias wrote to amuse an "Income Tax-paying" middle or upper class which asked "to be taken out of itself," unaware that to be taken out of itself was the very last thing it really desired. In *The Grand Babylon Hotel, Hugo* (1902), *The Gates of Wrath* (1903), *Buried Alive*, or *The Sinews of War* (1906, in collaboration with Eden Phillpotts), Bennett offered his readers romance in externals, conventionality in morals. His Continental sophisticates or American millionaires move opulently through event-crammed plots on their way to true love, domesticity, marriage, and the affirmation of English decencies in general. The fantasias may therefore be said to be playing with fire, as *Three Weeks* and other best-sellers do, but with less cynicism; Bennett was closer to his readership than Elinor Glyn was to hers, and shared both their sentimentality and their eagerness for monied delights. Indeed he elevated himself into the class of his readers by hard work, "by the help of God and strict attention to business," as he says in an unconscious parody of the ambitious provincial spirit.[32]

The romantic externals of the fantasias presuppose the characters' ability to move freely in space and time, to be unimpeded by the controls ordinarily preventing, in Richard Ellmann's phrase, "the sudden alteration of the self."[33] The emblem of this freedom is the hotel, where all things are available and movement is the rule of living. The *femme fatale* of *The Gates of Wrath*, Mrs. Cavalossi, likes hotels because they impose on her no restrictions, no attachments. They are her theater of operation, and notions of disguise, artifice, and play-acting are indeed never far in the background when Bennett writes of hotels, either here or in *The Grand Babylon Hotel*. Hotels allow characters both to seem and to become larger than themselves. The grandiose department store in *Hugo* has the same power. The owner of its limitless goods is freed from the tyranny of things and can indulge his romantic instincts at whim. This is a Great Place perhaps, but not a Good one in any Jamesian sense. Bennett's hotels and stores function superbly without order, tradition, the benefit of control over limited space, or anything else associated with the country houses of Edwardian fiction. In hotels one does not repossess the nation but samples goods, defeats enemies, and imagines further possibilities for the self.

Wells was hard on Bennett the author of fantasias, whom he accused of championing "surface values": "hotels are not luxurious, *trains de luxe* are full of coal grit, chefs and pianists are not marvellous persons, dramatic triumphs are silly uproars. But it isn't irony—you believe in these things."[34] This is not the judgment of a realist on a romancer, but the judgment of one romancer on another. Wells's romanticism simply inhered in different things, the gestures of Ann Veronica instead of Bennett's hotels and *trains de luxe*. Bennett may indeed have believed in surface values, but his belief was not expressed without irony. Moreover, it was accompanied by belief in a world where freedom was the exception and constraint of one kind or another the rule. The values of this other world were not on the surface. They lay deep in personal and cultural history. E. V. Lucas recalled that it was one of Bennett's peculiarities, when in restaurants or other people's homes, to look at the trade-marks beneath the plates to see from which factory in the Five Towns they had come.[35]

The fantasia *Buried Alive* marks an intermediate stage between the Grand Hotels and the Five Towns, because it rescues Priam Farll from artistic loneliness and gives him a loving homebody for a wife. "One little home, fixed and stable," it claims, "render[s] foolish the whole concourse of European hotels."[36] But this simple domestic opinion is uncharacteristic of the hard-headed, unsentimental Bennett who remembered his origins and wrote novels, not fantasias. *Anna of the Five Towns* (1902), *The Old Wives' Tale* (1908), and *Clayhanger* are about ordinary life in the Five Towns. Although grander claims are sometimes made —the Potteries are "England in little," while St. Luke's Square has an important place "in the scheme of the created universe"— Bennett's essential purpose is dispassionately to examine one particular region of the industrial Midlands, and to set his stories of personal development against this region.[37] Bennett takes "against" literally. In his fiction, as in the fiction of his fellow provincials George Eliot and D. H. Lawrence, individuals worth writing about are by definition born in environments too limiting for them. Anna is a Staffordshire Dorothea Brooke: "It seemed a face for the cloister, austere in contour, fervent in expression, the severity of it mollified by that resigned and spiritual melancholy peculiar to women who, through the error of destiny, have been born into a wrong environment." The wrongness is a matter of religious narrowness, petty mercantilism, and foolish provincial smugness; it is also a matter of failed perception. Beauty lies about characters and they fail to see it. Romance is "even here—the romance which, for those who have an eye to perceive it, ever dwells amid the seats of industrial manufacture, softening the coarseness, transfiguring the squalor, of these mighty alchemic operations."[38]

Anna is most directly concerned with the inability of characters to take proper account of their native landscape or culture, but the other novels add variations to the theme. *Clayhanger* laments Edwin's inability to see the exquisite "composition" of colors in Bursley ("Beauty was achieved, and none saw it"), not to mention his refusal to see romance in the family printing business.[39] *The Old Wives' Tale* redefines romance. It is not to be found in the mysterious locked room of the Baines house, nor in a guillotining, as Sophia discovers in Auxerre, nor even in Chirac's balloon ascent. These excitements are as artificial as anything offered by Bennett's fantasias. Genuine romance is located in a market field with tents, or the movement of characters from one shop to another in the square. In Bennett generally beauty and romance are for the taking—or making. The clog-dancing episode of *Clayhanger* shows how the emblem of servitude is made into the medium of grace.

Among the limits on individual development in Bennett are parents. These are all novels of generational conflict. *Anna of the Five Towns* ought to be *Anna Daughter of Ephraim Tellwright*, since her inability to love stems ultimately from her father's miserliness, brutality, and tyranny. Old Tellwright is the first in a series of crippled, manipulative fathers which includes John Baines the invalid and Darius Clayhanger with his softening of the brain. The old men enjoy at best a grim, dessicated happiness consisting largely of control over their progeny. But Bennett is not merely a Staffordshire version of Gosse or Butler. He is most original as a novelist in studying a constraint more limiting than any parents can impose, the constraint of time itself. Time changes the healthy young into the decrepit old. Time defeats adolescent expectations and contradicts the infinitely leisured hotel life of Bennett's fantasias. Time also prevents life from taking paradigmatic shape; its slow movement gives Bennett's novels their special quality and keeps them from becoming conventional *Bildungsromane*. In works of that genre, time is at the service of the young. They shape it to their purpose, forcing it to stand still at moments of symbolic importance, hastening it ahead when life is ordinary, and cutting it short when the moment of triumphant departure is reached. The curtain descends on Paul Morel and Stephen Dedalus when, freed from family ties, those two heroes set their faces firmly toward Life. No such abridgments of a lifetime are permitted in Bennett. The Baines sisters' story becomes an old wives' tale; Sophia and especially Constance are subjected to time. "The naive ecstasies of her girlhood had long since departed," Bennett writes of Constance, "—the price paid for experience and self-possession and a true vision of things. The vast inherent melancholy of the universe did not exempt her."[40] Prices are paid; routine is routine. Character is changed by the slowly accumulating weight of experience, as Edwin Clayhanger is changed "by the slow daily influence of a large number of trifling habitual duties . . . and the monotony of them, and the constant watchful conventionality of his deportment."[41]

Bennett makes change occur imperceptibly, in the midst of an environment hostile to drama and even to the idea of change. Ideals die while one's head is turned, he remarks in *The Old Wives' Tale*. The young of *Anna* think that Titus Price's suicide will forever shame the Methodist Society, but the old people are wiser, "foreseeing with certainty that in only a few days this all-engrossing phenomenon would lose its significance, and be as though it had never been."[42] To adapt John Gross's phrase for Bennett, he is almost unsurpassed at showing how nothing remains the same but everything goes on as usual.[43] One of the things that goes on as usual is the setting for individual lives—the house. The constant factor in Anna's girlhood is the house shutting her in, just as the constant factor in her dutiful marriage with Mynors is undoubtedly going to be their house. In Wellsian terms, Anna's house is the gaol of her ambitions. The Baines house is the starting and finishing point of *The Old Wives' Tale.* The opening pages of the work describe the bedroom where Constance uses one long and two short drawers, Sophia two long drawers. Hundreds of pages go by; the sisters lead separate lives in Bursley and Paris; finally they come together again in the same old space, utterly changed by their lifetimes apart but in another sense exactly the same. All the experience they have gained from life might be contained in the same long and short drawers in the same bedroom. They come home like many other Edwardian characters, but they do not repossess their home; it repossesses them.

About all this the Baines sisters are ignorant. No Bennett character understands the full importance of the place in which she lives, whether that importance has to do with the expression or the entrapment of the self. Entrapment is the case with Ephraim Tellwright: "Had he been capable of self-analysis, he would have discovered that his heart lightened whenever he left the house, and grew dark whenever he returned; but he was incapable of the feat."[44] With such judgments Bennett rises superior to his characters. He understands, as they do not, why they furnish rooms of their own but spend so much time looking out of windows, how they alter facades to suit the Five Towns' taste, why Edwin Clayhanger is so fascinated by architecture. Bennett also understands the private meaning that inheres, for himself as a novelist, in all the houses and house-buildings of his fiction: the making of a house symbolizes the making of a novel. "The portions already drafted seemed good," Bennett congratulates himself on *Anna of the Five Towns* in a journal entry of 1897, "more than satisfactory as the result of the 'first process' in the manufacture of my fiction. The 'first process' (imagine the building of a house on a hill) is to get the materials, pell-mell, intermixed, anyhow, to a certain height."[45] After *Anna* Bennett became a more conscientious workman. By the stage of *Clayhanger* he was unsatisfied with pell-mell intermixings and was fully justified in imagining his own creative effort, his "manufacture," as the deliberate, unhurried, brick-by-brick construction of a house. Edwin thinks his house will never get itself done:

> One brick at a time—and each brick cost a farthing—slow, careful; yes, and even finicking. But soon the brick-layers had to stand on plank-platforms in order to reach the raw top of a wall that was ever rising above them. The measurements, the rulings, the plumbings, the checkings! He was humbled and he was enlightened. He understood that a miracle is only the result of miraculous patience, miraculous nicety, miraculous honesty, miraculous perseverance. He understood that there was no golden and magic secret of building. It was just putting one brick on another and against another—but to a hair's breadth! It was just like anything else! For instance, printing![46]

Or, for instance, fiction. Bennett did not write novels about English country houses, although his fantasias touch on them occasionally, because he could not look at them as other novelists did. They saw centers of order, or emblems of national virtue, or vessels of tradition. Bennett saw brick placed on brick. This is only to say, finally, what Henry James says about Bennett's novels, that in spite of their allegiances to provincial landscapes, in spite of their lessons about parents and children, in spite of their determined antiromanticism, they are not really monuments to ideas, to "pursued and captured meaning." A Bennett novel is rather a monument *of* "the quarried and gathered material it happens to contain, the stones and bricks and rubble and cement and promiscuous constituents of every sort that have been heaped in it and thanks to which it quite massively piles itself up." For James, that piling-up is nearly its own justification: "Our perusal and our enjoyment are our watching of the growth of the pile and of the capacity, industry, energy with which the operation is directed."[47] The building of Bennett's house of fiction turns out to be more important than the significance of the house once built.

14

This Strange Loneliness of Millions in a Crowd

The Broken Men of a 1902 Kipling poem are criminals fled to South America ("Behind was dock and Dartmoor, / Ahead lay Callao!") who bless the "just Republics" that ask no foolish questions and permit men to prosper; but homesickness finally forces its way into their contentment:

> Ah, God! One sniff of England—
>> To greet our flesh and blood—
> To hear the traffic slurring
>> Once more through London mud!
> Our towns of wasted honour—
>> Our streets of lost delight!
> How stands the old Lord Warden?
> Are Dover's cliffs still white?[1]

The same longing for England from afar, a longing centered on England's imperial capital, strikes Shere Ali, the Moslem hero-villain of Mason's *The Broken Road*. He has been educated at Eton and Oxford, then feted in Town, and back in India it takes only his love for the Englishwoman Violet Oliver to bring the old images to mind: "Perhaps here and there a drum would begin to beat, the cries of children would rise up from the streets, and I would lie in my bed with my hands clenched, thinking of the jingle of a hansom cab along the streets of London, and the gas lamps paling as the grey light spread. Violet!"[2] That could be a prose rendition of the nostalgic, soft-toned Alvin Langdon Coburn photograph of a London cab that James used as a frontispiece to *The Golden Bowl* in the New York Edition. All these images belong to the poetry-of-London school, which in reaction to late Victorian outcries against the City of Dreadful Night took a loving view of familiar urban scenes. Adam Wayne, in Chesterton's *The Napoleon of Notting Hill*, is a professed adherent of this school. He is a draper's assistant, like Kipps, but also "a dumb poet from his cradle." His volume *Hymns on the Hill* praises the country by comparing it to the city, bringing in whatever urban similes it can, as in the "fine Nocturne, 'The Last Omnibus' ": "The wind round the old street corner/Swung sudden and quick as a cab." Nature means to Wayne "a line of violet roofs and lemon lamps, the chiaroscuro of the town."[3]

Set against this love affair with London is a wholly different Edwardian impression of the capital. The lemon lamps and hansoms vanish, replaced by soulless walls, monstrous iron cranes, cruel-looking hooks over the decks of lifeless ships—the emblems of an industrialized and terrifying metropolis—or by a vision which dispenses with incidentals altogether and presents London as a single thing, problematic, incomprehensible, crowded with anonymous miseries. The London unguessed of in Wayne's cosy impressionism is the London glimpsed late in *The Nigger of the "Narcissus,"* and if Conrad's view is not more truthful than Wayne's, it is at least more comprehensive. It takes in more of the actual London which greeted Edwardians when they went about their daily routines or returned to the city from abroad and saw its nature freshly, "for the first time," "as though it were a foreign city." Conrad imagines a city capable of defeating attempts to understand it and of swallowing up individual human beings who enter into its "great opalescent and tremulous cloud, that seemed to rise from the steaming brows of millions of men."[4]

This is what literally happens at the end of *The Nigger*, when the "Narcissus" docks at its warehouse and discharges its crew to the shipping office and hence to the Black Horse, where they are bilked of what the shipping office pays them, and to the streets, which deafen and distract them with a dull roar. The defeatism in a tale about heroism at sea trades on the established tradition of London as a wicked place—London the wen, the cesspit, the gull-trap, the paradise of fools—and on hard contemporary fact.

The authenticity of personal observation is unmistakable in vignettes such as Singleton hesitantly fingering the small pile of gold that is his wages, so soon to be lost; the sailors in their new shore togs, smart jackets that looked as if they had been shaped with an axe; and the woman screaming "Hallo, Jack!" at the silent ship without looking at anyone in particular. Conrad is as taken with London's incomprehensibility as with its wickedness. While the "Narcissus" is still at sea, he describes the coast of England as a "great ship" with an impossibly mixed cargo: "a ship carrying the burden of millions of lives—a ship freighted with dross and with jewels, with gold and with steel. She towered up immense and strong, guarding priceless traditions and untold suffering, sheltering glorious memories and base forgetfulness, ignoble virtues and splendid transgressions." How are these items to be reconciled on the manifest? As the "Narcissus" is towed upriver, the contradictions in terms and the disorienting similes multiply: from London comes the murmur of millions of lips "praying, cursing, sighing, jeering—the undying murmur of folly, regret, and hope"; the mad walls loom up "vaguely in the smoke, bewildering and mournful"; a bridge breaks in two before the ship "as if by enchantment," mooring lines become snakes, capstans turn themselves, "as though animated by a mysterious and unholy spell." From the warehouse comes a penetrating smell of "perfumes and dirt, of spices and hides, of things costly and things filthy . . . an atmosphere precious and disgusting."[5] A swarm of strange men inexplicably takes possession of the "Narcissus," and she ceases to live.

In subsequent years London was again and again stylistically assaulted like this, because it seemed too large for the understanding of men. There is a bewildered return to the city in E. V. Lucas' *Listener's Lure*, where Harberton complains that London oppresses him, robs him of individuality, makes him feel "damned anonymous."[6] An equally bewildered return-via-memory occurs in Gissing's *The Private Papers of Henry Ryecroft*. Thinking of his past threatens Ryecroft with engulfment all over again, so he retreats hastily from images of Grub Street to the natural scenery of Devon. The return to the city in Wells's *A Modern Utopia* is specifically reminiscent of Conrad's scenes in *The Nigger*. Wells's utopian visionary and the friend with whom he has been theorizing about the future while on a tour of the Alps come home abruptly to a sullen roar, "an iron seat of poor design in that grey and gawky waste of asphalt—Trafalgar Square," a lot of filthy, torn paper, a stupidly held umbrella, an incorrectly drawn Union Jack. Newspaper posters report the random violence of a dystopian world ("Massacre in Odessa . . . Shocking Lynching Outrage in New York State"); odd snatches of conversation break into the two men's discourse. They cannot finish their sentences, being defeated by "the great multitude of people, the great uproar of vehicles, streaming in all directions." This formidable world "has a glare, it has a tumult and vigour that shout one down . . . What good would it be to recommend Utopia in this driver's preoccupied ear?"[7] London thus defeats visionary planning as it defeated the heroism of Conrad's crew, and though in both works there is a last-minute assertion to the contrary—a ringing endorsement of Utopia and a brave valedictory to the "good crowd" of the "Narcissus," respectively—the damage has been done. The unmanageable "Thing in Being that roars so tremendously about Charing Cross Corner" proves larger than attempts to cope with it practically, tidy it scientifically, or moralize it.

The young curate Mitchell in Phyllis Bottome's *The Master Hope* (1904) aspires to a slum parish because in London "we form new and hideous possibilities; brains that have become machines, and machines in charge of depraved human passions . . . Think of the bodies and souls of London districts! Have you watched them pour out of factories, or seen them stagger into the only free Homes open to them, at the street corner?"[8] The curate first is perceptive about the dehumanization of the urban poor, but then casts the "new possibilities," lest they seem threatening, into the familiar language of a sermon: the poor are sinned against or sin themselves (in drinking). Social confusion becomes a moral problem, a not infrequent Edwardian evasion.

Without categories of good and evil Englishmen found it deeply unsettling to try to apprehend this city full of movements that could not be traced and millions of inhabitants who resisted generalization by the sheer force of their individuality.

Edwardians found it particularly difficult to cope with one urban phenomenon, the New Woman, "the contemporary London female, highly modern, inevitably battered." That is how James describes Kate Croy in *The Wings of the Dove*, adding that she is "honorably free" because, like Ann Veronica, she strenuously resists the exchange of personal independence for survival in the unfriendly city.[9] James portrays the same character on a much lower social level in Maud Blandy, the beer-drinking, cigarette-smoking journalist of "The Papers" (*The Better Sort*). Maud is a product of the day hard for James to reconcile with old understandings: "It was as if a past had been wasted on her and a future were not to be fitted."[10] All three women are of the city as much as they are against the city. They are part of what *Ann Veronica* calls London's "big diffused impulse towards change."[11] They resist entanglements, defy conventional notions of womanliness—Maud and Ann more so than the ladylike Kate —and so contribute to London's confusions and moral formlessness, even as they provoke oversimplified male reactions. Because of them, the "modern world is burthened with its sense of the immense, now half articulate, significance of women."[12]

Wells returned to the problem of London in *The New Machiavelli*. Among Remington's most pleasing recollections is the memory of visits to his uncle in Bursley. Remington liked the simple rich-and-poor, owner-and-worker topography of the Potteries: "It was like a very simplified diagram," and diagrams reassured him after "the untraceable confusion of London."[13] In London rich-and-poor, owner-and-worker distinctions yielded to the suspicion that no one was really in control. The city passively resisted its nominal leaders and laughed at reformers intent on probing its dark corners on slumming expeditions or in theorizing sessions. Leaving one of these intellectualizing discussions of London carried out by the Baileys, Remington says, with all this administrative fizzle, this pseudo-scientific administrative chatter, dying away in your head, out you went into the limitless grimy chaos of London streets and squares, roads and avenues lined with teeming houses . . . you saw the chaotic clamour of hoardings, the jumble of traffic, the coming and going of mysterious myriads, you heard the rumble of traffic like the noise of a torrent; a vague incessant murmur of cries and voices, wanton crimes and accidents bawled at you from placards; imperative unaccountable fashions swaggered triumphant in dazzling windows of the shops; and you found yourself swaying back to the opposite conviction that the huge formless spirit of the world it was that held the strings and danced the puppets of the Bailey stage.[14]

Wells was contemptuous of the reformers because they took such a narrow view of problematic London, defining it all as a matter of slum housing, or unemployment, or bad drains—in short, of poverty. In the view of Wells and other novelists, problematic London broke down into millions of individual impressions and crises, with which fiction as well equipped to deal. The London impressions in Remington's remark are the sort of thing Wells sketched at length in *Kipps* and *Tono-Bungay*, Galsworthy in *The Island Pharisees* and *Fraternity*. Novels could always deal with a wanton crime, like the murder of Verloc in *The Secret Agent*, or with swaggering fashions, like those Remington glimpses in the dazzling windows of the shops. But to indulge in incidentals was to evade the presentation of the whole city. London in its entirety was inimical to fiction and could be approached only with lists of contradictions. As Forster puts it in *Howards End*, "One visualizes [London] as a tract of quivering grey, intelligent without purpose, and excitable without love; as a spirit that has altered before it can be chronicled; as a heart that certainly beats, but with no pulsation of humanity."[15] Purpose, love, humanity—the elements of Forster's Liberal, humanistic fiction—are exactly what the city fails to offer.

While the novelists were collecting scattered images or looking for the right tone of quivering gray for their descriptions, the reformers were going ahead with their slumming. "The Dock Life in East London," published by Beatrice Webb in 1887 after she had gained experience by collecting rents for her father in the East End, might be narrow, but from its narrowness came progress—a better dock life, if nothing else.[16] Sociological investigators carried out many inquiries into poverty in the Edwardian decade, with a purpose and methodology adapted from the great Victorian Charles Booth, whose *Life and Labour of the People in London* had first appeared in 1889; the seventeenth volume of his massive study came out in 1902-1903. Products of this statistical compassion were B. Seebohm Rowntree's *Poverty: A Study of Town Life* (1901); E. G. Howarth and Mona Wilson's *West Ham: A Study in Social and Industrial Problems* (1907, the report of the Outer London Enquiry Committee, which included C. P. Sanger, C. F. G. Masterman, and Beatrice Webb); L. Chiozza Money's *Riches and Poverty* (1905); and in a less scientific, more imaginative style, Phyllis Bottome's *Raw Material*, Masterman's *From the Abyss* (1902), and Galsworthy's *A Commentary* (1908) and *A Motley* (1910). Publications of all sorts were casting light into a domestic heart of darkness. The parallel to Africa is not farfetched. General William Booth's *In Darkest London* (1890) was named specifically after Henry Stanley's *In Darkest Africa* of the same year, and phrases like "the jungle of dim streets" were current. Explorations into working-class life were often styled as explorations of or exiles into "another nation," after Disraeli, or another world. In Ian Hay's novel *Pip* (1907) the hero loses his money and must work under a pseudonym as a factory hand and chauffeur; his cover for this period as a working man is "being abroad."

The slum visitor was a familiar Edwardian type caricatured in the cheerful guide Richard Shelton meets in Galsworthy's *The Island Pharisees*: "There's a splendid drain just here . . . the people are dying like flies of typhoid in those three houses . . . If we were in the East End, I could show you other places quite as good."[17] The enthusiasm of the expert passes over into ghoulishness here, but there were even more trivial thrills to be gained from slumming. George Pendyce and Mrs. Bellew in *The Country House* are out for a drive and suddenly decide to visit the East End: "let's do something not quite proper!"[18] They need the stimulant of impropriety, hedged about as they are by the cruel divorce laws and the stuffiness of Pendyce's family.

Despite the simple jibes of these books, Galsworthy was deeply troubled about the rationale for intervening in the poverty of London. The characters of his books who intervene are insensitive and effective, or sensitive and ineffective. In the first class falls Martin in *Fraternity*, a callous but efficient doctor who grades slum neighborhoods in shades of darkness (purple, black, and so on). In the second class falls Gregory Vigil of *The Country House*. As his name suggests, Vigil is a chivalrous reformer and philanthropist; he devotes himself particularly to the cause of fallen women. He is also politically naive, a kind of virtuous fool who can pose searching moral questions that political wisdom cannot answer, especially questions about divorce. A woman's divorce suit falls through because she gives temporary shelter to her estranged, alcoholic husband, and Vigil is on the spot with his *J'accuse:* "Do you mean to tell me that because she acted like a Christian to that man she is to be punished for it in this way?" Yet Vigil does not appear to be helpful to the fallen women of the novel. The rooms of his society are located so high up in a London building that from them one can see chiefly the sky, and that is the direction to which Vigil's real attention is turned. When down on the ground, he is not particularly observant: "the men he met looked at Gregory, and Gregory looked at them, and neither saw the other, for so it is written of men, lest they pay attention to cares that are not their own."[19] "For so it is written of men" suggests Galsworthy's helpless pessimism. Wrapped up in his dreamy, impractical pity, Vigil is a failure of one sort; Martin, treating the poor as the raw data in a public health scheme, is a failure of another. Paying attention to cares not one's own is clearly an unsatisfactory business. Yet Galsworthy cannot really believe that men should not be altruistic. His conscience forces him to ever more unhappy confrontations between rich and poor. He steeps himself in the painful state of separation between social classes, suspecting that "only connect" is a mere ideal, not practical advice; and like Helen Schlegel, he devotes himself to a showy petulance when the suspicion becomes a certainty. Ford Madox Ford called Galsworthy's writing about the poor "the Literature of agonised materialism," and that agony may be defined as a set of emotions—pity, guilt, revulsion, and anger—that Galsworthy indulged in when he could not find a solution to his problem.[20] Superficially that problem was the well-to-do man's inability to help the poor; at heart it was the writer's inability to comprehend an unfamiliar and unresponsive body of data.[21]

All this is patent in the failure of Galsworthy's *A Commentary*, a collection of previously published articles. Some of these present impoverished virtue, some castigate middle-class indifference, some demonstrate the failure of the judicial system. But the most ambitious pieces dramatize the encounter between slum visitor and slum dweller, and these fail as both literature and social documentation. Galsworthy's earnestness shines through the gloominess of the encounters, persistent in its claim that strong feelings about suffering are enough. In "A Lost Dog" a disillusioned middle-class gentleman describes the hopelessness of an unemployed drunkard's lot. The drunkard replies only, in refrain, "I am a lost dog." "Demos," with its Gissingesque title, presents an argument between a violent, hard-drinking navvy and a man, presumably from a benevolent society, who has taken away the navvy's wife and children for their own safety. No pitiable refrains here; the navvy is angry and provokes in the social worker reactions like "the brute beast," "the chained monster"—dehumanizing labels that an earlier generation of writers had used to describe the workers of industrialized England. Finally, "A Commentary" hints how much Galsworthy's pity owes to self-pity, or how much his compassion is adulterated with the hopelessness of not being able to do anything personally. Galsworthy can only lament as a crippled old man laments: "This progress, or what do they call it, is destroyin' of us. You can't keep it back, no more than you could keep back that there roller if you pushed against it; all you can do 's to keep ahead of it, I suppose."[22] The old man and Galsworthy are together keeping only one step ahead of that steamroller.

Bennett, blunt as always, thought that *A Commentary* was monotonous because "chiefly governed by a strong prejudice against its own subjects."[23] The sense of beauty he was looking for appears at least intermittently in Galsworthy's *Fraternity*, in which hopelessness is poignant rather than irritating. Hilary Dallison, a poet and critic of private means, cannot "bear to force anyone to do anything; he seems to see both sides of every question, and he's not good at making up his mind." In short, he is a feckless Liberal, and the slum-visiting doctor's attack on him sounds like Henry Wilcox condemning the Schlegels and their talkative friends: "There's plenty of aestheticism about you and your people—plenty of good intentions—but not an ounce of real business . . . Hilary's got so much consciousness of what he *ought* to do that *he* never does anything."[24] The confrontation of types here is plain, but *Fraternity* rises superior to *A Commentary* in exact measure as it rises superior to plainness and typifying. The crudity of "you and your people" is balanced by the fineness of Hilary's portrayal. He has the fictional roundness to be classed among the characters of *Howards End:* perhaps a Tibby Schlegel grown up, given some energy, and made capable of noticing the lives of other people.

As the title suggests, noticing the lives of other people is Galsworthy's main theme in *Fraternity*. All the Liberal Dallisons of the book are conscientiously drawn to the poor, but one by one they back off, offended by the separation enforced by the sense of smell and the sense of sight, or merely distracted by other interests. Hilary alone makes a persistent effort, partially because he worries less than the others about what the upper orders might lose in mingling too intimately with the lower orders. Hilary and his wife—the diametric opposites of the Forsytes—have little or no sense of property. Furthermore, Hilary understands the cryptic imperative spoken by his aged and addled father, who urges that all the Dallisons become involved with the inhabitants of a poor home, because "each of us . . . has a shadow in those places—in those streets." The thought haunts Hilary, forcing him to realize his common humanity, his common passivity before the huge fact of London. He thinks himself as victimized as any one of the anonymous millions of urban poor, particularly at moments when Mr. Purcey, the City businessman, passes by in his A.1 Damyer: "Before him in the sunlight a little shadow fled; behind him the reek of petrol seemed to darken the road . . . The machine in the middle moving on its business; shadows like you and me skipping in front; oil and used-up stuff dropping behind."[25] Forster's "throbbing, stinking motor-car" is here blended with the steamroller juggernaut of *A Commentary* in an emblem of man subject to inhuman economic and social forces. London generalized in this way is more ominous than East End poverty by itself would ever be.

Hilary's particular "shadow" is a poor model whom his wife painted. As a real thing of poverty, she has been amply mistreated, but Galsworthy is not so sentimental as to make her pure in spite of mistreatment. He is frank about her degradation, showing how she sets out to make Hilary fall in love with her and then put her in a compromising position. She succeeds with the first part of her plan but fails with the second, since Hilary is, after all, not good at making up his mind. In the end Hilary renounces her and breaks up his marriage as well, going abroad just to get out of England; to Galsworthy's credit, no convenient African explorer, as in *Multitude and Solitude* or *The Edwardians,* makes his appearance here. The finale openly declares that the gulf between classes cannot be effectively bridged. This theme of failure-to-connect is nothing new for Galsworthy, but in *Fraternity* it is conveyed with an absence of mawkishness and an inventiveness both in realistic particulars and metaphorical language surprising after the awkwardness of *A Commentary.* The critical lesson would seem to be that Galsworthy wrote best when he was writing least personally, most fictionally.

Hilary keeps a bust of Socrates and thinks of the philosopher as urging the Dallisons to fraternity: "He's telling us . . . to drink deep, to dive down and live with mermaids, to lie out on the hills under the sun, to sweat with helots, to know all things and all men. No seat, he says, among the Wise, unless we've been through it all before we climb!"[26] To dive down and live with mermaids is an invitation to experience passion wherever it may be found; it is what Strether might have said to Little Bilham if he had been more imaginative. The actual metaphor Hilary uses touches on an important longing of the period—or an important fear, since it is not easy to distinguish between the two emotions. Edwardians were drawn to thoughts of undersea dreaminess, of dim movement and looming distorted shapes. They did not have to be urged to dive down underwater as a duty or as a preparation for seats "among the Wise." They simply looked about them and let their favorite metaphor shape itself. "Under the fog of snow high up in the heaven the whole atmosphere of the city was turned to a very queer kind of green twilight, as of men under the sea," writes G. K. Chesterton in *The Man Who Was Thursday*. "It was a very trying day, choked in raw fog to begin with, and now drowned in cold rain. The flickering, blurred flames of gaslamps seemed to be dissolving in a watery atmosphere," writes Conrad in *The Secret Agent*, and later, slightly varying the image, "His descent into the street was like the descent into a slimy aquarium from which the water had been run off. A murky, gloomy dampness enveloped him."[27] In "The Remarkable Case of Davidson's Eyes" (*The Country of the Blind*, 1911) Wells describes a man suffering from the persistent hallucination that he is not walking about his own home but on the bottom of the sea, and that the familiar chairs and tables of his rooms have been metamorphosed into sea-creatures and water-weeds. Wells's *The Sea Lady* is about a literal sea-creature, a mermaid who portrays the deep-sea world as "a green luminous fluidity . . . lit by great shining monsters that drift athwart it and by waving forests of nebulous luminosity amidst which the little fishes drift like netted stars."[28] The star simile effectively puts the sea into the open air and makes the dreaminess general. Later the submerged life is straightforwardly taken as "this dream we are all dreaming," the life of men in cities.

The underwater metaphor in *The Sea Lady* aims to suggest the normal conditions of urban life—its passivity, its lack of sharp outlines, its strange unpredictability, its random cases of being stifled or escaping to the air. For more conventional understandings, being "submerged" might simply mean the same thing as being over the edge, or in the abyss, or at the bottom of a gulf, or in any of the other places symbolizing the fall into penury. But this is too limited and too sociological a view for Wells, Conrad, and the other Edwardians who noticed that even the employed and the intellectual might be "submerged" in a London oppressively incomprehensible. The undersea life they portray is not acutely threatening until it is apprehended. At that moment there comes an awakening from passivity and a symbolic drowning. Hilary Dallison finds his life tolerable until he realizes the exact state of his passionless marriage and the impossibility of reaching the model's heart. Then he is shocked into awaking and walking out of his life for good. Winnie Verloc in *The Secret Agent* is protected by the dreaminess of her existence in a London drowned in rain or dissolving in a watery atmosphere. Then she kills her husband, is plunged into a city full of nightmares, and escapes, but only to drown herself literally. Chatteris, the rising young politician in *The Sea Lady*, falls in love with the mermaid, then recalls himself to duty and earthly love, and finally realizes the stifling conventionality of his fiancée and his "brilliant" future career, at which point he walks into the sea with his mermaid. In each case the result of awakening from delusion is ambiguous: it is a radical loss that may be a way of gaining knowledge denied the submerged millions, who remain asleep among the water-weeds. This is not far from the romantic symbolism of a poem written at the end of the Edwardian period:

> We have lingered in the chambers of the sea
> By sea-girls wreathed with seaweed red and brown
> Till human voices wake us, and we drown.

Earlier lines from Eliot's poem are a reminder of another aspect of London:

> Shall I say, I have gone at dusk through narrow streets
> And watched the smoke that rises from the pipes
> Of lonely men in shirt-sleeves, leaning out of windows?[29]

Prufrock's vision could be of Conrad's Mr. Baker, chief mate of the "Narcissus," waiting in a London lodging for his next billet and having no one to think about, now that the ship is deserted; or of any of Conrad's "lost alone forgetful doomed" sailors once they lurch separately out of the Black Horse; or of one of the passersby who encounter Gregory Vigil and fail to see him. Loneliness was an inescapable fact of Edwardian London, and it appeared in the particularly harrowing form that is felt in crowds. Novels of the period note this fact no less often than they note poverty or incomprehensible size: "All around me stretched an immense town—an immense blackness. People— thousands of people hurried past me, had errands, had aims, had others to talk to, to trifle with. But I had nobody. This immense city, this immense blackness, had no interiors for me."[30] "These shadowy figures, wrapped each in his own little shroud of fog, took no notice of each other. In the great warren, each rabbit for himself."[31] Men and women moved about London living and dying, and no one cared, as Galsworthy notes in *The Island Pharisees*, since men and women are merely "human weeds" flourishing and fading under the fresh, impartial skies of London.[32] In this sense he shares the vision of the first great English novelist to write about the modern city, Charles Dickens, who in *Little Dorrit* (1856) had sent his joyous hero and heroine out into oblivious crowds, into streets that fretted and chafed and made their "usual" uproar.

The best Edwardian phrases for loneliness were Chesterton's: "this horrible silence of modernity . . . this strange indifference, this strange dreamy egotism, this strange loneliness of millions in a crowd." He hated the loneliness of the city and fought it in *The Napoleon of Notting Hill* by imposing on the city a fantastic transformation. It is provided with a "new religion of mankind," romanticized, medievalized. Random events and encounters in city streets become the glorious charades of warring armies. War does away with their loneliness forever. "Whatever makes men feel young is great—a great war or a love story."[33] Chesterton was supremely buoyant among Edwardians because he was supremely antimaterialistic:

> My madness . . . was more and more moving in the direction of some vague and visionary revolt against the prosaic flatness of a nineteenth-century city and civilization; an imaginative impatience with the cylindrical hats and the rectangular houses . . . I had perhaps got no further than the feeling that those imprisoned in these inhuman outlines were human beings; that it was a bad thing that living souls should be thus feebly and crudely represented by houses like ill-drawn diagrams of Euclid, or streets and railways like dingy sections of machinery . . . I never doubted that the human beings inside the houses were themselves almost miraculous; like magic and talismanic dolls, in whatever ugly dolls'-houses. For me, those brown brick boxes were really Christmas boxes.[34]

Not even Chesterton, however, could take comfort for long in the tinselly magic of *The Napoleon of Noting Hill.* Four years after that novel, in *The Man Who Was Thursday,* he again struck at the prosaic flatness of London, his "madness" this time turning him toward anarchism. It was a timely choice. Londoners were learning about anarchists from sixpenny novels, from tradesmen's newspapers, from *Ally Sloper's Half-Holiday* and the *Sporting Times.*[35] All journalistic and fictional sources agreed that this sinister form of political violence was arriving, like influenza, from the Continent. David Rossi, half-English, half-Italian, is the anarchist in Hall Caine's *The Eternal City* (1901), and in Guy Boothby's *The League of Twelve* (1903) the villains are the millionaire anarchist D'Alvaro and his henchmen. They have the temerity to invade the heart of the English countryside but are defeated by a stout-hearted young squire and his plucky friends. D'Alvaro, it turns out, who is really "Carlitz," unites Latin treachery with Slavic fanaticism; eventually the Tsar's police send him to Siberia.

Gabriel Syme, the antianarchist philosophical policeman in *The Man Who Was Thursday*, takes his enemies as seriously as Caine and Boothby do. For him anarchism is a huge and pitiless peril, a time bomb ticking away, a mass of kindling waiting for a match. Chesterton himself makes anarchism serve his own purposes: the events of an immensely complicated plot eventually transform the secret anarchist conspiracy into a sort of divine council, with the much-feared anarchist chairman, Sunday, revealed as God himself, come to earth to show there is a ruling intelligence in the universe after all. Chesterton's anarchism is essentially a form of magic; it expresses itself in secret rituals, underground meeting places, and all the mystification that the Christmas-box side of Chesterton could wish for the vicarious excitement of human beings imprisoned in their brown brick houses. But as Chesterton sees it, anarchism is also radically isolating. It keeps conspirator apart from conspirator and secret policeman apart from secret policeman. It generates puzzles. It decries governance by law and governance by rationality; hence the senseless messages about trouser-stretchers and Martin Tupper that Sunday dispatches to his pursuers. In dramatizing the meaninglessness of events, at least before divine authority manifests itself, and such separations between men as the inability of city-dwellers to penetrate the disguises of passersby, Chesterton's anarchism simply intensifies the city itself—its loneliness, chaos, incomprehensibility. By threatening London with the anarchist bogeyman, Chesterton is really showing what London is.

The same thing had been shown a year earlier. Conrad dedicated his novel of anarchism, *The Secret Agent*, "affectionately" to H. G. Wells as a "Simple Tale of the XIX Century." Admittedly the novel fictionalizes an actual incident of 1894, but in all other respects it is a book of its time, 1907, the year before *The Man Who Was Thursday* and the year after the magazine publication of two antianarchist tales by Conrad, "The Informer" and "An Anarchist" (both later collected in *A Set of Six*, 1908). Conrad wrote the book after "coming home" from the distant setting of *Nostromo*, and it owes more to what he saw about him in London during that period of mental change than to the facts of the incident. *The Secret Agent* originates in what had concluded *The Nigger of the "Narcissus,"* a vision of London: "a monstrous town more populous than some continents and in its man-made might as if indifferent to heaven's frowns and smiles; a cruel devourer of the world's light. There was room enough there to place any story, depth enough there for any passion, variety enough there for any setting, darkness enough to bury five millions of lives."[36]

The formlessness of the city is a challenge to Conrad the artist in roughly the same way that the indifference of its masses is a challenge to the bomb-manufacturing Professor: they must shock if they are to succeed. In *The Secret Agent* Conrad tries out new and ever more violent stylistic devices, ironies couched so destructively that they disrupt meaning, daring metaphors that take life away from human beings and give it to inanimate objects. The secret agent and informer Verloc gets "rusty" or becomes a soft kind of rock. A police constable, "part of inorganic nature," surges apparently out of a lamppost. A newspaper is flushed by the warmth of its own convictions; a couch is unhappy and homeless; a player piano executes all by itself a valse tune with aggressive virtuosity. These devices disorient the reader and prepare the way for a London in which inexplicable things may happen at any time. A child may carry a bomb, a meek wife may suddenly turn against her husband.

In his imagination Verloc undresses at night as a man might undress in the solitude of a "vast and hopeless desert." Fear of exposure as a double agent produces this image, or perhaps merely the circumstances of his life. Like the Professor, Verloc carries an impenetrable loneliness about him wherever he goes. His indolence has the same effect as the Professor's fanaticism. Although Verloc has a secret not to be shared with his anarchist "comrades," Conrad keeps his novel from being a thriller about the individual against the group by spreading secrecies and loneliness and indolence widely among his characters. He makes London a place of universal loneliness. The police scheme against each other in sour jurisdictional campaigns, the anarchists are locked up within their individual fantasies, the Professor stays hidden in his room or the Silenus, and Winnie is trapped in a loveless and childless marriage. Her loneliness is the price paid not only for renouncing happiness and accepting Verloc's aid, but simply for being poor in London, where material interests are even more determinative of affection than in Costaguana. Winnie is as impoverished in words as Emilia Gould, but unlike Emilia, she is one of the voiceless poor of the city, the silent millions. Unlike Leonard Bast, who tries to pattern his prose style on Ruskin's, Winnie lacks even the will to search for a voice not her own. The poor represented by Winnie might as well stay silent in the face of the surroundings they would have to convey: "the enormity of cold, black, wet, muddy, inhospitable accumulation of bricks, slates, and stones, things in themselves unlovely and unfriendly to man."[37]

Who would care, Conrad asks, if an anarchist blew up this particular London? Is the damage not done? Is the city not already fragmented into bricks, slates, and stones?[38] Because his own way of looking at the monstrous city is so bleak, Conrad contemptuously dismisses the superfluous plotting of Michaelis, Yundt, and Ossipon in the anarchist cell. They would like to be active, as vigorously (if not as virtuously) active as the Four Just Men of Edgar Wallace's best-seller, who two years before *The Secret Agent* stalked "tragically through the world," "vague shadowy figures . . . condemning and executing the capitalist, the corner maker, the tyrant, evil forces all, and all beyond reach of the law."[39] But having all the words that Winnie lacks, Conrad's "vague shadowy figures" talk rather than act, and their talk fails to achieve unanimity. Around and around the isolating obsessions go, Michaelis envisioning historical progress, Yundt yearning for bloodshed, Ossipon "scientifically" theorizing, all of them plotting circles as solipsistic and meaningless as those the good, quiet, moronic Stevie draws on his deal table. When Michaelis reaches the peroration of his address ("art, philosophy, love, virtue—truth itself!"), the coals on the grate settle down with a "slight" crash, commenting on his performance just as the popping bottle of stout comments on Irish eloquence in James Joyce's "Ivy Day in the Committee Room." Stevie is more dangerous than any of the anarchists, because he really can feel pain in others and because, trusting Verloc, he can be made to carry Verloc's bomb. Stevie's retardation is useful to Conrad. It is at once an invitation to pity and a check on its excessive indulgence. Stevie is grotesque and slightly forbidding, but never so grotesque as to stop being representative of a whole silent populace—the "army of the Ignorantly Innocent," as Bennett had called them in a journal entry of 1896.[40]

That Conrad's novel deflates the anarchists' pretentiousness does not mean he takes their theory lightly. In the abstract, the theory is the contradiction of everything Conrad values— accepted morality, discipline, restraint, the dignity of toil—so he allows Inspector Heat a little heroism, of the same sort allowed Captain MacWhirr, and Verloc more than a little evil, which if not strictly due to anarchism is at least provoked by the anarchists' admiration for violence. *The Secret Agent* is not morally nihilistic; such a novel could not have been serialized in *Ridgeway's: A Militant Weekly for God and Country*. It is merely realistic in that it refuses to finish the story of the Professor, who is Conrad's version of the perfect technocrat: intelligent, completely indifferent to the natural world and other people, lonely by choice, embracing ruin and destruction as the expected conclusions to arduous research. When asked what he wants, the Professor responds with a description of what he is, the perfect detonator. He confirms the view of the curate in *The Master Hope* that London is a place where brains have become machines. Not even a brilliant Heat, a Heat drawn by Edgar Wallace, could find the Professor in the city drawn by Conrad. The city hides the Professor perfectly. Yet if no one looks at him as he passes through the streets unsuspected and deadly, that is not Conrad's fault, who gives ample warning of the Professor and the detonator in his pocket—or the fault of fellow Edwardian novelists, who saw London as a devourer equally of the world's light and of such novelistic expectations as that wickedness is punished, innocence preserved, England protected from anarchy, sense made of city life.

15

The Condition of England and the Condition of Fiction

The history of the English novel from 1900 to 1910 is the history of a movement in imaginative sympathy. To put it in paradigmatic form, the novelist stops writing adventures abroad and starts writing about the experience of coming home. He transfers his imagined locales from the Congo to a country house, his thematic interests from the probing of heroism to the cultivation of English virtues and the exploration of a great and mysterious city. He puts aside myths and begins to notice facts. In a crude way Conrad fits the paradigm, moving from *Lord Jim* and *Nostromo* to "The Informer" and *The Secret Agent,* as do Kipling, Wells, Forster, and even Bennett, who moves from *The Grand Babylon Hotel* with its cosmopolitanism of the Strand to *The Old Wives' Tale* with its provincialism of the Five Towns. But no one novelist perfectly demonstrates the movement or captures, in his published Edwardian work, all of its shiftings and turnings. General patterns must be built up out of the individual movements of many novelists, as well as out of their fixities, for there were writers who remained resolutely unchanged over the decade—including those who kept abroad, such as Buchan and Shiel, those who stayed at home, such as Galsworthy, De la Mare, and Lucas, and those who resisted all categorization, such as James.

Toward the end of the period one pattern in particular emerged from the stubborn individualities of Edwardian fiction. That was the pattern formed by attempts to put all of England within the covers of a book, to anatomize contemporary Englishness and be compendiously factual in the study of the national situation. Writers coming figuratively home from abroad were obliged to consider exactly what "home" was, to whom it belonged, and what its destiny would be. They carried on in a professional, rigorous way that examination of the realm begun by the fictional amateurs of E. V. Lucas, Lynn Harberton and Kent Falconer. Such writers could not escape from "the meaning and progress of the actual life around them"; the question before them was "the present: the past but furnishing material through which that present [could] rightly be interpreted, the future appearing as a present which [was] hurrying towards them—impatient to be born." They asked for "fact; not make-believe."[1] These phrases come from C. F. G. Masterman's *The Condition of England* (1909), a work with which the most comprehensive novels of Englishness, above all *Tono-Bungay*, have much in common (*The Condition of England* alludes more than once to Wells's book).[2] The theorist Masterman and the novelist Wells attacked the same "encompassing problem," to some extent by the same methods of reportage, satire, and direct commentary, just as fifty or sixty years before them Carlyle and Dickens, the two chief investigators of the mid-Victorian condition of England, had worked by roughly the same methods of sarcasm, hyperbole, and symbolic description. In 1854 and in 1908 the condition of England was a topic that drew discursive and imaginative writers together.

In the Edwardian period condition-of-England fiction employed, to begin with, emblems of the country. Conrad thought of England as a great ship carrying a hopelessly mixed cargo; Bennett saw it as a macrocosmic version of the Potteries' landscape, with open spaces, rows of houses, and belching chimneys. In "The Mother Hive" from *Actions and Reactions*, Kipling makes England into a beehive. The story represents Kipling nearly at his worst, but also at his most revealing, in that it employs all the sharply turned effects of his art—the gift for parody, the ironic reversals, the insistent cleverness—in a few resentful pages.

Forging realism for political allegory, observation for satire, the story is the work of a Kipling weary of patient encouragement, contemptuous of the spirit of the age, and ready for a slashing attack on avant-garde thought. More than a decade has gone by since "Recessional," and the English are still complacent, still ignorant of their responsibilities, and still deluded by pride, though the pride is now not militaristic but arrogantly intellectual. The idealism of "An Habitation Enforced" and the history lessons of *Puck* and *Rewards and Fairies* have proved inadequate. Only the determined symbolism of the beast fable may help. An old and overcrowded beehive is invaded by a Wax-moth ("where bees are too thick on the comb there must be sickness or parasites"), who hides in the brood-comb and subverts the insect youth ("young bees will tolerate any sort of stranger"). That is, the English commonwealth is under attack from radical reformers. The Wax-moth raises a generation of malformed bees, part worker and part drone, then stirs up trouble among the genuine workers by intensifying their class consciousness ("Swarming was invented to cheat a worker out of her proper comforts") and by replacing experience with abstract social theory and sensual temptation ("One [accomplice] proved that if every bee only gathered honey for seven and three-quarter minutes a day, she would have the rest of the time to herself, and could accompany the drones on their mating flights"). Finally, political-sexual-economic wickedness leads to the collapse of the whole society. The beekeeper opens the hive, giving the Wax-moth one last chance for rhetoric ("That's our work. Look up, and you'll see the dawn of the New Day"), then burns everything out.[3] A mere remnant of the old swarm survives, with its new queen, to inhabit the purified hive.

John Galsworthy's condition-of-England novel, *The Island Pharisees*, though as packed with feeling as Kipling's short story, dispenses with Kipling's violence. It is, in fact, "unable to go beyond feelings to questions of causes and remedies" and therefore shrinks from the idea of a solution, whether apocalyptic or Fabian.[4] Praised in Masterman's *The Condition of England* as a "rather fierce" indictment of conventional society, Galsworthy's book might more accurately be classed with the literature of sentimental Liberalism, that is, with the habit of mind Masterman both describes and exemplifies: "critical rather than invigorating: sceptical, questioning, sometimes with an appearance of frivolity, sometimes torturing itself with angers and despairs."[5]

The Island Pharisees and "The Mother Hive" are equally far removed from the norm of conventional fiction, the novel because it is loosely constructed and thematically unresolved, the short story because it is minutely contrived and all too resolved. In generalizing on England, both Galsworthy and Kipling had to revise the normal methods of the realistic storyteller. Galsworthy, indeed, had to revise the work itself. He first published *The Island Pharisees* in 1904, then brought it out again with changes in 1908. Defining his purposes may have required an unusually prolonged effort because he felt within himself, as a writer, a battle between "All things that are, are right" and "All things that are, are wrong," that is, between literary complacency and rebelliousness. The cost of breaking away from the conventional journey of life is high. Of ten men who enter upon that journey, Galsworthy maintains, only one turns aside from it, and only one in ten of those survives. But now and then a man finds himself "near that thing which has no breadth, the middle line," and from that position he may watch both the complacent and the rebellious and smile to see the fun.[6] The middle line is Galsworthy's position exactly, the line reached after revisions and battlings within himself, after giving up any attempt to commit himself fully to complacency or rebellion. He neither turns aside from the journey nor goes along blithely with it. He neither breaks cleanly from the conventional novel, inventing to replace it some new composite form more accommodating to his interests, nor accepts that conventional form with all its aesthetic assumptions and strictures.

The Island Pharisees fictionalizes the articles collected in *A Commentary*, extending the investigation of phariseeism to the whole of the island of Britain and various social classes. The observation of sufferings and hypocrisies is carried out by Richard Shelton, yet another Englishman returned home from travel abroad ("The streets . . . after his long absence in the East, afforded him much food for thought"). Shelton is awaiting marriage to the ultraconventional Antonia, who carries with her "a taste of home . . . the very image of an English day." Antonia *is* England. But before the joining of man with woman or man with nation, there must be some inward and outward exploring. A chance acquaintance, the vagabond Louis Ferrand, introduces Shelton to poverty in London; they encounter a prostitute, they hear a monologue from a drunken actor. The returnee is confused and troubled ("My respectability is only luck") but feels no better when he inspects, using a familiar image of submergence, middle-class life: "It was like knocking at a never-opened door, looking at a circle—couple after couple all the same. No heads, toes, angles of their souls stuck out anywhere. In the sea of their environments they were drowned." His middle-class relatives fail utterly to understand his uneasiness. His uncle has "a touching muddle in his optimism—a muddle of tenderness and of intolerance, of truth and second-handedness"; his mother is "full of the sympathy that has no insight."[7]

The large, helpless liberality of Shelton's relations answers none of his questions, so he sets off, a latter-day William Cobbett or W. H. Davies, on a tour of the countryside; this is a condition-of-*England*, not a condition-of-*London* novel. Perhaps the heart of the nation is to be found not in the grimy city but in "The soft air, the drawling voices, the shapes and murmurs, the rising smell of wood-smoke from fresh-kindled fires." Under the influence of these rural clichés, Shelton grows nostalgically insular: "The outside world was far indeed. Typical of some island nation was this nest of refuge—where men grew quietly tall, fattened, and without fuss dropped off their perches; where contentment flourished, as sunflowers flourished in the sun."[8] Not surprisingly, he is accused of being a Little Englander; but he denies it, and at the end of the novel he denies country sentiment altogether. Shelton admits that he cannot, after all, be a supertramp; he will have to make something of himself, and take his place in society. But he will have to take it without Antonia, for his championing of Ferrand, his pleasantness to a fallen woman, and above all his attempt to put ideas into Antonia's head, to question her prejudices about class and privilege, have permanently alienated him from her and her family. The only reward Shelton has at the end is knowledge. What value is to be attached to that knowledge is unclear.

Richard Shelton is less a character than a recording consciousness; *The Island Pharisees* is less a conventionally plotted novel than an anthology of Edwardian emotions about and images for a painfully divided England. Galsworthy's comprehensive sentitivity gathers into one book what other writers had touched on in a more scattered way: the meaninglessness of social change, the helplessness of the poor, the fatuity of country-house life, the horror of London, and the merely nostalgic prettiness of rural life. But Galsworthy makes no real attempt to connect one part of the divided nation with the other—to connect, say, selfishness at Antonia's Holm Oaks causally with suffering in the East End —or to suggest what personal actions ought to follow on an understanding of the condition of England. Shelton feels everything and does nothing. The lesson of the book is that there is no lesson. Galsworthy's Liberalism consistently pushes him away from large-scale judgments and toward emotional impressionism.[9] His book is really a study of the condition of English feelings.

Galsworthy was not the only Liberal to approach the encompassing problem of England in the first decade of the twentieth century. There were studies by the young Winston Churchill (*Liberalism and the Social Problem*, 1909), Forster's friend Goldsworthy Lowes Dickinson (*Liberty and Justice*, 1908), the economist J. A. Hobson (*The Social Problem*, 1901, and *The Crisis of Liberalism*, 1909), and even Wells in a non-Radical mood (*Liberalism and Its Party*, 1913). Perhaps the most useful Liberal self-definition comes from L. T. Hobhouse's *Liberalism* (1911), published as part of the "Home University Library of Modern Knowledge," one of those inexpensive series for self-improvement which were themselves an expression of the Liberal faith in education. Hobhouse traces contemporary Liberalism back to the libertarian doctrines of Mill and defines the essence of the faith as a belief in personal expressiveness: "To find vent for the capacities of feeling, of emotion, of thought, of action, is to find oneself." That might be the motto of innumerable Edwardian connoisseurs of right feeling or searchers after the self—George Ponderevo, Lambert Strether, Philip Herriton. The result of self-expression or self-definition, Hobhouse continues, is not anarchy but rather the introduction of "some unity into life, some harmony into thought, action and feeling." The central achievement of Liberalism consequently is an awareness that parts of one person's life are lived in relation to other parts, and that lives are lived in relation to other lives. Society is guided by the rules of the relation between constituent members. The point of finding oneself turns out to be the "sense of ultimate oneness," which is "the real meaning of equality, as it is the foundation of social solidarity and the bond which, if genuinely experienced, resists the disruptive force of all conflict."[10]

Exactly how one gets from the expression of feeling, thought, and action to the sense of ultimate oneness is left unexplained by Hobhouse, and that omitted step is one subject of *Howards End* (1910), a novel much more subtly "about" English society than anything in Kipling or Galsworthy. Forster's personal connections with Liberalism, especially political Liberalism, are important but not very distinct. On the one hand, he was an early contributor to the *Independent Review,* a Liberal journal, and Cambridge and the Apostles introduced him to such thinkers as Dickinson and G. M. Trevelyan; but on the other hand he liked to keep aloof from party affairs and was not greatly interested in political theory. Yet Forster's work is unquestionably engaged by Liberal problems. All his novels show characters trying to "find vent for the capacities of feeling, of emotion, of thought, of action," and thereafter trying to connect themselves with others, if not in an ultimate oneness, then in the more prosaic achievements of friendship or marriage. The "only connect" on the title page of *Howards End* insists on some unity in life and some unity between lives, both goals being essential to Liberal hopes.

Forster's book is at the start a comic rescue novel, as Mrs. Munt rushes to undo the hasty engagement of Helen Schlegel and Paul Wilcox, but quickly passes on to more far-reaching issues. The Liberal Schlegels are set to arguing with the Conservative Henry Wilcox about the Social Question. Wilcox, who sees "a good deal behind the scenes," thinks that the Social Question is concocted by journalists. There are just rich and poor, as there always have been and always will be. Helen and her sister Margaret know better: the poor are increasingly different from the rich, and the nation is increasingly divided. The very integrity of England as a single definable commonwealth is under attack. The case of the struggling clerk Leonard Bast alone has shown Helen that much. His spiritual poverty is a sign that all is not well, that goblins are walking quietly over the universe. In their Liberal way the Schlegels for a moment achieve the desired connection to Bast: "Somehow the barriers of wealth had fallen, and there had been—he could not phrase it—a general assertion of the wonder of the world." That is, Bast sees his essential identity with these articulate and knowledgeable sisters, and he proceeds from that fact to a realization of his place in the world. At this point Forster quotes the same sentence from Novalis which Conrad used as the epigraph to *Lord Jim*, "My conviction . . . gains infinitely the moment another soul will believe in it."[11] This may be taken as yet another version of the central idea of Liberalism. Belief within is fostered by belief without. Individuals are most free at the moment when they realize their dependence on others. After the moment of connection in *Howards End*, problems arise. The Schlegels mishandle the Bast situation by passing on bad information about his job; they tend to mishandle all the practical affairs of their life. But their intellectual achievement is clear: they have understood that finding oneself is a matter of finding connections to others. The refinement of Helen and Margaret needs to be joined with the restless ambition of Bast; the Schlegel life of personal relations needs to be joined with the Wilcox life of telegrams and anger. The condition of England results first from an unequal distribution of money, and then from connections made badly or not at all, too conventionally interpreted or too timorously pursued.

The plot of *Howards End* involves an inheritance, and that too leads Forster outward to national questions. The first Mrs. Wilcox bequeaths her home to Margaret, but does Margaret deserve Howards End? What has she done to earn its comforts or pay off its mortgages? By extension, does England belong "to those who have moulded her and made her feared by other lands, or to those who have added nothing to her power, but have somehow seen her, seen the whole island at once, lying as a jewel in a silver sea, sailing as a ship of souls, with all the brave world's fleet accompanying her toward eternity?" To whom does the future belong—the half-German Schlegels, the aggressively English Wilcoxes, or perhaps Leonard Bast, who has walked across England in the dark? Forster's first answer to these questions is that nature is plenteously turning out Wilcoxes "so that they may inherit the earth." Henry's energy overwhelms Margaret. She marries into his family and expectations, though with hopes she may help him "to the building of the rainbow bridge that should connect the prose in us with the passion." Their marriage, like the marriages in E. V. Lucas' novels, implies that the nation will belong to the middle-aged and young together. All is well—life is to be lived in fragments no longer, the beast of sensualism and the monk of asceticism are to die—as long as the Schlegel-Wilcox alliance holds; but then circumstances intervene, the alliance dissolves, and in Henry's collapse and Margaret's new-found strength are created an entirely different situation. Toward the end of the novel England recedes, Howards End comes to the fore. The issue of the national future is held in abeyance, there being more pressing personal issues to consider, namely the needs of the characters to retreat to a place that will heal them. The hope for unity yields to the triumph of the life of personal relations. On farms in the neighborhood of

Howards End, Forster says, "one might see life steadily and see it whole, group in one vision its transitoriness and its eternal youth, connect."[12] But the fact of the matter is that the Schlegel life is not going to be connected with the Wilcox life. It has overcome it.

In a 1907 lecture on "Pessimism in Literature" delivered to the Working Men's College in London, Forster testifies that as a modern, as a witness of rapidly altering social feelings, he can no longer accept the old fictional formula for a happy ending—the sound of wedding bells ushering in a marriage: "We of today know that whatever marriage is, it is not an end. We know that it is rather a beginning, and that the lovers enter upon life's real problems when those wedding bells are silent." Following his own precept, Forster gives the married couple of Howards End real problems to be dealt with in the future. He is clear-sighted about Henry's state of brokenness, Margaret's state of ascendancy, and their passionless and fruitless union. But Forster hardly follows his own advice to end a novel with a scene of separation—"the erection of a barrier, spiritual or physical, between the people in his book."[13] At the end of Howards End no separations impend. The tone is celebratory rather than ironic or pessimistic: the hay harvest is coming, Helen's child is flourishing, old enmities are softened. Henry may be in his inner room sneezing, but he is joined with his wife in a place that allows him to survive. "Only connect" matters less than that people should be happy. In spite of diligent intentions to be modern, Forster proves old-fashioned enough to end this novel on a note of permanence. "Salvation"—not just hope or progress—lies round the characters in the wych-elm tree and superbly proportioned rooms of the house and narrowing circles of the field. They have only to recognize it as salvation.

This ending helps to explain why Howards End, though it describes English life in 1910, is not exactly a condition-of-England novel. The resolution of the plot Forster provides runs counter to the unresolvable questions which must be part of any ongoing examination of England; the narrowing down of his focus to one house, and beyond that to the sacred center of one field, necessarily keeps him from surveying the nation as a whole. "System after system of our island would roll together" under the feet of someone standing on a summit in the Purbeck Hills, but such panoramas are in the end not what interest Forster.[14] His vision is more selective. He is occupied with only some of the important issues of the day: motoring, but not women's suffrage; the growth of London, but not labor unrest. He undertakes no investigation of different social classes because his business, as he admits, is with gentlefolk or those obliged to pretend they are gentlefolk. More generally, Forster's business with his middle-class characters is always the clear exposition of their diversity as individuals, and then the possibility of connection between them. About such a possibility he is guardedly optimistic, whereas he has few hopes that the larger social questions can be solved or even put in such terms as would allow him to investigate them thoroughly. In this sense Forster is as much a Liberal pessimist as Masterman.

The whole bent of Forster's art is toward the life of personal relations, to use Margaret's phrase, and away from the impersonal forces molding English civilization, to use Henry's phrase. Edwardian England was indeed being molded by great impersonal forces—the economic force, for example, that deprives Bast of his job—and Forster's relative neglect of these keeps *Howards End* from being as comprehensively about England as it seems, at first, to be. But this only means that *Howards End* is a novel, "the distinctive art form of liberalism," that faith which has as its controlling center "an acknowledgement of the plenitude, diversity, and individuality of human beings in society, together with the belief that such characteristics are good as ends in themselves."[15] Believing that, how could Forster write about social forces that were making individuals seem faceless and powerless? How could he write anything but a finely drawn, persuasive, controlled novel about the condition of Englishmen?

In *Tono-Bungay*, which is unquestionably a condition-of-England novel, Wells takes for granted the relative powerless-

ness of individual human beings, and he makes their powerlessness more emphatic by presenting it as a bitter lesson to his hero
and narrator.[16] George Ponderevo begins his adult life, like all
heroes of *Bildungsromane,* with a firm belief in his ability to do
significant things in a large and important world, but events
teach him that, "when you most think you're doing things,
they're being done right over your head. *You're* being done." At
every point in the novel—George's random ordering of his life,
his uncle Teddy's fall, Susan Ponderevo's passivity in circumstances she knows she cannot control—men and women are sub-
servient to "great new forces, blind forces of invasion, of
growth."[17] Though Wells might have described himself at times
as a Liberal or a Socialist, his book is without a Liberal faith in
individual responsibility or a Socialist faith in meaningful collective action. It is, instead, attuned to the impersonality of contemporary English life: the multitudinous, limitless, unchange-
able fact of London, with its faceless crowds and sense of vast
irrelevant movement, and behind London swarming hinterlands
of humanity with whom it is possible to have no dealings, of
whom it is possible to know nothing. Whereas *Howards End* is
given to narrowing, *Tono-Bungay* is given to enlarging and
broadening. It reaches out to events that individuals can neither
control nor understand.

The exploration of England takes the form of George's history.
He starts with a below-stairs upbringing at Bladesover, the great
house which as a child he accepts on trust "as a complete authentic microcosm" of the world. Yet its fine appearance of order is
already compromised; and George discovers that Bladesovery is
doomed, from the senile helplessness of its owner to the pointless
extravagance of the house itself. The great-house system, even
when modified by those who take over and vulgarize Bladesover, is simply not relevant to the condition of contemporary
England. What Bladesover does represent is a troubled inheritance. Somewhere within its ancestry it contains leisure, spaciousness, comfort, a sense of how things may be done with
grace, but no one quite understands how to value these qualities

246

or adapt them to present conditions. It is as though the past has left all its enormous wealth to the present, but without instructions for use. The wealth cannot be forgotten—nor can George simply forget Bladesover, which remains a "social datum" for him wherever he goes—and it is consequently a troubling factor throughout the novel.

From Bladesover George proceeds through his schooling to a scientific education in London. The city is stimulating to the young man, for Wells is writing an ordinary coming-of-age tale as well as a study of contemporary England. But London is also symbolically valuable because it is a place "disproportionately large" and "morbidly expanded," without plan or intention. It stands for everything in modern life that cannot easily be comprehended. For George to comprehend it at all he must impose arbitrary structures on it. He invents a theory making London's streets and squares a geographic development of the Bladesover system, or more importantly, he romanticizes the city as the arena of modern commerce, where advertising signs cry out ceaselessly from the hoardings and Tono-Bungay has its birth. George joins his uncle Teddy's campaign to publicize the patented tonic, and they are successful beyond even Teddy's dreams. Tono-Bungay becomes a national institution, then an empire, and all the time it is resting on the flimsiest financial and moral structure. That is what Wells detects in modern capitalism —not just its rapaciousness, or the worthlessness of the goods it foists off on the public, but an essential fraudulence. Tono-Bungay is a faith to which men blindly give their devotion, and the condition of England represented in the success of the nostrum is simply a state of willed self-deception. Modern men cannot make sense of their existence, so they choose a cause that will at least absorb their energies and give them a material reward. "You perceive now," George informs the reader, "the nature of the services for which this fantastic community gave [Teddy] unmanageable wealth and power and real respect. It was all a monstrous payment for courageous fiction, a gratuity in return for the one reality of human life—illusion."[18]

247

In the course of time the "courageous fiction" of Tono-Bungay proves unequal to its inventor; Teddy needs another outlet for his energies, and that is provided by the series of houses he builds, each grander than the one before, but all unconsciously emulating Bladesover. From an unpretentious suburban dwelling the Ponderevos pass to Lady Grove, "a still and gracious place, whose age-long seclusion was only effectively broken with the toot of the coming of the motor-car." There Teddy wants to have "Merrymakings. Lads and lasses dancing on the village green. Harvest home. Fairings. Yule Log—all the rest of it." It is as though he has read all the nostalgic Edwardian country-house novels, not just Kipling's "Below the Mill Dam." He soon has grander notions—a new house built in the dimensions of his commercial achievement. "Crest Hill" is to turn its back on Lady Grove and assert the megalomania of its owner. But Teddy falls into bankruptcy and disgrace before the house can be completed. Crest Hill, the "replacement" for Bladesover, signifies the failure of the present to translate the richness of the past into current terms. In Wells's novel the "multitude of economically ascendant people who are learning how to spend money" never master their lessons, and the result is "quite an important element in the confusion of our world."[19]

Meanwhile, George's outlets for surplus energy are first the Socialism he likes to discuss with his friend Ewart, then the love of women, and finally scientific research. Ewart is an amateur political theorist whose Socialism is a beautifully shaped ideal, but otherwise useless, as any theory based on mere aesthetic appeal must be. George hardly agrees with Ewart when he describes the reality of life as "Chromatic Conflict" and "Form"; the reality of life is what the novel as a whole is laboring to reproduce. Still less does George believe in the efficacy of Ewart's scheme for dealing with the pressures of sexuality: women are to inhabit a city of their own, walled in and self-sufficient, and are to let down silken ladders to those men they choose as lovers. Women, that is, will remain untroubled by men, and men will remain untempted by women. George knows this could never work because he is so constantly and irresistibly tempted by the women in his life. One and all they distract him from the cares and guilts of Tono-Bungay, but only by entangling him in further problems of jealousy, mismatched sexual appetites, and betrayal. Love is the "queerest thing in all this network of misunderstandings and misstatements and faulty and ramshackle conventions which makes up our social order as the individual meets it." His mistress Beatrice in particular threatens to infect him with her melodramatic, fin-de-siècle fatalism: "the whole world *is* blotted out—it's dead and gone, and we're in this place. This dark wild place . . . We're dead. Or all the world is dead. No! We're dead."[20]

George's research into flight allows him to resist such thoughts by reassuring him he is alive. Science in general regulates his haphazard existence. After the collapse of the Tono-Bungay empire and the failure of the expedition to Mordet Island, George needs all the order he can get. He pours his resources into the design of ever more complicated flying machines, which lift him, when they work, above the half-completed shell of Crest Hill, above the landscape of England itself. Flight supplies the panoramic overview suitable to a condition-of-England novel, and Wells makes the last flight into a resumé of the whole work. What was examined before in fragments and in progress is now examined, as if from a great distance, in a single finished image: "I saw the whole business of my uncle's life as something familiar and completed. It was done, like a play one leaves, like a book one closes."[21] The flying machine succeeds in getting George and Teddy to the Continent, but it crashes in France, answering to the metaphor about up like a rocket and down like a stick which George introduced, in the opening pages, as a guide to the history of Tono-Bungay.

On the Continent Teddy dies and George must return to the ruins of his career in England. There he contemplates the meaning of the whole experience. This story of "activity and urgency and sterility," he thinks, should really be called *Waste*. The word links him with Granville-Barker, who called one of his plays *Waste,* and with Forster, who entertained the notion in *A Room with a View:* "Waste! That word seemed to sum up the whole of life."[22] "Waste" is an Edwardian word because it encapsulates a guilty knowledge of riches being meaninglessly spent, of an inheritance like that of Bladesover being thoughtlessly dissipated. George takes stock of the "forest of scaffold poles" in the half-built structure of Crest Hill, the "waste of walls and bricks and plaster and shaped stones," and sees the most distressing emblem yet of the condition of England, "the compactest image and sample of all that passes for Progress, of all the advertisement-inflated spending, the aimless building up and pulling down, the enterprise and promise of my age. This was our fruit, this was what we had done, I and my uncle, in the fashion of our time."[23]

Wells cannot end his novel in quite this deadening mood, though neither can he end it happily, with anything like Forster's retreat to redemptive personal relations, let alone wedding bells. As though he had been convinced by Forster's advocacy of impermanence as the right mood for the end of a modern novel, Wells sends George off into an indistinct future of more scientific research—this time on destroyers. In one sense George manifests a longing for apocalypse, a violent cleansing of corruption and waste. He judges the condition of England irremediable and turns his attention to faster, more efficient mechanisms of destruction. In another sense, George simply turns his attention to the abstract ideas of change, impermanence, and flux, alluring and valuable in themselves. The warship George takes on time-trials in the Thames estuary conveys him to the trackless, indeterminate space of the sea. As he steams downriver, George passes England in review—one last comprehensive image, one last chance to recapitulate the present and the past which has led to the present before he reaches the unknown future. The last few pages of *Tono-Bungay,* like the concluding *stretto* of a fugue, gather together all of the previous themes and play them again at a faster tempo. "This is England," George perceives, ". . . what I wanted to give in my book. This!" He goes past grimy suburbs and the Victorian houses of Parliament, where the landlords and lawyers, the railway men and the magnates of commerce go to and fro "in their incurable tradition of commercialised Bladesovery"; behind him are Kew and Hampton Court "with their memories of Kings and Cardinals," ahead newer developments and dingy industrialism; then the "essential London" of Charing Cross railway station, "heart of the world"; then St Paul's, "the very figure of whatever fineness the old Anglican culture achieved"; then bridges and warehouses; and then finally the world of accident and nature, the seaport and the sea: George's ship passes London County Council steamboats named *Caxton, Pepys, Shakespeare,* and he laughs; they seem "wildly out of place, splashing about in that confusion." History is out of place in the great gray space of the future that George and the destroyer reach: "Out to the open we go, to windy freedom and trackless ways. Light after light goes down. England and the Kingdom, Britain and the Empire, the old prides and old devotions, glide abeam, astern, sink down upon the horizon, pass—pass. The river passes—London passes, England passes."[24]

Trackless ways versus narrowing circles. The passing of England versus its preservation in a house and a field. *Tono-Bungay* and *Howards Ends* provide as sharply contrasted a view of the contemporary situation as possible. The pairing of the two works suggests the condition of fiction itself in the last few years of the Edwardian decade. Their achievements show how, in radically different ways, the novel responded to tasks before it.

Howards End is based on an art of exclusion. Forster eliminates irrelevancies and even less important relevancies in the effort to get to the essence of experience, the center of a house or of a personal relation. Exclusion allows him to see life steadily, in terms of the apothegm borrowed from Matthew Arnold; from beginning to end the life of his novel is under his regulating, selecting control as omniscient narrator. He only feints when he begins the narrative with the words "One may as well begin." Nothing is as improvised as that, as casual. In small matters, such as the dresses worn at the first dinner in Howards End, and in large matters, such as statements of moral truth, Forster commands what shall be omitted and what proclaimed.

What he does not do, nor claim to do, is to see life whole. The empire he dismisses, with the confident judgment that its problems are peripheral to his study of England in 1910. London he may visualize, briefly, as a tract of quivering gray, intelligent without purpose and excitable without love, but precisely because its formlessness is inimical to his controlling intelligence as author, he quickly turns away from London as a whole and passes to smaller, more understandable regions—Wickham Place, Ducie Street, the Queen's Hall. There he can get on with his work of fine discriminations, between those who live in flats and those who live in houses, those who can joke about the loss of an umbrella and those who cannot, those who readily admit that Beethoven's Fifth Symphony is the most sublime noise that has ever penetrated the ear of man and those who fall silent because they do not know how to pronounce *Tannhäuser*. There is no reason to expand the spaces of one's fiction when one's most intelligent characters can open up imaginative spaces for themselves, as Margaret "doubles her kingdom" merely by opening a door in Howards End.

Forster excludes from consideration not merely certain places but certain people: "We are not concerned with the very poor. They are unthinkable, and only to be approached by the statistician or the poet. This story deals with gentlefolk, or with those who are obliged to pretend that they are gentlefolk."[25] The "we" in that sentence forms a community between author and readers, and the bond uniting the community is the tacit agreement that only some matters may properly be dealt with in the individualizing domain of fiction. The "we" signifies a body of shared assumptions—that personal relations matter, that personal relations require a minimum of material comfort, and that existences entirely deprived of that comfort are outside of the novelist's ken. In an odd way the "we" of *Howards End* is reminiscent of the "one of us" in *Lord Jim:* Forster's cultural community corresponds to Conrad's equally restricted moral community. But

Forster's pronoun, with all its implications of consensus and limitation, is vastly different in meaning from the one appearing in the last sentence of *Tono-Bungay*, with all its implications of universality: "We are all things that make and pass, striving upon a hidden mission, out to the open sea."

Tono-Bungay is based on an art of inclusion. It admits the randomness of real life and talk generously into its plot, following the theory of novel-writing Wells had devised as early as 1900 in his letter to Bennett: "I want to write novels and before God I *will* write novels. They are the proper stuff for my everyday work, a methodical careful distillation of one's thoughts and sentiments and experiences and impressions."[26] To the young writer the novel held out a promise not of greater artfulness or greater realism or greater contemporaneity—all the things that might have been expected—but rather of greater roominess. The novel was capacious and therefore valuable. This idea Wells elaborated over the course of a decade's writing. He neglected the tightly plotted scientific romance, with its strained, intense visions (*The First Men in the Moon* supplies a metaphor for such visions: "to have the picture of our impression complete, you must bear in mind that we saw it all through a thick bent glass, distorting it as things are distorted by a lens, acute only in the centre of the picture, and very bright there, and towards the edges magnified and unreal").[27] He worked instead to perfect the naturalistic novel of middle-class life, with its leisurely tempo and plentiful opportunities for digression. After *Kipps* and *Tono-Bungay*, at the end of the decade, Wells knew once and for all that the novel he was particularly equipped to write was a discursive thing. Such works were not a mere license for self-indulgence. Wells thought freedom from Jamesian rules and restrictions, freedom to respect his own intellectual waywardness, gave him his best chance to answer "the great moral challenge of the novel," namely to bring people to take a greater interest in each other. Almost as much as Forster, Wells believed in an ideal of connection, "this tremendous work of human reconciliation and elucidation."[28]

In *Tono-Bungay*, which Bennett thought united the verifiable naturalism of novels like *Kipps* with the large manner of the scientific romances, the novel's inclusiveness is an open concern of the narrator.[29] In order to present "the spectacle of man whole," in Bennett's phrase, George Ponderevo wishes to tell the full truth about himself, and to include as much peripheral life as possible. He regrets never having made the acquaintance of royalty, nor of navvies or stokers, nor of "that dusty but attractive class of people who go about on the high-roads drunk but *en famille*." No "we are not concerned" here. Wells specifically chooses to represent Ponderevo as writing a novel, rather than an autobiography or a history, because the novel as Ponderevo defines it is an appealingly open form: "My ideas of the novel all through are comprehensive rather than austere . . . I've reached the criticizing, novel-writing age, and here I am writing mine— my own novel—without having any of the discipline to refrain and omit that I suppose the regular novel-writer acquires." The restraints and rules of the art are impossible for Ponderevo; he must be a "lax, undisciplined story-teller," he must "sprawl and flounder, comment and theorize." The novel is the best place for what are described as Teddy Ponderevo's "novel and incredible ideas." George does speculate about more contrived forms of art, the seventeenth-century pictorial style, say, with its long scrolls of dialogue coming out of the mouths of woodcut figures. For such a symbolic picture George would pose himself and Teddy at work after midnight, elaborating ideas. Or he wishes he could arrange the story of his life in two parallel columns of unequal width, one for the business of Tono-Bungay, the other for home and wife. Or he dreams of a symbolic painting of Teddy as Napoleonic businessman. But in the end, George and Wells realize together that the novel-as-a-discursive-thing is the form best suited to their ambitions. It is inclusive of all they wish to say about England and at the same time inconclusive in the manner they deliberately choose. At one point George reminds his readers that this is "a novel, not a treatise. Don't imagine that I am coming presently to any sort of solution of my difficulties."[30] That hint leads directly to the irresolute ending of *Tono-Bungay*, its final opening outward into the sea and the future.

There was no satisfactory Edwardian synthesis of the kinds of novel-writing demonstrated in *Howards End* and *Tono-Bungay*. On the one hand was Forster's art of control, of character exactly delineated, of moral acuity, of careful ambitions and admitted limits. On the other hand was Wells's art of imaginative power, of fluid characterization, of relative formlessness and artistic courage passing imperceptibly into recklessness. There was a slightly contrived resolution on one side and a slightly brazen irresolution on the other, and no way of connecting the extremes. This failure of connection represents the relative failure of Edwardian fiction. No single novelist put into his work the virtues separately associated with a Forster or a Wells, a James or a Galsworthy, a Conrad or a Bennett. No single novelist managed perfectly to balance his art between the counterclaims of discipline and energy, or to become an ideal mediator between the poet and the statisticiah, those two alternative respondents to England's condition Forster suggests in *Howards End*. In the formal perfection of his art the poet hints that beauty may be achieved; in his random comprehensiveness the statistician describes how men really live. The novelist partakes of both efforts and so, inevitably, seems always to be compromising. But there are compromises and compromises. If the Edwardians are blamed for not producing some amalgam of Wells and Forster, it must in justice be admitted that they did, after all, produce those two novelists with all the disparate excellences of their work, and all the other novelists whose work defines the achievement of Edwardian fiction.

Notes

1. A BALFOURIAN AGE

1. *Westminster Gazette*, Sept. 28, 1908: "That the Edwardian age is more placidly disposed towards such a threat ['your beer will cost you more'] than the times of the King's great grandfather, George III." *Oxford English Dictionary*, Supplement (1933), s.v. "Edwardian." "Georgian" as referring to George V appears promptly in 1910.

2. For attempts to define the "complex and elusive" character of the Edwardian age, see Samuel Hynes, *The Edwardian Turn of Mind* (Princeton: Princeton University Press, 1968), pp. 3-14; Hynes, *Edwardian Occasions* (New York: Oxford University Press, 1972), pp. 1-12; Richard Ellmann, "The Two Faces of Edward," in *Edwardians and Late Victorians*, ed. Ellmann, English Institute Essays 1959 (New York and London: Columbia University Press, 1960), pp. 188-210; Frank Swinnerton, *The Georgian Scene: A Literary Panorama* (New York: Farrar and Rinehart, 1934), pp. 3-16; Lascelles Abercrombie, "Literature," in *Edwardian England*, ed. F. J. C. Hearnshaw (London: Benn, 1933), pp. 185-203. Abercrombie stubbornly attempts to deny that the decade's literature had a spirit of its own.

3. H. G. Wells, "The Scope of the Novel," in *Henry James and H. G. Wells*, ed. Leon Edel and Gordon N. Ray (Urbana: University of Illinois Press, 1958), p. 145.

4. Barbara Tuchman, *The Guns of August* (New York: Macmillan, 1962), p. 46, quoting Haldane's autobiography.

5. Wells, "The Scope of the Novel," *Henry James and H. G. Wells*, p. 147.

6. H. G. Wells, *The New Machiavelli* (New York: Duffield, 1910), p. 122.

7. See C. S. Lewis, *Studies in Words* (Cambridge: Cambridge University Press, 1960).

8. Quoted in Amy Cruse, *After the Victorians* (London: George Allen & Unwin, 1938), p. 15. Canon Bartlett was typically Victorian in his tireless work of slum settlement, expansion of university studies to the working class, and art appreciation among the poor; he authored *Practicable Socialism* in 1907.

9. H. G. Wells, *Experiment in Autobiography* (New York: Macmillan, 1934), p. 523.

10. Wells, *Experiment in Autobiography*, p. 398.

11. Wells, *The New Machiavelli*, p. 458.

12. Arnold Bennett, *The Journals*, ed. Frank Swinnerton (Harmondsworth: Penguin, 1971), p. 236. The anecdote was told to Bennett by Wells.

13. Richard Burton, *Forces in Fiction and Other Essays* (London: Stevens and Brown, 1902), p. 20.

14. John Galsworthy, *The Man of Property* (London: Heinemann, 1906), p. 76. The ungrammatical comparison is not typical.

2. FROM PERSONALITY TO PERSONALITY

1. See Hynes, *The Edwardian Turn of Mind*, pp. 15-17.

2. Arthur Conan Doyle, *The Great Boer War* (London: Smith, Elder, 1900); Doyle, *War in South Africa* (London: Smith, Elder, 1902); Rudyard Kipling, *Traffics and Discoveries* (London: Macmillan, 1904). See also the poems of Kipling, *The Five Nations* (London: Methuen, 1903).

3. Osbert Burdett, *The Last Ten Years of English Literature* (London: Spottiswode, 1907), p. 1.

4. Leon Edel, *Henry James*, vol. IV: *The Treacherous Years* (Philadelphia: Lippincott, 1969), p. 50; Rudyard Kipling, *Something of Myself* (London: Macmillan, 1937), p. 65. See also Charles Carrington, *Rudyard Kipling* (Harmondsworth: Penguin, 1970), pp. 119-120.

5. Quoted in A. St. John Adcock, *Gods of Modern Grub Street* (London: Sampson Low, Marston, 1923), p. 224. Mrs. Braddon was in fact the most popular novelist of all in Edwardian libraries, having an average of 109 works in each of twenty-one lending institutions throughout the nation. See Derek Hudson, "Reading," in *Edwardian England, 1901-1914*, ed. Simon Nowell-Smith (London: Oxford University Press, 1964), p. 310.

6. G. K. Chesterton, *The Napoleon of Notting Hill* (London and New York: John Lane, The Bodley Head, 1904), p. 14.

7. Quoted in Gordon N. Ray, "H. G. Wells Tries to Be a Novelist," *Edwardians and Late Victorians*, p. 131.

8. Wells to Bennett, June 1, 1901, in *Arnold Bennett and H. G. Wells*, ed. Harris Wilson (London: Rupert Hart-Davis, 1960), p. 54.

9. The novel *The Well-Beloved* appeared in 1897 but had previously been published as *The Pursuit of the Well-Beloved* in the *Illustrated London News* and *Harper's Bazar* (sic) of 1892.

10. Bennett to Wells, Feb. 7, 1905, *Arnold Bennett and H. G. Wells*, p. 117. The next year Bennett collaborated with Phillpotts on *The Sinews of War*.

11. Eden Phillpotts, *The Secret Woman* (London: Methuen, 1905), pp. 3-4, 13-14.

12. Bennett to Wells, Nov. 23, 1901, *Arnold Bennett and H. G. Wells*, pp. 66-67.

3. CONTINUITIES OF FORM

1. Mary P. Willcocks, *A Man of Genius* (London and New York: John Lane, 1908), p. 350.

2. Similarly atypical is the Edwardian novel which refers to "the Novel" in general. Such references tend to be weak excuses for some stereotyped turn of plot, as when Jack Trowbridge, at the opening of Guy Boothby's *The League of Twelve*, tells his sister he has just met a mysterious foreigner, the most beautiful woman he has ever seen, and she responds "This is most interesting . . . It is like the commencement of a novel" (London: F. V. White, 1903), p. 32.

3. Gordon N. Ray has demonstrated Wells's authorship of these book reviews in "H. G. Wells Tries to Be a Novelist," *Edwardians and Late Victorians*, pp. 106-159.

4. Alexander Maxwell, Oxford Chancellor's Essay (Oxford: Basil Blackwell, 1905), pp. 3, 5, 11-13.

5. Gordon N. Ray proposes *Kipps* instead as Wells's *Great Expectations* in "H. G. Wells Tries to Be a Novelist," *Edwardians and Late Victorians*, p. 140.

6. Walter Benjamin, "The Storyteller: Reflections on the Works of Nikolai Leskov," in *Illuminations*, ed. Hannah Arendt, trans. Harry Zohn (New York: Harcourt Brace, 1968), pp. 83-84, 87.

7. Reprinted in *The Art of the Novel: Critical Prefaces by Henry James* (New York: Scribner's, 1934), pp. 169, 171, 172.

8. "Normyx," *Unprofessional Tales* (London: T. Fisher Unwin, 1901), p. 151.

9. Joseph Conrad, *Typhoon and Other Stories* (London: Heinemann, 1903), p. 151.

10. Joseph Conrad, *Youth: A Narrative and Two Other Stories* (Edinburgh and London: Blackwood, 1902), pp. 93-94. *Heart of Darkness* was first published in *Blackwood's Magazine*, 1899; "Youth" in *Blackwood's*, 1898.

4. THE UNCRITICAL ATTITUDE

1. Frederick T. Cooper, *Some English Story Tellers* (London: Grant Richards, 1912), p. 10.

2. For a typical attack on the form, see J. M. Kennedy, *English Literature, 1880-1905* (Boston: Small, Maynard, 1913). Kennedy puts it

bluntly ("The novel is one of the lowest forms, if not the lowest form, of creative art," p. 219) and attacks Wells in particular; but his criticism is vitiated by snobbism. For a defense of the novel by an American, see William Lyon Phelps, *The Advance of the English Novel* (New York: Dodd, Mead, 1916), pp. 1-11.

3. The *English Review* was rivaled in seriousness of intention by Orage's *New Age*, for which Arnold Bennett wrote excellent criticism under the name "Jacob Tonson," by Vernon Rendall's *Athenaeum*, and by Lewis Hind's and Lord Alfred Douglas' *Academy*.

4. F. M. Ford, *The Critical Attitude* (London: Duckworth, 1911), p. 33.

5. Walter Besant, *The Art of Fiction* (London: Chatto & Windus, 1902), p. 6.

6. Henry James, "The Art of Fiction," in *The Future of the Novel*, ed. Leon Edel (New York: Vintage, 1956), pp. 5, 20, 12, 25. James's essay was first reprinted in *Partial Portraits* (1888).

7. Henry James, "The Future of the Novel," *The Future of the Novel*, pp. 30, 35, 41.

8. James, "The Future of the Novel," *The Future of the Novel*, p. 32.

9. James, "The Future of the Novel," *The Future of the Novel*, pp. 37-38.

10. Edel, *Henry James*, IV, 350.

11. James to Wells, Nov. 19, 1905, *Henry James and H. G. Wells*, p. 105.

12. James to Wells, Mar. 3, 1911, *Henry James and H. G. Wells*, p. 127.

13. James to Wells, Oct. 11, 1906, *Henry James and H. G. Wells*, p. 111.

14. Edel, *Henry James*, IV, 50.

15. James to Wells, Sept. 23, 1902, *Henry James and H. G. Wells*, p. 81.

16. Wells to Bennett, Sept. 9, 1902, *Arnold Bennett and H. G. Wells*, p. 84.

17. Arnold Bennett, review of *The Finer Grain*, *New Age* 7 (Oct. 27, 1910), reprinted in *The Author's Craft and Other Critical Writings of Arnold Bennett*, ed. Samuel Hynes (Lincoln: University of Nebraska Press, 1969), pp. 130-131.

18. Leon Edel, *Henry James*, vol. V: *The Master* (Philadelphia: Lippincott, 1972), 119.

19. The notice of *The Wings of the Dove* in the young *TLS* (founded 1902) conveys, chiefly by metaphor, an admirable sense of that novel's ambitiousness.

20. Burton, *Forces in Fiction*, p. 8.

21. W. L. Courtney, *The Feminine Note in Fiction* (London: Chapman & Hall, 1904), p. xxx.

5. EDWARDIAN BEST-SELLERS

1. James Joyce, *Ulysses* (New York: Random House, 1961), p. 590.

2. Roger Fulford, "The King," *Edwardian England, 1901-1914*, p. 15, quoting Prince Albert; Cruse, *After the Victorians*, p. 181.

3. George Dangerfield, *The Strange Death of Liberal England* (London: Macgibbon & Kee, 1966 [1935]), p. 348. For an Edwardian confirmation of this opinion, see E. V. Lucas, *Listener's Lure* (London: Methuen, 1906), pp. 32-33.

4. Marie Corelli, *The Devil's Motor* (London: Hodder & Stoughton, 1910), unpaged.

5. On the issue of motoring, see also a reference to Corelli in a 1910 review of C. E. Byles's *Cornish Breakers and Other Poems* (1909): "Though the wild words of the father, on seeing his little son apparently slain by a motor, are natural enough, we cannot help feeling that the attributes of motoring are not wholly Satanic." *Edwardian England, 1901-1914*, p. 308. The *locus classicus* of Edwardian admiration for motoring is Shaw's *Man and Superman*.

6. H. G. Wells, *Anticipations*, 2nd ed. (London: Chapman & Hall, 1902), p. 139.

7. Wells, *Anticipations*, p. 139.

8. Lovat Dickson, *H. G. Wells* (Harmondsworth: Penguin, 1972), p. 171.

9. James, *The Art of the Novel*, pp. 169, 172, 175. See also the preface to Vol. XVII, pp. 241-266.

10. The favorite reading of Ann Veronica's father. H. G. Wells, *Ann Veronica* (London: T. Fisher Unwin, 1901), p. 16.

11. Arnold Bennett, *How to Become an Author* (London: C. Arthur Pearson, 1903), pp. 150-151.

12. Elinor Glyn, *Three Weeks* (London: Duckworth, 1907), pp. 50, 93, 154.

13. George Orwell, "Such, Such Were the Joys," *Collected Essays, Journalism and Letters*, ed. Sonia Orwell and Ian Angus (New York: Harcourt Brace Jovanovich, 1968), IV, 357.

14. Arnold Bennett, *The Grand Babylon Hotel*, 2nd ed. (London: Chatto & Windus, 1902), p. 326.

15. Bennett, *How to Become an Author*, p. 21.

16. Walter Besant, *The Pen and the Book* (London: Burleigh, 1899), pp. 19, 24.

17. Bennett, *How to Become an Author*, p. 149. On the best-seller in general, see Q. D. Leavis, *Fiction and the Reading Public* (London: Chatto & Windus, 1932), pp. 205-273; Claud Cockburn, *Bestseller: The Books That Everyone Read, 1900-1939* (London: Sidgwick & Jackson, 1972).

18. Chesterton, *The Napoleon of Notting Hill*, p. 125.

19. Jeffrey Farnol, *The Broad Highway* (London: Sampson Low, Marston, 1910), pp. 1-2.

20. Swinnerton, *The Georgian Scene*, p. 15.

21. Elinor Glyn, *Romantic Adventure* (New York: Dutton, 1937), p. 131.

22. Glyn, *Three Weeks*, p. 302.

23. H. G. Wells, *Kipps* (London: Macmillan, 1905), p. 241.

24. E. M. Forster, *Howards End* (London: Edward Arnold, 1910), p. 38.

25. Robert Hichens, *The Garden of Allah* (London: Methuen, 1904), p. 520. Another return-to-faith best-seller is Braddon's *The Conflict* (1903).

26. Marie Corelli, *The Master Christian* (London: Methuen, 1900), p. 88.

27. G. K. Chesterton, *The Ball and the Cross* (London: Wells, Gardner, 1909), p. 148.

28. On the secularism of Edwardian literature and its paradoxical liking for religious phraseology, see Ellmann, "The Two Faces of Edward," *Edwardians and Late Victorians*, pp. 191-196.

6. DEPARTURE

1. Edmund Gosse, *Questions at Issue* (London: Heinemann, 1893), p. 31.

2. James, "The Future of the Novel," in *The Future of the Novel*, p. 40.

3. *Complete Tales of Henry James*, ed. Leon Edel (Philadelphia: Lippincott, 1964), XI, 315-16.

4. Frank Swinnerton, *Background with Chorus* (London: Hutchinson, 1956), pp. 16, 18.

5. Swinnerton, *Background with Chorus*, p. 26.

6. Forster, *Howards End*, p. 43.

7. R. A. Scott-James, *Modernism and Romance* (London: John Lane, The Bodley Head, 1908), pp. 16, 86.

8. Wells, *Ann Veronica*, p. 30. Mr. Stanley has in mind Grant Allen's *The Woman Who Did* (1895).

9. Dickson, *H. G. Wells*, pp. 235, 239.

10. On Edwardian censorship, see Hynes, *The Edwardian Turn of Mind*, pp. 212-253, 254-306.

11. James to Wells, June 17, 1900, *Henry James and H. G. Wells*, p. 67.

12. Wells to Bennett, June 15, 1900, *Arnold Bennett and H. G. Wells*, p. 45.

13. Wells, "The Scope of the Novel," *Henry James and H. G. Wells*, pp. 136-137.

14. Arnold Bennett, "Herbert George Wells and his Work," *Arnold Bennett and H. G. Wells*, p. 267. The essay was first published in *Cosmopolitan Magazine* 33 (August 1902): 465-471.

15. Arnold Bennett, "The 'Average Reader' and the Recipe for Popularity," *The Author's Craft*, p. 55. This article became the first chapter of *Fame and Fiction* (1901).

16. Arnold Bennett, "The Fallow Fields of Fiction," *The Author's Craft*, pp. 61-62.

17. Bennett, "The Fallow Fields of Fiction," *The Author's Craft*, pp. 65-66.

18. Bennett, *Journals*, p. 28.

19. Bennett to Wells, Oct. 10, 1897, *Arnold Bennett and H. G. Wells*, p. 36.

20. Virginia Woolf, "Mr. Bennett and Mrs. Brown," reprinted in *The Author's Craft*, p. 270. Woolf's essay first appeared in the *Nation and Athenaeum* 34 (Dec. 1, 1923). Bennett's comment came in "Is the Novel Decaying?" *Cassell's Weekly*, Mar. 28, 1923, p. 47; reprinted in *Things That Have Interested Me*, 3rd ser. (New York: Doran, 1926), pp. 160-163. See also Samuel Hynes, "The Whole Contention Between Mr. Bennett and Mrs. Woolf," *Edwardian Occasions*, pp. 24-38.

21. These remarks come from the second, revised version of "Mr. Bennett and Mrs. Brown," which was given as a paper at Girton College, Cambridge, in May 1924; reprinted in Virginia Woolf, *Collected Essays*, ed. Leonard Woolf (New York: Harcourt Brace, 1967), I, 331, 332.

22. Woolf, *Collected Essays*, pp. 320-321, 327-328.

23. See e.g. the American critic Clayton Hamilton, *The Materials and Methods of Fiction* (New York: Baker & Taylor, 1908), pp. 23-41. Cf. A. St. John Adcock, *Gods of Modern Grub Street*, p. 123.

24. James, *The Art of the Novel*, pp. 31-32. For Edwardian romance and realism, see Hynes, *Edwardian Occasions*, pp. 73-74.

25. Wells, *Ann Veronica*, p. 326.

7. THE ADVENTURE AND ROMANCE AGENCY

1. Erskine Childers, *The Riddle of the Sands* (London: Smith, Elder, 1903), pp. 13, 93-94.

2. Hichens, *The Garden of Allah*, p. 6.

3. H. G. Wells, *Tono-Bungay* (London: Macmillan, 1909), pp. 279-281. Reprinted by permission of the Estate of H. G. Wells.

4. Joseph Conrad and F. M. Hueffer [F. M. Ford], *Romance* (London: Smith, Elder, 1903), pp. 50-51.

5. G. K. Chesterton, *The Club of Queer Trades* (New York and London: Harper, 1905), pp. 44-45.

6. F. M. Ford, *The Benefactor: A Tale of a Small Circle* (London:

Brown, Langham, 1905), p. 50. The sentence quoted refers to the hero Moffat, whose need for vicarious living, via fiction or philanthropy, is described as being like a craving for drink.

7. Ford, *The Benefactor*, p. 173.

8. Wells, *Tono-Bungay*, p. 31.

9. Childers, *The Riddle of the Sands*, p. 1.

10. See e.g. John Halverson and Ian Watt, "The Original Nostromo: Conrad's Source," *Review of English Studies* 10 (1959): 45-52; Jocelyn Baines, *Joseph Conrad* (London: Weidenfeld & Nicolson, 1960), pp. 294-297.

11. R. B. Cunninghame Graham, *Faith* (London: Duckworth, 1909), p. xv.

12. For the figure of the faithful retainer, see David Thorburn, *Conrad's Romanticism* (New Haven: Yale University Press, 1974), pp. 43-54.

13. Conrad and Ford, *Romance*, p. 356.

14. H. G. Wells, *In the Days of the Comet* (London: Macmillan, 1906), p. 194; Conrad, *Youth*, p. 108.

15. Joseph Conrad, *Nostromo* (London: Blackwood, 1904), p. 347.

16. Childers, *The Riddle of the Sands*, pp. 97, 259, 106.

17. John Masefield, *Multitude and Solitude* (London & Edinburgh: T. Nelson, 1909), pp. 104, 150, 147.

18. Masefield, *Multitude and Solitude*, pp. 171, 256, 259.

19. Masefield, *Multitude and Solitude*, p. 47.

20. Paul Zweig, *The Adventurer* (New York: Basic Books, 1974), pp. 34-36.

21. Rudyard Kipling, "On the Great Wall," *Puck of Pook's Hill* (London: Macmillan, 1906), p. 178.

22. Rudyard Kipling, "The Ballad of East and West," *Rudyard Kipling's Verse: Definitive Edition* (New York: Doubleday, Doran, 1940), p. 233. Poems by Kipling, copyright 1909, 1910, reprinted by permission of the National Trust and Doubleday & Company, Inc.

23. *Rudyard Kipling's Verse*, pp. 380, 107, 306, 321.

24. Rudyard Kipling, *Actions and Reactions* (London: Macmillan, 1909), p. 136.

25. G. K. Chesterton, *Heretics* (London: John Lane, The Bodley Head, 1905), pp. 45-46.

26. H. G. Wells, *A Modern Utopia* (London: Chapman & Hall, 1905), pp. 283-284.

27. H. G. Wells, *Discovery of the Future* (London: T. Fisher Unwin, 1902), p. 86.

28. Bennett's fantasias reveal "a faint trace of megalomania in their conception and development, a hugeness of setting and environment, an unparalleled and inexhaustible opulence of color and light, of ostentation and gaiety, of thronging men and women, and the glitter of

jewels and the sheen of priceless fabrics." Cooper, *Some English Story Tellers*, pp. 214-215.

29. Wells, *Tono-Bungay*, pp. 327, 185, 262.

30. H. G. Wells, *The Food of the Gods* (London: Macmillan, 1904), p. 228.

31. Wells, *The Food of the Gods*, p. 317.

32. Wells, *The Food of the Gods*, p. 105.

8. COMPLICATIONS OF IMPERIALISM

1. *Rudyard Kipling's Verse*, p. 524.

2. See Paul Fussell, *The Great War and Modern Memory* (New York and London: Oxford University Press, 1975).

3. A. E. W. Mason, *The Broken Road* (New York: Scribner's, 1908), pp. 27, 355.

4. G. K. Chesterton, *Autobiography* (New York: Sheed & Ward, 1936), p. 145.

5. Arthur Conan Doyle, *The Crime of the Congo* (London: Hutchinson, 1909), p. 8.

6. Joyce, *Ulysses*, p. 335.

7. Brian Inglis, *Roger Casement* (London: Hodder & Stoughton, 1973), p. 92.

8. Joseph Conrad and F. M. Hueffer [F. M. Ford], *The Inheritors* (London: Wm. Heinemann, 1901), pp. 117, 148. On the flyleaf of the copy of *The Inheritors* in the Conrad Collection at Yale is a signed note by Conrad: "There is very little of my actual writing in this work. Discussion there has been in plenty. F. M. H. held the pen."

9. Kipling, *Traffics and Discoveries*, p. 81.

10. Asa Briggs, "The Political Scene," *Edwardian England, 1901-1914*, p. 85; Inglis, *Roger Casement*, p. 125.

11. Kipling, *Traffics and Discoveries*, p. 21.

12. *Rudyard Kipling's Verse*, pp. 299-300, 301; first collected in *The Five Nations* (1903).

13. L. T. Hobhouse, *Liberalism* (London: Williams & Norgate, 1911), pp. 216-217.

14. Chesterton, *Heretics*, p. 265.

15. Barbara Tuchman, *The Proud Tower* (London: Hamish Hamilton, 1966), p. 351.

16. Kipling, *Actions and Reactions*, p. 244.

17. John Buchan, *A Lodge in the Wilderness* (Edinburgh and London: Wm. Blackwood, 1906), pp. 3, 32, 5-6.

18. Buchan, *A Lodge in the Wilderness*, pp. 28-29, 44, 287, 290, 204.

19. Buchan, *A Lodge in the Wilderness*, pp. 248, 136, 148, 258.

9. THE BLACK PANTHER

1. Wells, "The Scope of the Novel," *Henry James and H. G. Wells*, p. 133. On fiction and imperialism, see Alan Sandison, *The Wheel of Empire* (London: Macmillan, 1967); Susanne Howe, *Novels of Empire* (New York: Columbia University Press, 1949).

2. Richard Ellmann, *James Joyce* (New York: Oxford University Press, 1965), pp. 178-181.

3. M. P. Shiel, *The Purple Cloud* (London: Chatto & Windus, 1901), pp. 78, 70.

4. Wells, *Tono-Bungay*, p. 417.

5. Wells, *Tono-Bungay*, p. 418.

6. Still more extraneous is Wells's curious description of the sea-captain who conveys Ponderevo to Africa—a portrait of Conrad in all probability. See Bernard Bergonzi, *The Turn of a Century* (London: Macmillan, 1973), pp. 95-98.

7. Dickson, *H. G. Wells*, p. 123.

8. H. G. Wells, *First and Last Things* (London: Archibald Constable, 1908), pp. 135-136.

9. Wells, *In the Days of the Comet*, p. 232.

10. Bennett, "Herbert George Wells and His Work," *Arnold Bennett and H. G. Wells*, p. 265.

11. H. G. Wells, *The First Men in the Moon* (London: George Newnes, 1901), pp. 47, 114.

12. Wells, *The First Men in the Moon*, pp. 129, 233.

13. W. H. Hudson, *Green Mansions: A Romance of the Tropical Forest* (London: Duckworth, 1904), pp. 60-61.

14. J. M. Barrie's *Peter Pan in Kensington Gardens* appeared in 1904, the year of *Green Mansions.*

15. John Buchan, *Prester John* (London: T. Nelson, 1910), p. 350.

10. CONRAD AND ADVENTURE

1. See E. K. Hay, *The Political Novels of Joseph Conrad* (Chicago and London: University of Chicago Press, 1963); R. F. Lee, *Conrad's Colonialism* (The Hague: Mouton, 1969); Avrom Fleishman, *Conrad's Politics* (Baltimore: Johns Hopkins University Press, 1967).

2. Thorburn, *Conrad's Romanticism*, pp. 26-30.

3. Conrad and Ford, *Romance*, pp. 30, 212, 182, 250.

4. Conrad and Ford, *Romance*, p. 132.

5. Joseph Conrad, *Lord Jim* (London: Blackwood, 1900), p. 230.

6. Conrad, *Lord Jim*, pp. 233-34, 242-43. The same stylistic deflation is visible on p. 2: expansive remarks about the loving devotion of a ship-chandler's clerk to a visiting captain are followed by the sentence, "Later on the bill is sent in."

7. Conrad, *Lord Jim,* p. 184.

8. A. E. W. Mason, *The Four Feathers* (London: Smith, Elder, 1902), pp. 39, 53. Not all adventure fictions were as sanguine about the redemptive value of action abroad. In Somerset Maugham's *The Explorer* (1907) the coward George Allerton signally fails to redeem himself during an antislavery expedition in Africa.

9. Mason, *The Four Feathers,* p. 51.

10. See Baines, *Joseph Conrad,* pp. 212, 223, 235, 241.

11. Conrad, *Youth,* p. 58.

12. Henry James, *The Golden Bowl* (London: Methuen, 1905), p. 1.

13. Hynes, *The Edwardian Turn of Mind,* pp. 24-32.

14. Wells, *The First Men in the Moon,* p. 5.

15. Quoted in David D. Harvey, *Ford Madox Ford, 1873-1939: A Bibliography of Works and Criticism* (copyright © 1962 by Princeton University Press), pp. 147-148. Reprinted by permission of Princeton University Press. Ford's poem first appeared in the *Daily Mail* (1907).

16. Conrad, *Youth,* pp. 54, 56-57.

17. Conrad, *Youth,* pp. 70, 72, 107, 104.

18. Conrad, *Youth,* p. 121.

19. Conrad, *Youth,* pp. 151, 61-62.

20. Conrad, *Youth,* p. 141.

21. Conrad, *Lord Jim,* p. 364.

22. Conrad, *Youth,* p. 109.

23. Conrad, *Nostromo,* p. 21.

24. Conrad, *Nostromo,* p. 434.

25. Conrad, *Nostromo,* pp. 70, 137, 311.

26. Edward Said, *Beginnings* (New York: Basic Books, 1971), pp. 115-116.

27. Hobhouse, *Liberalism,* pp. 42-43. See also George Orwell in "Shooting an Elephant" (1936): "when the white man turns tyrant it is his own freedom that he destroys. He becomes a sort of hollow, posing dummy, the conventionalized figure of a sahib . . . He wears a mask, and his face grows to fit it." *Collected Essays, Journalism and Letters,* I, 239.

28. Conrad, *Nostromo,* p. 40.

29. Conrad, *Nostromo,* pp. 175, 37, 90, 89.

30. Conrad, *Nostromo,* pp. 123, 185-186, 42-43.

31. Antonia was elaborated, one suspects, with the aid of Ford. In the MS of *Nostromo,* now at Yale, a fragment from Part II, Chapter 5, is in Ford's hand (pp. 145-154 of the published text), and it is probable that Ford composed these pages. See Conrad to Pinker, Aug. 22, 1903, quoted in Baines, *Joseph Conrad,* pp. 291-292; Arthur Mizener, *The Saddest Story* (New York and Cleveland: World, 1971), pp. 89-91. The fragment involves Decoud and Antonia; whether or not Ford wrote it, his notion of idealistic young womanhood (as in Nancy of *The Good Soldier*) seems to influence Antonia here and elsewhere in *Nostromo.*

32. Conrad, *Nostromo*, p. 172.
33. Conrad, *Nostromo*, p. 443. Cf. a similar vision in Wells, *Love and Mr. Lewisham* (London and New York: Harper, 1900), p. 139: "She saw the grandiose vision of the future she had cherished, suddenly rolled aside and vanishing, more and more splendid as it grew more and more remote—like a dream at a waking moment. The vision of her inevitable loneliness came to replace it, clear and acute. She saw herself alone and small in a huge desolation—infinitely pitiful, Lewisham callously receding."
34. Joseph Conrad, *The Secret Agent* (London: Methuen, 1907), pp. 346-347.
35. Joseph Conrad, *Lord Jim: A Tale* (London and Toronto: J. M. Dent, 1917), p. ix. Conrad is here also making the Jamesian point that the artistic imagination needs silence or mystery. Just as James preferred not to hear the conclusions of the anecdotes which were to become the "germs" of his fiction, Conrad prefers that the real-life Jim be silent—to give the novelist room to work in.
36. Conrad, *Nostromo*, p. 215.

11. THE THEME OF RECESSIONAL

1. Dec. 6, and Sept. 10, 1897, Bennett, *The Journals*, pp. 42, 33-34.
2. *The Poems of William Watson* (New York: John Lane; London: John Lane, The Bodley Head, 1905), II, 95-96. The lines here and in epigraph to Part Two are used by permission of Harrap Limited.
3. Kipling, *Actions and Reactions*, p. 176.
4. Carrington, *Rudyard Kipling*, p. 434.
5. *Rudyard Kipling's Verse*, p. 293.
6. Kipling, *Something of Myself*, p. 178.
7. Carrington, *Rudyard Kipling*, p. 433.
8. Carrington, *Rudyard Kipling*, p. 383. Cf. Kipling to James Conland, July 24, 1900: "Now we are putting up a tin drill-shed where they [rifle club members] can drill and practice Morris-tube shooting in the winter. An American workman would have run it up in a week. I've had to wait five—for non-delivery of materials and their slack laziness. The contractor who supplies the ironwork invited me to look around his forge the other day. Says I: 'Yes it would be all right if we lived in Queen Elizabeth's time. It's only three hundred years out of date—all your machinery.' " Carrington, *Rudyard Kipling*, pp. 376-377. See also the poem "Chant-Pagan" from *The Five Nations*, where a Tommy explains why he cannot stay in England after having known the greater freedoms of South Africa.
9. Wells, *Tono-Bungay*, p. 328.
10. Kipling, *Puck of Pook's Hill*, pp. 12, 13, 14.
11. Kipling, *Something of Myself*, p. 190.

12. Rudyard Kipling, *Rewards and Fairies* (London: Macmillan, 1910), pp. 140, 263.

13. Kipling, *Something of Myself*, p. 186.

14. James, "The Third Person," *Complete Tales of Henry James*, XI, 137.

15. C. F. G. Masterman et al., *To Colonise England: A Plea for a Policy* (London: T. Fisher Unwin, 1907), p. 3.

16. Asa Briggs, "The Political Scene," *Edwardian England, 1901-1914*, p. 47.

17. Arnold Bennett, *Clayhanger* (New York: Doran, 1910), p. 456.

18. Henry James, *The Wings of the Dove* (Westminster: Archibald Constable, 1902), p. 46.

19. In *Howards End* Leonard Bast walks all night long in an attempt to capture the essence of nature. For a review of Edward Thomas' countryside books, see Hynes, *Edwardian Occasions*, pp. 91-97.

20. Frank Howes, "Music," *Edwardian England, 1901-1914*, p. 422.

21. E. V. Lucas, *Reading, Writing, and Remembering: A Literary Record* (London: Methuen, 1932), p. 180.

22. Edel, *Henry James*, IV, 160, 251.

23. Edel, *Henry James*, IV, 242; Edel, *Henry James*, V, 152; Edel, *Henry James*, IV, 239.

24. James to Wells, Dec. 9, 1900, *Henry James and H. G. Wells*, p. 68.

25. Wells, *Experiment in Autobiography*, p. 393.

26. Wells, *Experiment in Autobiography*, p. 488.

27. George Gissing, *The Private Papers of Henry Ryecroft* (Westminster: Archibald Constable, 1904), p. 60.

28. Gissing, *The Private Papers of Henry Ryecroft*, pp. 82, 96-97, 150.

12. CONTINENTAL RESCUES AND AUTUMNAL AFFAIRS

1. Henry Harland, *My Friend Prospero* (New York and London: John Lane, The Bodley Head, 1904), p. 17.

2. E. M. Forster, *Where Angels Fear to Tread* (Edinburgh and London: Blackwood, 1905), p. 41.

3. Cf. James, "Broken Wings": "they gave themselves so to the great irony—the vision of the comic in contrasts—that precedes surrenders and extinctions" (*Complete Tales of Henry James*, XI, 236).

4. E. M. Forster, *A Room with a View* (London: Edward Arnold, 1977), pp. 161, 55, 85. Miss Lavish is apparently modeled on Emily Spender, great-aunt of Stephen Spender, whom Forster and his mother encountered in Perugia in 1901. *Soldier for a Day* is one of her Italian novels. See P. N. Furbank, *E. M. Forster: A Life* (New York: Harcourt Brace Jovanovich, 1976), I, 87.

5. Forster, *A Room with a View*, pp. 154, 166, 26, 156.

6. Forster, *Where Angels Fear to Tread*, pp. 235, 196.

7. E. M. Forster, *Where Angels Fear to Tread*, ed. Oliver Stallybrass (London: Edward Arnold, 1975), p. ix. The present title was supplied by E. J. Dent.

8. Forster, *Where Angels Fear to Tread* (1905), p. 256.

9. Henry James, *The Ambassadors* (London: Methuen, 1903), p. 251.

10. James, *The Ambassadors*, pp. 216, 161, 357.

11. James, *The Ambassadors*, pp. 457-458.

12. Hugh Walpole, *Maradick at Forty* (New York: Doran, 1914), pp. 196, 241; first published London: Smith, Elder, 1910.

13. Walpole, *Maradick at Forty*, pp. 302, 283.

14. Walpole, *Maradick at Forty*, pp. 369, 377.

15. James, "Broken Wings," *Complete Tales of Henry James*, XI, 233.

16. James, "The Beast in the Jungle," *Complete Tales of Henry James*, XI, 397.

17. Ford, *The Benefactor*, p. 349.

18. Leonard Merrick, *Conrad in Quest of his Youth* (London: Grant Richards, 1903), p. 291.

19. Lucas, *Listener's Lure*, pp. 204, 38. Sir Herbert is a stock figure. Cf. Alexander MacKenzie, the returned traveler in Somerset Maugham's *The Explorer*, whose "pride in the great empire which had sprung from that small island, a greater Rome in a greater world, dissolved into love as his wandering thoughts took him to green meadows and rippling streams" (New York: Burt, 1909), p. 178. MacKenzie falls in love with a young woman, encounters difficulties, and departs for the Congo Free State. Other returning men-of-affairs appear in Ian Hay's novels, such as *A Man's Man* (1909).

20. E. V. Lucas, *Over Bemerton's* (London: Methuen, 1908), pp. 21-22.

21. Lucas, *Over Bemerton's*, p. 7.

22. James, "The Bench of Desolation," *Complete Tales of Henry James*, XII, 372.

23. Wells, *The New Machiavelli*, p. 283.

13. THE BACKWARD HUNT FOR THE HOMELY

1. John Galsworthy, *The Country House* (London: Heinemann, 1907), pp. 133-134.

2. For the English country house in fiction from James to Waugh see Richard Gill, *Happy Rural Seat* (New Haven and London: Yale University Press, 1972), esp. pp. 95-132.

3. Galsworthy, *The Country House*, p. 49.

4. Arnold Bennett, *The Grand Babylon Hotel*, p. 49.

5. Hugh Walpole, *The Wooden Horse* (London: Smith, Elder, 1909), p. 19.

6. Bennett, review of *Actions and Reactions* in *New Age* 6 (November 1909), *The Author's Craft*, pp. 182-185.

7. *Rudyard Kipling's Verse*, p. 485.

8. Kipling, *Traffics and Discoveries*, p. 327. It is these lines that underlie T. S. Eliot's images of quick hidden movement in "Burnt Norton."

9. "They" is autobiographical insofar as it draws on Kipling's grief at the death of his daughter Josephine.

10. *The Notebooks of Henry James*, ed. F. O. Matthiessen and K. B. Murdock (New York: Oxford University Press, 1961), p. 200.

11. James, "The Great Good Place," *Complete Tales of Henry James*, XI, 32.

12. Henry James, *The Outcry* (New York: Scribner's, 1911), p. 47.

13. James, "Broken Wings," *Complete Tales of Henry James*, XI, 219.

14. James, *The Outcry*, p. 25.

15. James, "Flickerbridge," *Complete Tales of Henry James*, XI, 335, 337.

16. Phyllis Bottome, *The Master Hope* (London: Hurst & Blackett, 1904), p. 16.

17. James, "Broken Wings," *Complete Tales of Henry James*, XI, 218.

18. Galsworthy, *The Country House*, p. 10.

19. Galsworthy, *The Country House*, p. 128.

20. Galsworthy, *The Man of Property*, p. 264.

21. Galsworthy, *The Man of Property*, p. 102.

22. Wells, *Experiment in Autobiography*, pp. 6-7.

23. Wells, *In the Days of the Comet*, p. 3.

24. Wells, *The First Men in the Moon*, p. 52.

25. James, "Julia Bride," *Complete Tales of Henry James*, XII, 160.

26. Wells, *Love and Mr. Lewisham*, p. 74.

27. H. G. Wells, *Twelve Stories and a Dream* (London: Macmillan, 1903), p. 4.

28. Wells, *Experiment in Autobiography*, p. 393.

29. Wells, *The Food of the Gods*, p. 237; Wells, *In the Days of the Comet*, pp. 220, 297.

30. Wells, *Ann Veronica*, pp. 10, 34, 47, 64.

31. Wells, *The Food of the Gods*, pp. 159, 161.

32. Arnold Bennett, "The Novel-Reading Public," *The Author's Craft*, pp. 81, 76.

33. The "sudden alteration of the self" is a central miracle for the Ed-

wardians. See Ellmann, *Edwardians and Late Victorians*, pp. 198-199.

34. Wells to Bennett, Sept. 25, 1905, *Arnold Bennett and H. G. Wells*, p. 121.

35. Lucas, *Reading, Writing, and Remembering*, p. 194.

36. Arnold Bennett, *Buried Alive* (London: Chapman & Hall, 1908), p. 117.

37. Arnold Bennett, *The Old Wives' Tale* (London: Chapman & Hall, 1908), pp. 2, 4.

38. Arnold Bennett, *Anna of the Five Towns* (London: Chatto & Windus, 1902), pp. 8, 17.

39. Bennett, *Clayhanger*, pp. 8, 24.

40. Bennett, *The Old Wives' Tale*, p. 161.

41. Bennett, *Clayhanger*, p. 137.

42. Bennett, *Anna of the Five Towns*, p. 285.

43. John Gross, *The Rise and Fall of the Man of Letters* (New York: Macmillan, 1969), p. 215.

44. Bennett, *Anna of the Five Towns*, p. 186.

45. Jan. 12, 1897, Bennett, *Journals*, p. 28.

46. Bennett, *Clayhanger*, p. 207.

47. Henry James, *Notes on Novelists* (New York: Scribner's, 1914), p. 331.

14. THIS STRANGE LONELINESS OF MILLIONS IN A CROWD

1. *Rudyard Kipling's Verse*, pp. 96, 98, first collected in *The Five Nations*, 1903.

2. Mason, *The Broken Road*, p. 151.

3. Chesterton, *The Napoleon of Notting Hill*, pp. 126-132.

4. Joseph Conrad, *The Nigger of the "Narcissus"* (London: Heinemann, 1898 [for 1897]), p. 244.

5. Conrad, *The Nigger of the "Narcissus,"* pp. 242-243, 244-246.

6. E. V. Lucas, *Listener's Lure*, p. 13.

7. Wells, *A Modern Utopia*, pp. 317-325.

8. Bottome, *The Master Hope*, p. 28.

9. James, *The Wings of the Dove*, p. 48.

10. James, "The Papers," *Complete Tales of Henry James*, XII, 14.

11. Wells, *Ann Veronica*, p. 144.

12. Wells, *The New Machiavelli*, p. 9.

13. Wells, *The New Machiavelli*, p. 154.

14. Wells, *The New Machiavelli*, p. 203.

15. Forster, *Howards End*, p. 105.

16. Dickson, *H. G. Wells*, p. 117.

17. John Galsworthy, *The Island Pharisees* (London: Heinemann, 1908), p. 112.

18. Galsworthy, *The Country House*, p. 123.

19. Galsworthy, *The Country House*, pp. 85, 261.

20. Ford, *The Critical Attitude*, p. 96.

21. See Hynes, *The Edwardian Turn of Mind*, pp. 77, 83.

22. John Galsworthy, *A Commentary* (London: Grant Richards, 1908), p. 18.

23. Arnold Bennett, review of *A Commentary* in *New Age* 3 (June 1908), reprinted in *The Author's Craft*, p. 203.

24. John Galsworthy, *Fraternity* (London: Heinemann, 1909), pp. 115, 128.

25. Galsworthy, *Fraternity*, pp. 26, 144.

26. Galsworthy, *Fraternity*, p. 32.

27. G. K. Chesterton, *The Man Who Was Thursday* (Bristol: Arrowsmith; London: Simpkin, Marshall, 1908), pp. 134-135; Conrad, *The Secret Agent*, pp. 141, 208.

28. H. G. Wells, *The Sea Lady* (London: Methuen, 1902), pp. 41, 240. In *Experiment in Autobiography* Wells offers submergence as a formal simile for the oppressive state of contemporary living: "We are like early amphibians, so to speak, struggling out of the waters that have covered our kind, into the air, seeking to breathe in a new fashion and emancipate ourselves from long-questioned necessities. At last it becomes for us a case of air or nothing. But the new land has not yet definitely emerged from the waters, and we swim distressfully in an element we wish to abandon" (p. 3).

29. T. S. Eliot, "The Love Song of J. Alfred Prufrock," *Collected Poems, 1909-1962* (New York: Harcourt, Brace & World, 1963), pp. 7, 5. Reprinted by permission of Harcourt Brace Jovanovich, Inc., and Faber and Faber, Ltd.

30. Ford and Conrad, *The Inheritors*, p. 68.

31. Galsworthy, *The Man of Property*, p. 317.

32. Galsworthy, *The Island Pharisees*, p. 41.

33. Chesterton, *The Napoleon of Notting Hill*, pp. 149, 291.

34. Chesterton, *Autobiography*, pp. 136-137.

35. Chesterton, *The Man Who Was Thursday*, p. 53.

36. *Conrad's Prefaces*, ed. Edward Garnett (London: Dent, 1937), p. 108.

37. Conrad, *The Secret Agent*, p. 78.

38. See the discussion of the theme of fragmentation in Fleishman, *Conrad's Politics*, pp. 187-214.

39. Edgar Wallace, *The Four Just Men* (London: Tallis, 1905), p. 146.

40. "Judging from the ordinary occupants of the streets one is apt to think of London as a city solely made up of the acute, the knowing, the worldly, the blasé. But hidden away behind sun-blinds in quiet squares and crescents, there dwells another vast population . . . an army of the Ignorantly Innocent, in whose sheltered seclusion a bus-ride is an event, and a day spent amongst the traffic of the West End an occasion long to be remembered." July 22, 1896, Bennett, *Journals*, p. 20.

15. THE CONDITION OF ENGLAND AND THE CONDITION OF FICTION

1. C. F. G. Masterman, *The Condition of England* (London: Methuen, 1909), p. vii.

2. See e.g. pp. 236-237. Masterman read Wells's novel in proof.

3. Kipling, *Actions and Reactions*, pp. 83-84, 93, 95-96, 101.

4. Hynes, *The Edwardian Turn of Mind*, p. 74.

5. Masterman, *The Condition of England*, pp. 49-50, 230.

6. Galsworthy, *The Island Pharisees*, pp. ix, xi.

7. Galsworthy, *The Island Pharisees*, pp. 22, 17, 30, 32, 56, 87.

8. Galsworthy, *The Island Pharisees*, p. 136.

9. See Hynes, *The Edwardian Turn of Mind*, pp. 72-86.

10. Hobhouse, *Liberalism*, pp. 111, 121.

11. Forster, *Howards End*, p. 121.

12. Forster, *Howards End*, pp. 172, 182-183, 267.

13. E. M. Forster, "Pessimism in Literature," in *Albergo Empedocle and Other Writings*, ed. George H. Thomson (New York: Liveright, 1971), pp. 135, 137.

14. Forster, *Howards End*, p. 164.

15. W. H. Harvey, *Character and the Novel* (London: Chatto & Windus, 1965), p. 24.

16. For a discussion of *Tono-Bungay* as a condition-of-England novel, see David Lodge, *The Language of Fiction* (London: Routledge & Kegan Paul; New York: Columbia University Press, 1966), pp. 214-242.

17. Wells, *Tono-Bungay*, pp. 98, 121.

18. Wells, *Tono-Bungay*, p. 275.

19. Wells, *Tono-Bungay*, pp. 310, 317, 306.

20. Wells, *Tono-Bungay*, pp. 199, 398.

21. Wells, *Tono-Bungay*, p. 462.

22. Forster, *A Room with a View*, p. 195.

23. Wells, *Tono-Bungay*, pp. 437-438.

24. Wells, *Tono-Bungay*, pp. 484-490.

25. Forster, *Howards End*, p. 43.

26. Wells to Bennett, June 15, 1900, *Arnold Bennett and H. G. Wells*, p. 45.

27. Wells, *The First Men in the Moon*, p. 91.

28. Wells, "The Scope of the Novel," *Henry James and H. G. Wells*, p. 152.

29. Arnold Bennett, review of *Tono-Bungay* in *New Age* 4 (Mar. 4, 1909), reprinted in *The Author's Craft*, p. 200.

30. Wells, *Tono-Bungay*, pp. 4, 6, 8, 79, 252.

Index

Adventurism, myth of, 83, 97, 98, 100
Anarchism as fictional topic, 229-234
Austen, Jane, 16, 202
Austin, Alfred, 1

Bailey, Henry Christopher, 49
Balfour, Arthur James, 4
Ballantyne, R. M., 79, 122
Balzac, Honoré de, 63, 71
Barclay, Florence, 189, 200
Baring, Maurice, 22
Barnett, Canon Samuel, 7
Barrie, J. M., 20, 161
Beerbohm, Max, 23, 48
Belgian Congo, 103-105, 133-139, 145
Belloc, Hilaire: *Emmanuel Burden*, 104; "The South Country," 168
Benjamin, Walter, 28-29
Bennett, Arnold, 12, 16-17, 18, 20, 22, 37, 49, 66, 69, 70, 80, 117, 192, 235, 236; on James, 43-44; and romance of manufacture, 68, 156; on Galsworthy, 224; on *Tono-Bungay*, 254; *Anna of the Five Towns*, 155-156, 210-213; *Buried Alive*, 184, 185, 208, 210; *Clayhanger*, 8, 68, 74, 165-166, 210-214; "The Fallow Fields of Fiction," 66-68; *The Gates of Wrath*, 208, 209; *The Grand Babylon Hotel*, 23, 51, 94, 191, 208, 209; *Hilda Lessways*, 8, 70; *Hugo*, 208-209; *Journals*, 9, 67, 155-156, 213-214, 233; *The Old Wives' Tale*, 23, 24, 71, 210-213; *The Sinews of*

War (with Phillpotts), 208
Besant, Walter, 35; *All in a Garden Fair*, 14; *The Art of Fiction*, 37-38; *The Pen and the Book*, 22, 51-52
Best-sellers, 10, 45-57
Bildungsromane, 212, 246
Blackwood, Algernon, 48, 61
Boer War, 5-6, 12, 103, 105-108
Booth, Charles, 221
Booth, General William, 221
Boothby, Guy, 229-230
Borrow, George, 167
Bottome, Phyllis: *The Master Hope*, 73, 200, 218, 233; *Raw Material*, 73, 221
Bowen, Marjorie, 49
Braddon, M. E., 14
Bramah, Ernest, 48
Briggs, Asa, 165
Buchan, John, 165, 235; *A Lodge in the Wilderness*, 109-111, 192; "No-Man's Land," 113-114; *Prester John*, 122-123; *The Watcher by the Threshold*, 84
Burdett, Osbert, 13
Burton, Richard, 10, 44
Butler, Samuel, 14, 171

Caine, Hall, 12, 43, 52; *The Eternal City*, 229
Campbell-Bannerman, Sir Henry, 164
Carlyle, Thomas, 236
Casement, Roger, 103, 104
Censorship, 63-64
Chesterton, G. K., 13, 15, 53; and anti-imperialism, 107-108; *Autobiography*, 103, 229; *The Ball and*

the Cross, 56-57; *The Club of Queer Trades*, 80-81, 82; *Heretics*, 56, 92, 93; *The Man Who Was Thursday*, 82, 166, 226, 229-230; *The Napoleon of Notting Hill*, 15, 26, 216, 228-229
Childers, Erskine, 61, 77, 83, 86-87, 90, 141
Churchill, Winston, 240
Cobbett, William, 239
Coburn, Alvin Langdon, 215
Collins, Wilkie, 14
Condition-of-England fiction, 235-251
Conrad, Joseph, 11, 12, 36, 57, 84, 170, 235, 236; and frame-tale, 31-34; and imperialism, 124-125; "Amy Foster," 33, 195; "An Anarchist," 231; *Heart of Darkness*, 33-34, 35, 85, 89, 104, 119, 121, 128, 133-142, 147, 152, 167; "The Informer," 231; *The Inheritors* (with Ford), 104, 228; *Lord Jim*, 18, 32, 35, 83, 86, 87, 89, 124-125, 128-133, 134, 140, 147, 149, 152, 167, 242, 252; *The Nigger of the "Narcissus,"* 20, 32, 155, 216-218, 228, 231; *Nostromo*, 26, 85-86, 90, 101, 115, 125, 128, 142-152, 201, 231, 232; "An Outpost of Progress," 104, 134; *Romance* (with Ford), 80, 85, 125-127, 128, 133, 152; *The Rover*, 127; *The Secret Agent*, 7, 23, 82, 84, 149, 167, 220, 226, 227, 230-234; *Typhoon*, 127, 146; *Under Western Eyes*, 50; *Victory*, 127; "Youth," 33, 126, 134, 167
Conservatism in fictional methods, 5, 13, 20-34
Corelli, Marie, 45, 52; *The Devil's Motor*, 46-47; *The Master Christian*, 56; *The Sorrows of Satan*, 55
Country houses, 7, 8, 109, 189-214, 246-247
Courtney, W. L., 44
Craigie, Pearl M. T. *See* "Hobbes, John Oliver"
Crane, Stephen and Cora, 8, 170
Crockett, S. R., 20

Cust, Harry, 9

"Danby, Frank" (Julia Frankau), 82
Dangerfield, George, 45
Davies, W. H., 239
De la Mare, Walter, 235; *Henry Brocken*, 167; *The Return*, 25, 182
De Morgan, William, 15
Dickens, Charles, 27, 95, 110, 202, 205, 236; influence of, 14-17; *Little Dorrit*, 228
Dickinson, Goldsworthy Lowes, 109, 240, 241
Disraeli, Benjamin, 221
Douglas, George ("Normyx"), 19-20
Douglas, Norman, 31
Doyle, Arthur Conan, 12, 49; *The Crime of the Congo*, 103; *The Hound of the Baskervilles*, 191

Edward VII, King, 5, 12, 45
"Edwardian," meaning of term, 3-4, 6-7
Eliot, George, 16, 38, 210
Eliot, T. S., 13; "The Love Song of J. Alfred Prufrock," 227-228; *The Waste Land*, 69
Ellis, Havelock, 155
Ellmann, Richard, 209
Englishness, as fictional topic, 167, 168, 190, 192, 195
English Review, The, 36

Fantasy, 48
Farnol, Jeffrey, 53, 168
Ficelles, 24
Firbank, Ronald, 48
First World War, 100, 159
Folk Song Society, 168
Ford, Ford Madox, 22, 28, 170; and "impressionism," 25; on Galsworthy, 223; *The Benefactor*, 82, 183-184; *The Critical Attitude*, 36-37; *The Fifth Queen* trilogy, 49; *The Good Soldier*, 130; *The "Half Moon,"* 82; *The Inheritors* (with Conrad), 104, 228; "The Pro-Consuls," 136; *Romance* (with Conrad), 80, 85, 125-127, 128, 152

Forster, E. M., 11, 23, 24, 164, 235; *Howards End*, 26, 47, 55, 61, 69, 72-73, 165, 170, 174, 175, 194, 196, 201, 202, 220, 224, 241-245, 246, 251-253, 255; *The Longest Journey*, 171; *A Passage to India*, 23, 102; "Pessimism in Literature," 244; *A Room with a View*, 173-176, 186, 250; *Where Angels Fear to Tread*, 173, 174, 176-177, 183
Frame-tale, 28-34, 162-163
Frankau, Julia. *See* "Danby, Frank"

Galsworthy, John, 5, 12, 23, 24, 36, 37, 60, 69, 70, 71, 167, 235; *A Commentary*, 7, 221, 223-224, 225, 238; *The Country House*, 182, 189, 190-191, 195, 200-202, 203, 222; *Fraternity*, 182, 183-184, 220, 222, 224-226, 227; *The Island Pharisees*, 8, 26, 73, 220, 221, 228, 232-240; *The Man of Property*, 10-11, 68, 202-204, 228; *A Motley*, 221
Gardiner, A. G., 164
Garnett, Richard, 35
Gaskell, Elizabeth, 110
Georgian period, 13, 68, 69
Ghost-stories, 48-49
Gissing, George, 15; *The Private Papers of Henry Ryecroft*, 25, 171-172, 217-218
Glyn, Elinor, 81; *Three Weeks*, 49-50, 53, 54-55, 208
Gosse, Edmund, 58, 60; *Father and Son*, 14, 171
Graham, R. B. Cunninghame, 84
Grahame, Kenneth, 48
Granville-Barker, Harley, 249-250
Greene, Graham, 94-95
Griffith, George Chetwynd, 13-14
Gross, John, 212

Haggard, Rider, 79, 168
Haldane, Viscount, 4
Hardy, Thomas, 17-20, 21, 29, 57, 155
Harland, Henry, 59, 173
Hay, Ian, 221

Henley, W. E., 1, 93
Hewlett, Maurice, 49, 63, 168
Hichens, Robert, 56, 78, 99, 141
Historical romances, 49
"Hobbes, John Oliver" (Pearl M. T. Craigie), 74
Hobhouse, L. T., 107; *Liberalism*, 240-241
Hobson, J. A., 101, 240
Hodgson, W. B., 164
Hope, Anthony, 127, 190; *The God in the Car*, 94; *The Great Miss Driver*, 27
Howarth, E. G., 221
Hudson, W. H., 137; *Green Mansions*, 120-121
Hynes, Samuel, 3, 135

Imperialism, 12, 46, 60, 90-92, 99-111, 112-123, 124-125, 130-131, 133-140, 143-146
Impressionism, 21, 25
Inheritance and repossession as fictional themes, 157, 191-195, 196, 209, 243
Initiation as fictional theme, 86-89, 102, 129
Innovation in fictional methods, 13, 40, 58, 60-63, 71-72; seeing "for the first time," 20, 67; freshness in Edwardian fiction, 66
Insularity, 47, 165, 190, 195
Ireland, issue of Home Rule in, 25, 101, 106, 113

James, Henry, 11, 12, 16, 22, 24, 36, 57, 127, 169-170, 235; correspondence with Wells, 41-43, 64-65; isolation of, 41-44; and Lamb House, 156; on imperialism, 170; and Walpole, 180-181; on Bennett, 214; "The Altar of the Dead," 30; *The Ambassadors*, 27, 49, 177-180, 183, 199; "The Art of Fiction," 38-39, 64; *The Awkward Age*, 169, 187; "The Beast in the Jungle," 182-183; "The Bench of Desolation," 183, 187; "Broken Wings," 167, 182, 184, 198, 200, 201; *The Finer Grain*, 43; "Flickerbridge," 199; "The Future of the Novel," 39-41, 64; *The Golden Bowl*, 27, 135, 167, 215; "The Great Good Place," 165, 197, 204, 209; "The Jolly Corner," 48, 49, 184; "Julia Bride," 205; "Maud-Evelyn," 30, 31; "Mrs. Medwin," 199; *The Outcry*, 197-198; "The Papers," 167, 219; Prefaces to the New York Edition, 27, 29-30, 48, 72; *The Spoils of Poynton*, 156, 196, 198; "The Story in It," 58-59; "The Third Person," 163-164; "The Two Faces," 199; "The Turn of the Screw," 29-30; *What Maisie Knew*, 13, 156; *The Wings of the Dove*, 13, 27, 43, 166, 167, 219

James, M. R., 48

Jefferies, Richard, 167

Joyce, James: "The Dead," 182; *Dubliners*, 63, 64; "Ivy Day in the Committee Room," 233; *Portrait of the Artist*, 171; *Stephen Hero*, 171; *Ulysses*, 45, 103, 113

Kailyard School, 20

Kaye-Smith, Sheila, 168

Kenner, Hugh, 3

Kidd, Benjamin, 101

Kipling, John Lockwood, 14

Kipling, Rudyard, 14, 36-37, 73, 80, 100, 129, 135; and frame-tale, 31-33; settlement in England, 159-161; "The Absent-Minded Begger," 59; "The Army of a Dream," 106; "The Ballad of East and West," 91; "The Bell Buoy," 158; "Below the Mill Dam," 160-161, 248; Boer War stories, 12; "The Bonds of Discipline," 32, 159; "The Broken Men," 215; "Brother Square Toes," 162; *Captains Courageous*, 87; "The Captive," 32, 106; "A Centurion of the Thirtieth," 91-92; "A Charm," 153; "Cold Iron," 162; "The Comprehension of Private Copper," 106; "A Deal in Cotton," 32, 158; "A Doctor of Medicine," 163; "The Dykes," 153; *The Five Nations*,

105, 158; "Gloriana," 161-162; "An Habitation Enforced," 68, 192-195, 196, 237; Hadrian's Wall stories, 159; "The House Surgeon," 159-160; "If," 162; "The Islanders," 107; *Kim*, 90, 102; "The Knife and the Naked Chalk," 162-163; "The Knights of the Joyous Venture," 122, 162; "The Land," 159; "The Lesson (1899-1902)," 105; "Little Foxes," 91, 108; "The Mother Hive," 236-237, 238; "Mrs. Bathurst," 32; "The New Knighthood," 99, 100; "On Greenhow Hill," 32-33; "On the Great Wall," 91-92; "The Proconsuls," 92; *Puck of Pook's Hill*, 32, 122, 161, 237; "The Recall," 194; "Recessional," 59, 156-158, 160, 237; "The Return of the Children," 195; *Rewards and Fairies*, 32, 161, 162, 237; "A Sahib's War," 105-106; "Simple Simon," 162; *Something of Myself*, 163; "Sons of Martha," 92; "Steam Tactics," 159; "Sussex," 160; "Their Lawful Occasions," 159; "They," 48, 195-196; *Traffics and Discoveries*, 105; "The Wage-Slaves," 92; "Weland's Sword," 161; "The White Man's Burden," 92; "The Winged Hats," 91-92; "With the Night Mail," 92, 93; "The Wrong Thing," 162, 163; "Young Men at the Manor," 193

Klein, Georges Antoine, 134

Labour Party, 5

Law, Bonar, 106

Lawrence, D. H., 13, 23, 206, 210

Le Gallienne, Richard, 59

Lewis, C. S., 6

Liberalism, 35, 104, 164, 220, 224, 238, 240-241, 245, 246

Liberal Party, 4, 6, 103, 108-111

Little Englandism, 59, 101, 108, 165, 239

Locke, W. J., 82-83, 90

London as fictional topic, 67, 186, 187, 215-234, 245, 246, 247, 252

Lubbock, Percy, 24
Lucas, E. V., 25, 210, 235, 236, 243; *Listener's Lure*, 27, 185-186, 187, 217; *Over Bemerton's*, 185, 186-188

Maclaren, Ian, 20
Macmillan, Frederick, 48
Marryat, Frederick, 79, 127
Masefield, John, 165; *Multitude and Solitude*, 8, 87-89, 101, 141, 225
Mason, A. E. W.: *The Broken Road*, 101-103, 115, 141, 142, 215; *The Four Feathers*, 132-133
Masterman, C. F. G., 111, 221, 245; *The Condition of England*, 236, 237, 238; *From the Abyss*, 221; *To Colonise England*, 164
Maugham, Somerset, 155
Maxwell, Alexander, 25
Maxwell, William Babington, 14
Merrick, Leonard, 25; *Conrad in Quest of His Youth*, 184-185, 186, 188
Merriman, Henry Seton, 49
Milner, Lord, 109
Money, L. Chiozza, 221
Money-consciousness, 51
Moore, George, 22, 36
Morel, E. D., 103
Morrison, Arthur, 155
Motoring and the motor-car as fictional topics, 5, 36, 46-47, 186, 225, 245

Nesbit, E., 48
New Woman as fictional topics, 10, 60, 219
"Normyx." *See* Douglas, Norman
Novalis, 132, 242
Novel, status of, 10, 22, 35

Onions, Oliver, 48
Oppenheim, E. Phillips, 14
Orwell, George, 50

Phillpotts, Eden: Dartmoor novels, 18-19; *The Sinews of War* (with Bennett), 208
Plot: in the best-seller, 54; struggle

against its tyranny, 25-27
Pound, Ezra, 13, 26

Reeves, Amber, 63
Regeneration as fictional theme, 182-188
Reid, Thomas Mayne, 79
Rescue novels, 176-177, 180, 184, 242
Rhodes, Cecil, 109, 160
Romance: of manufacture, 68, 156, 211; and realism, 72-73, 79, 209
Roman Empire, allusions to, 88, 91, 110, 135-137, 159
Rosebery, Earl of, 94
Rowntree, B. Seebohm, 221

Sackville-West, Victoria, 51, 201; *The Edwardians*, 7-8, 19, 69, 190, 225
Said, Edward, 146
"Saki," 48
Sanger, C. P., 221
Science and technology as fictional topics, 95-96, 249, 250
Scott-James, R. A., 62
Sharp, Cecil, 168
Shaw, G. Bernard, 16, 26, 40, 93
Shiel, M. P., 235; *The Lord of the Sea*, 61, 93-94; *The Purple Cloud*, 93, 114
Short-story and experimentation with form, 28
Small-group loyalty as fictional topic, 159, 165, 166-167
Spencer, Herbert, 146
Stacpoole, H. De Vere, 99; *The Blue Lagoon*, 85, 86
Stanley, Henry, 221
Stephens, James, 48
Stevenson, Robert Louis, 79, 127; *The New Arabian Nights*, 81
Strachey, Lytton, 13
Submergence, metaphor of, 226-227
Suffrage, women's, 5-6, 25, 245
Swinnerton, Frank, 59-60

Thorburn, David, 125
Thorne, Guy, 55
Tomlinson, H. M., 84

Traditions, English, as fictional topic, 159-161, 165, 167, 168
Trench, Samuel Chenevix, 112
Trevelyan, G. M., 241
Turgenev, Ivan, 16

Vaughan Williams, Ralph, 168
Victoria, Queen, 12, 156

Wallace, Edgar, 232, 233
Walpole, Hugh: and Henry James, 180-181; *Maradick at Forty*, 180-182, 185; *The Wooden Horse*, 191-192, 194
Ward, Mrs. Humphry, 56, 60, 63
Watson, William, 75, 157
Webb, Sidney and Beatrice, 60, 63, 155, 221
Wells, H.G., 11, 12, 25, 36, 37, 38, 52, 57, 58, 60, 70, 80, 82, 112, 235; on the Balfourian age, 4-6; at Brede, 8; and Dickens, 16; on fictional form, 23-24, 65, 253; correspondence with James, 41-43, 64-65; at Spade House, Sandgate, 170-171; on Gissing, 171; on Bennett's fantasias, 209; *Anne Veronica*, 49, 62-63, 73-74, 79, 207-208, 209, 219; *Anticipations*, 5, 47, 60; *Boon*, 43; *Experiment in Autobiography*, 8, 204; "Filmer," 206; *First and Last Things*, 117; *The First Men in the Moon*, 42, 62, 101, 117-120, 123, 135-136, 205, 253; *The Food of the Gods*, 62, 96-98, 206, 208; *The History of Mr. Polly*, 63, 72, 185, 205, 208;

In the Days of the Comet, 42, 62, 85, 93, 117, 204, 205, 206-207; *The Invisible Man*, 155; *Kipps*, 16, 41, 55, 69, 205-206, 220, 253, 254; *Liberalism and Its Party*, 240; *Love and Mr. Lewisham*, 64, 205, 206; *The Misery of Boots*, 170; *A Modern Utopia*, 23, 93, 97, 101, 218; *The New Machiavelli*, 6, 8, 9, 42, 62-63, 171, 185, 188, 219-220; *New Worlds for Old*, 104; "The Remarkable Case of Davidson's Eyes," 226; "The Scope of the Novel," 5; *The Sea Lady*, 66, 226-227; *The Time Machine*, 63, 113-114; *Tono-Bungay*, 8, 27, 36, 48, 62, 68, 78-79, 83, 95, 101, 115-117, 123, 160-161, 166, 195, 220, 236, 245-251, 253-255; *The War in the Air*, 13-14; *The Wonderful Visit*, 66
Weyman, Stanley, 49
Wilde, Oscar, 13
Willcocks, Mary P., 17-18, 19, 21, 25
Wilson, Mona, 221
Withdrawal or retreat as fictional theme, 158-172
Woolf, Virginia, 23; "Mr. Bennett and Mrs. Brown," 68-71, 207
Wordsworth, William, 155

Yeats, W. B., 171, 201, 202

Zangwill, Israel, 155, 168
Zola, Emile, 25, 38, 63
Zweig, Paul, 89-90